ANTHONY AND THE
MAGIC PICTURE FRAME

by Michael S. Class

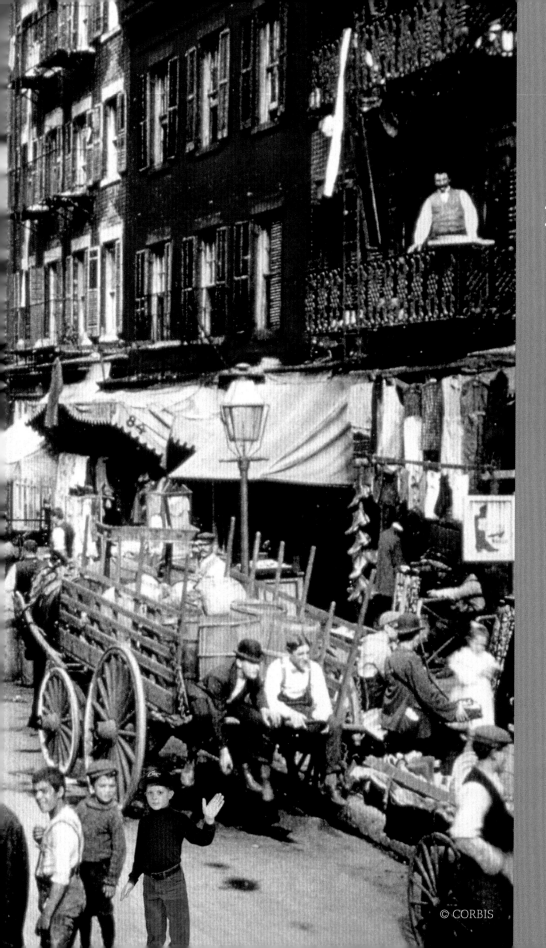

ANTHONY AND THE MAGIC PICTURE FRAME

Michael S. Class

The Story of the Boy Who Traveled into the Past
by Stepping through the Picture Frame on His Bedroom Wall
and Returned to See His Own Time in a New Light

www.magicpictureframe.com

Anthony and the Magic Picture Frame: The Story of the Boy Who Traveled into the Past by Stepping through the Picture Frame on His Bedroom Wall and Returned to See His Own Time in a New Light.

Library of Congress Control Number: 2004100453
ISBN: 978-0-9749269-0-2 [0-9749269-0-6]

First edition
06 05 04 03 02   5 4 3 2 1

Published by Magic Picture Frame Studio LLC, P.O. Box 2603, Issaquah, WA 98027–0119. For more information, contact the publisher at www.magicpictureframe.com.

NOTICE: *This book is a work of the author's imagination and is not intended to authentically reproduce actual events. While many of the events, places, and characters portrayed in this book are factual and a matter of public record, the conversations held between the historical/ public figures and the fictional characters are completely fabricated. Wherever possible, the author has attempted to use actual phrases of the speaker and to keep to the known facts, but literary license has been taken with context and motivation. All opinions expressed by Anthony (and the author) are solely those of the author and do not represent the opinions of any of the historical/public figures in this book. This book provides lists of books, movies, music, and places for further learning: Recommended reading levels are the opinion of the author, and other content ratings are provided only as a basic guide, not as a replacement for parental review and approval. Never let a minor buy anything, go anywhere, or make a phone call without parental approval or adult supervision.*

Edited by Maryann Karinch
Design by Andrea Thomas and Michael S. Class
Cover design by Michael S. Class
Composite photography by Michael S. Class
Separations by iocolor, Seattle
Produced by Marquand Books, Inc., Seattle
    www.marquand.com
Printed and bound in China by C&C Offset Printing Co., Ltd.

DEDICATION

This book is dedicated to my wife and children. They are the light in my life, and they shine brightly.

This book is dedicated to America's children. May the light of other days shine down around them, and show them the way.

This book is dedicated to the teachers of America's children. May they be reminded of that which they once knew.

This book is dedicated to all who dream. May they find the courage to make their dreams come true.

This book is dedicated to America and all those who dream of it.

Michael S. Class, 2005

ACKNOWLEDGMENTS

The biggest "thank you" goes to my wife, who believed in this book—and in me—even when I did not. She convinces me that mountains are only small bumps in the road. Marrying her was the best thing I ever did.

Thanks also go to my children, who laughed and smiled through the whole project and always had more ideas for the story.

Thanks go to my parents and grandparents—my parents for life, my grandparents for coming to America.

Thanks go to Doug V., Nick C., Lori D., Vince S., Susan M., Mark I., Uncle Joe, Uncle Frank, and so many others, friends and family all, who agreed to read this book and comment on it, even in its earliest forms.

Thanks go to Maryann K., my editor and friend; she has more positive energy than anyone I know.

And thanks to God. He knows what for.

Michael S. Class, 2005

CONTENTS

PRESIDENT ABRAHAM LINCOLN VISITS THE HEADQUARTERS OF THE ARMY OF THE
POTOMAC. Location: Sharpsburg, MD. Date: 10/3/1862. After the Battle of Antietam,
President Lincoln visited General George McClellan to persuade him to attack Lee's
Confederate Army while he had the advantage. McClellan declined to attack, and
Lincoln dismissed McClellan from command a few days later.
© Bettmann/CORBIS

AUTHOR'S INTRODUCTION ⚜

This book is based on my interviews with Anthony, the twelve-year-old boy who traveled into the past by stepping through the picture frame on his bedroom wall. Anthony's story is told in Anthony's own words, transcribed from taped interviews. This book is the only written record of the young time traveler's extraordinary adventures.

The part of Anthony's story that has surfaced is the "Philadelphia Textbook Mystery," which made national news in early 2005. Angela Rosen, a diligent seventh-grade student at Harry S. Truman Middle School in Philadelphia, Pennsylvania, said she saw the image of a boy appear in a photograph of Alexander Graham Bell as she paged through her history textbook. The boy was speaking into Bell's first telephone, she said. Ms. Rosen also reported that she saw the boy's image appear in a photograph of Henry Ford. The boy sat in the driver's seat of the first Model T automobile to come off the assembly line, she insisted. No one could verify Angela Rosen's claims because the photographs did not contain the boy's image when examined by her teachers.

Angela Rosen's claims would have been dismissed as foolishness, if it weren't for an incident at a nearby high school. Twenty-seven students in a ninth-grade history class simultaneously saw a boy's image appear in a photograph of Abraham Lincoln. The teacher had instructed the students to open their history textbooks to the chapter on the American Civil War. All of the students—and their teacher—watched the boy's image fade and disappear from the photograph five minutes later. But one student in the class used a camera-phone to record the phenomenon.

News of the high school students' sighting—with the photographic evidence—spread wildly. Television news reporters swarmed the high school and interviewed dozens of students, who swore they saw the boy's image in dozens of other historical photographs that day: the attack on Pearl Harbor, the Hindenburg disaster, the Wright brothers at Kitty Hawk, and Martin Luther King, Jr., during the March on Washington. But in every case, the boy's image could not be found in the photographs when later examined under scientific scrutiny. Nevertheless, the Philadelphia Textbook Mystery became a topic of national discussion, and Anthony learned that he had been seen—that his secret was out. When Anthony announced that he was the boy in the photographs, scientists from around the world converged on his home to examine the Picture Frame. I got the exclusive chance to interview Anthony and tell his story to the world in his own words.

Time travel should not really surprise us. Way back in 1915, Albert Einstein showed us that space is curved and time is relative. We know that astronauts orbiting the earth at high speed travel forward in time by tiny fractions of a second. We think nothing of the fact that computer clocks on orbiting communications satellites have to be corrected every year for a time travel effect: The length of a year that an orbiting satellite's clock experiences is shorter than the length of a year experienced by clocks on Earth.

We know these things, but it is only now, in the 21st century, that we are beginning to study the dimension of time seriously. On April 24, 2004, NASA launched a satellite into Earth orbit specially designed to measure distortions in the fabric of "space-time." And in the laboratory, physicists now attempt to warp space and time and propel atomic particles into the future—the first experiments that might one day lead to the invention of a time machine.

The odd photographic phenomena witnessed by so many students in Philadelphia resulted from a distortion in the fabric of space-time. Each time Anthony stepped through the Picture Frame on his bedroom wall, temporary space-time discontinuities led to Anthony's appearances in the photographs. Visible in the historical photographs while he traveled in the past, Anthony disappeared from the photographs when he returned to the present day—scientists now call this the "Magic Picture Frame Effect."

But because our understanding of time travel is limited, exactly how the Picture Frame works remains something of a mystery and a matter of heated scientific debate. Astrophysicists theorize that the Picture Frame creates tunnels of swirling light powerful enough to warp space and time into a loop, temporarily connecting the present with the past. Black holes, they say, exhibit the same phenomenon ironically called "frame dragging." Experts in quantum physics, however, insist that the Picture Frame is not a time machine at all. They claim that the Picture Frame merely creates a temporary bridge between alternate realities, and that we interpret the alternate realities as past and present.

I prefer a simpler explanation. I've heard that photographs are the "captured light" of other days. I think that the Picture Frame released the captured light of the photographs that Anthony viewed, allowing the light to envelop and transport him to the time and place the photograph was taken. Anthony's narrative seems to support my theory. I think Anthony hitched a ride on the "light of other days."

One final note: When I first interviewed Anthony, I was skeptical of his story. Like many others, I thought it was an elaborate hoax. But, I took the time to carefully check what Anthony said during his interviews against the known historical record. What I found out may surprise you. It surprised me. You can review my research for yourself: When you see a footnote number in "Anthony's Story," simply refer to the part of the book entitled "The Rest Of Anthony's Story" and read the note. I think you will agree with me that the places Anthony went were real, the events Anthony witnessed actually happened, and the words spoken by the people Anthony met were actually spoken by them.

I am convinced that Anthony traveled into the past. It's my hope that *Anthony and the Magic Picture Frame* will take you there, too.

Michael S. Class, 2005

"Everything's got a moral, if only you can find it."

THE DUCHESS,
ALICE'S ADVENTURES IN WONDERLAND (1865),
BY LEWIS CARROLL

"Oft, in the stilly night,
Ere slumber's chain
has bound me,
Fond memory brings
the light
Of other days
around me . . ."

THOMAS MOORE (1779–1852),
IRISH POET, COMPOSER, AND MUSICIAN

CHAPTER 1

THE MAGIC PICTURE FRAME

I walked on the moon with Neil Armstrong and Buzz Aldrin. I played baseball with Lou Gehrig and Babe Ruth. I flew from New York to Paris with Charles Lindbergh. I saw brave soldiers storm the beaches of Normandy on D-Day. I cried with survivors of the Holocaust. I watched proud and weary marines raise the American flag on Iwo Jima. I heard the first words to come out of Thomas Edison's talking machine. I saw the glow of Edison's first electric lamp. I met FDR. I saw Doctor Jonas Salk conquer polio and counted the dimes that made it possible. I crouched in the trenches during World War I. I stood in a breadline during the Great Depression. I crossed the Atlantic Ocean on a steamship one hundred years ago, when my great-grandfather first came to America; I walked with him through the doors to America on Ellis Island. And I was with him the day he became an American.

I did it all by stepping through the Picture Frame on my bedroom wall.

My name is Anthony and I am twelve years old.[1]

This is my story.

I don't exactly know where the Picture Frame came from. It's hung on my bedroom wall as long as I can remember. My father told me that his grandfather gave him the Picture Frame with specific instructions to pass it down to me. My great-grandfather, my father said, insisted on that. But where did it come from? My father could only tell me that my great-grandfather got the Picture Frame as a gift when he was young. Someone traveling through town gave it to him.

I don't really know how the Picture Frame works, but I know how to use it. Someday, scientists will figure out the physics behind it, I guess. I just place a photograph into the Picture Frame and wait. In a little while, the photograph becomes three-dimensional—almost real—like a scene on the other side of an open window. Then, beams of light from the Picture Frame pour into my room, like the sunbeams on a summer evening that make everything in my room glow. I step through the Picture Frame as if it really was an open window in the summertime, and I follow the beams of light into the world of the photograph—the world of the past. I've done it a lot. And when I want to come home, I just step back through the Picture Frame from the other side.

It's simple. Except that's not how it happened the first time. I mean, who would ever think of putting a photograph into a picture frame and then stepping through it? Not me. I only tried it because of what happened the first time. That night, the Picture Frame had its own plan. I didn't choose where or when to go, and I didn't even get to decide when to come home. Everyone knows about my later trips because I took them in the daytime and showed up in pictures in history books. But nobody knows the story of my first trip through the Picture Frame.

It was late at night and I was in my bed and sound asleep. I woke up and saw that a bright white light took over my whole room. At first, I thought that I was dreaming that the sun was rising in my room! But the light stung my eyes and I knew that I was awake. I squinted and I saw that it was coming from the Picture Frame on my bedroom wall.

And then the light came alive! Beams of the light moved around my room as if they were searching for something.

The light is searching for me!

I pulled the covers over my head. But the light beams found me. They bored through my blankets until the last bit of darkness disappeared.

I have to put out that light! Or . . . run!

From under my blankets, I slipped my hand to the floor and grabbed my football. Then I jumped up, threw my blankets off, and hurled my football at the Picture Frame. I wanted to knock it from the wall and put out that weird light. I expected a crash.

But the sound never came. My football flew right through the center of the Picture Frame and disappeared into the light.

Whoa!

Somehow, I got some courage, or maybe I just got so curious that I forgot that I was scared. I didn't run away. I climbed out of my bed and tiptoed toward the Picture Frame. I took some books and stacked them near the Picture Frame and then I climbed up. Then, I held my hands in front of my eyes to block out some of the light and looked into the Picture Frame.

There was another world on the other side! It had steep white and gray mountains, deep and dark craters, and sharp-edged jagged rocks. The sky was the blackest black I had ever seen. There were stars in the sky, but they didn't twinkle. The stars just hung in the black sky like tiny white Christmas tree lights. And the whole place was quiet—so quiet that I could actually hear my heart beat.

It can't be! But, it looks like . . .

I saw my football a few feet below me. It was at rest in the gray soil.

Then, I saw the earth—my home—rise above the horizon.

I know this place!

I wasn't afraid anymore. I climbed through the Picture Frame to get my football.

"Life is either a daring adventure or nothing."

HELEN KELLER (1880–1968),
AMERICAN AUTHOR AND EDUCATOR

CHAPTER 2

THE MEN ON THE MOON

Itook a deep breath, held it, and put one foot, then the other one, through the Picture Frame. Then I fell. What I thought would be a small step to the ground turned out to be more like a giant leap! I bounced and tumbled down a rocky slope, kicking up a cloud of powdery gray dust. When I came to a stop, I was on my back, staring up at a jet-black sky filled with stars that didn't twinkle. When the dust settled around me, I realized I wasn't hurt at all.[1]

When I stood up, I noticed something weird about the way the dust particles moved. Instead of scattering in all directions the way I thought they would, each particle floated in a pattern. It moved in a curve away from where it had been kicked up— a graceful parabolic motion. I kicked up more dust and watched even the tiniest particles do the same thing.

Of course! I'm on the moon!

The dust particles had a perfect trajectory because there was no wind to blow them off course! There was no wind because, on the moon, there's no air.

No air! Then how am I breathing? What am I breathing? How can I possibly stay alive without a spacesuit?

I panicked. I took a deep breath, and then another. Obviously, I was breathing something—but what? I was in a vacuum! Not only that, but I wasn't hot or cold. I felt fine! I was standing on the surface of the moon without a spacesuit and I felt fine!

How is this possible? Can it be that the Picture Frame is protecting me?

I looked back toward the Picture Frame. It was at the top of the hill, about four feet above the ground, just floating in midair—floating in space, actually. Inside the Picture Frame, I could see my bed, my dresser, and my desk—my home on Earth.

I decided that the Picture Frame had to be some kind of a doorway between distant places, or a transporter mechanism like the ones I had seen in old science fiction movies. But the Picture Frame could also protect me—at least temporarily, I figured. After all, the moon's harsh environment didn't bother me one bit.[2]

The Picture Frame protects me! What other explanation can there be? But, still, I'd better be careful. Maybe I shouldn't wander too far . . .

I was thinking that I should pick up my football and jump back through the Picture Frame and go home before anything could go wrong. And then I saw the earth rising above the moon's horizon. It was beautiful! I had only seen a view like that in pictures, and the pictures didn't compare. I totally forgot about the risk and the danger. For a long time, I just stared at the amazing blue and white planet that hung in the black sky above me—my home. That's when the incredible power of the Picture Frame really sunk in: To my left, my bedroom was only a few steps away, but above me, my home was more than a quarter of a million miles away![3]

I took a deep breath of nothing and smiled. I no longer wanted to go home. I wanted to see more. I wanted to explore. I wanted to travel to distant places. I wanted to discover all of the Picture Frame's secrets.

Can the Picture Frame take me anywhere I want to go?

I got so excited thinking about all the places the Picture Frame could take me, and then all of a sudden, I heard voices.

First voice: "Beautiful view!"
Second voice: "Isn't that something? Magnificent sight out here."
First voice, again: "Magnificent desolation."[4]

Two astronauts were walking toward me. A gold aluminum foil-covered spacecraft was behind them. I knew it wasn't there before. The astronauts were close enough for me to see their mission patches and read their nametags: "E. Aldrin" and "N. Armstrong."[5]

In a heartbeat, I knew I was wrong about what the Picture Frame did. The Picture Frame wasn't a doorway to other places—it was a doorway to other times! The question wasn't where the Picture Frame could take me—it was when! I had just traveled thirty-four years into the past. It was July 20, 1969! Apollo 11 had just landed on the moon! It was Neil Armstrong and Buzz Aldrin who were walking toward me!

Aldrin: "And, Neil, didn't I say we might see some purple rocks?"
Armstrong: "Find a purple rock?"
Aldrin: "Yes. They are small, sparkly *** fragments *** places *** would make a first guess that some sort of biotite *** We'll leave that to further analysis ***"[6]

I waved to the astronauts. But when I started to jog toward them, it turned out to be a big mistake! I forgot that the gravity on the moon was only one-sixth of the gravity on the earth. Because of the low gravity, my running launched me into space! I floated right by the two Apollo 11 astronauts, tumbling out of control two feet above the ground. And when I finally did hit the ground, I bounced up again and floated another ten feet.

Buzz Aldrin called out to me as I passed him. He tried to offer advice, but his radio kept cutting out and I heard only some of his words. I think he said: "About two or three or maybe four easy paces can bring you to a nearly smooth stop. *** change directions, like a football player, you just have to to *** foot out to the side and cut a little bit."[7]

So, what I learned in science class is true!

I was fooled by physics! Because I weighed less on the moon, my leg muscles had easily propelled me off the lunar surface. It's a good thing that the moon had a little bit of gravity, because I would have floated away! I soon realized that I had to be careful. My mass was still the same as on Earth, and any momentum and inertia I generated would be a lot more difficult to counteract without the usual

HERE MEN FROM THE PLANET EARTH
FIRST SET FOOT UPON THE MOON
JULY 1969, A. D.
WE CAME IN PEACE FOR ALL MANKIND

NEIL A. ARMSTRONG
ASTRONAUT

MICHAEL COLLINS
ASTRONAUT

EDWIN E. ALDRIN, JR.
ASTRONAUT

RICHARD NIXON
PRESIDENT, UNITED STATES OF AMERICA

Anthony

REPLICA OF THE PLAQUE LEFT ON THE
MOON BY THE APOLLO 11 ASTRONAUTS.
Date: 1969.
© Bettmann/CORBIS

help of Earth's gravity. I found that it was harder to stop and change direction on the moon without falling over![8]

"It's hard saying what a sane pace might be," Buzz Aldrin said. "I think it's the one that I'm using now—would get rather tiring after several hundred *** but this may be a function of this suit, as well as lack of gravity forces."[9]

In the end, I decided to adopt the kind of "kangaroo hop" that the astronauts were using to get around. For me, it was just fun to hop and cover large distances in a single leap, but the astronauts hopped because the mass of their backpacks had shifted their center-of-mass behind them; it was easy for the astronauts to lose their balance.

"You do have to be rather careful to keep track of where your center-of-mass is," Buzz Aldrin said. "Sometimes, it takes about two or three paces to make sure you've got your feet underneath you ... So-called kangaroo hop does work, but it seems that your forward mobility is not quite as good as—it is in the conventional—more conventional one foot after another."[10]

For the next few minutes, I hopped all over Tranquility Base as Neil and Buzz gathered their rock samples, took photographs, and set up their TV camera.

Armstrong: "Okay, Houston. Tell me if you're getting a new picture."

Houston: "Neil, this is Houston. That's affirmative. We're getting a new picture. You can tell it's a longer focal length lens. And for your information, all LM systems are GO. Over."

Aldrin: "We appreciate that. Thank you."

Aldrin: "Neil is now unveiling the plaque *** gear."

Houston: "Roger. We got you boresighted, but back under one track."

Armstrong: "For those who haven't read the plaque, we'll read the plaque that's on the front landing gear of this LM [Lunar Module]. First there's two hemispheres, one showing each of the two hemispheres of the earth. Underneath it says 'Here Man from the planet Earth first set foot upon the moon, July 1969 A.D. We came in peace for all mankind.' It has the crew members' signatures and the signature of the President of the United States."[11]

I hopped over to the Lunar Module and added my signature to the plaque.

APOLLO 11 COMMANDER NEIL ARMSTRONG
PLANTS HIS BOOT IN THE LUNAR SURFACE.
Location: Tranquility Base on
the moon. Date: 7/20/1969.
© Bettmann/CORBIS

Houston: "Columbia, this is Houston. Reading you loud and clear. Over."

Collins: "Yes. Reading you loud and clear. How's it going?"

Houston: "Roger. The EVA [Extravehicular Activity] is progressing beautifully. I believe they are setting up the flag now."

Collins: "Great."

Houston: "I guess you're the only person around who doesn't have TV coverage of the scene."

Collins: "That's all right. I don't mind a bit."

Collins: "How is the quality of the TV?"

Houston: "Oh, it's beautiful, Mike. It really is."

Collins: "Oh, gee, that's great! Is the lighting halfway decent?"

Houston: "Yes, indeed. They've got the flag up now and you can see the stars and stripes on the lunar surface."

Collins: "Beautiful. Just beautiful."[12]

It was a proud moment: The American flag was on the moon! But did you know that there was a time when it didn't seem likely that America would be successful in space? That's because, when people looked up into the night skies of October 1957, they saw the Soviet Union's satellite, Sputnik, orbiting the earth. Then on television, just two months later, they watched America's first attempt at putting a satellite into space end in disaster: The Vanguard rocket carrying the satellite exploded and burned on the launch pad at Cape Canaveral. It was a humiliating failure that millions of people saw.[13]

Even worse, Sputnik turned out to be just the beginning of a string of Soviet achievements in space. The first spacecraft to leave Earth's gravity was the Soviet Luna 1, in 1959. The first probe to reach the moon's surface was the Soviet Luna 2. That was also in 1959. In 1961, the Soviets put their first astronaut (actually, they called them cosmonauts) in space—Yuri Gagarin. Two years later, they put the first woman in space—Valentina Tereshkova. And the first astronaut to leave the capsule and "walk in space" was cosmonaut Alexei Leonov, in 1965.[14]

There was something else, too. The Soviet Union's early success in space sent an upsetting message to the rest of the world, especially to Americans: that people living under tyranny and communism could outperform free people living within a system of capitalism and democracy. After orbiting the earth on April 12, 1961, Yuri Gagarin said: "Now let the other countries try to catch us." Then, as if anybody missed that jab, Soviet Premier Nikita Khrushchev made the point even clearer when he said: "Let the capitalist countries catch up with our country, which has blazed the trail into outer space."[15]

In response to the Soviet challenge, President John F. Kennedy began thinking about ways for the United States to beat the Soviets and take the lead in space. On April 20, 1961, he wrote a memo to Vice President Lyndon Johnson: "Do we have a chance of beating the Soviets by putting a laboratory in space, or by a trip around the moon, or by a rocket to land on the moon, or by a rocket to go to the moon and back with a man? Is there any other space program which promises dramatic results in which we could win?"[16]

Then, on May 25, 1961, President Kennedy addressed the American people and told them that the "space race" had become part of the battle between freedom and tyranny, between capitalism and communism. He said: ". . . if we are to win the battle that is now going on around the world between freedom and tyranny, the dramatic achievements in space which occurred in recent weeks should have made clear to us all, as did the Sputnik in 1957, the impact of this adventure on the minds of men everywhere, who are attempting to make a determination of which road they should take." America had to take the lead in space, President Kennedy insisted, because, ". . . whatever mankind must undertake, free men must fully share."[17]

President Kennedy's words were bold, considering that the U.S. had only succeeded in putting its first astronaut, Alan Shepard, into space twenty days before—for a fifteen-minute ride. The Soviets had taken the lead in the space race, and President Kennedy knew it. But he said: "Recognizing the head start obtained by the Soviets with their large rocket engines, which gives them many months of lead-time, and recognizing the likelihood that they will exploit this lead for some time to come in still more impressive successes, we nevertheless are required to make new efforts of our own. For while we cannot guarantee that we shall one day be the first, we can guarantee that any failure to make this effort will make us last."[18]

Then, President Kennedy issued a fantastic challenge to the American people. He said: "I believe that this nation should commit itself to achieving the goal, before the decade is out, of landing a man on the moon and returning him safely to the earth." It would no longer be a space race between the United States and the Soviet Union—it would be a race to the moon.[19]

There I was standing on the moon on July 20, 1969, only eight years after President Kennedy had issued his historic challenge, and not ten. The American flag stood proudly in the lunar dust. What President Kennedy had hoped for had come true. The free people of the world had claimed the moon in the name of peace. "For the eyes of the world now look into space, to the moon and to the planets beyond," President Kennedy had said, "and we have vowed that we will not see it governed by a hostile flag of conquest, but by a banner of freedom and peace."[20]

I placed my hand over my heart as Astronaut Buzz Aldrin saluted the American flag on the moon. Neil Armstrong took our photograph.[21]

Houston: "Tranquility Base, this is Houston. Could we get both of you on the camera for a minute, please?"

Armstrong: "Say again, Houston."

Houston: "Roger. We'd like to get both of you in the field of view of the camera for a minute."

Houston: "Neil and Buzz, the President of the United States is in his office now and would like to say a few words to you. Over."

Armstrong: "That would be an honor."

Houston: "Go ahead Mr. President. This is Houston. Out."

President Nixon: "Neil and Buzz, I am talking to you by telephone from the Oval Room at the White House, and this certainly has to be the most historic telephone call ever made. I just can't tell you how proud we all are of what you *** for every American. This has to be the proudest day of our lives. And for people all over the world, I am sure they, too, join with Americans in recognizing what an immense feat this is. Because of what you have done, the heavens have become a part of man's world. And as you talk to us from the Sea of Tranquility, it inspires us to redouble our efforts to bring peace and tranquility to Earth. For one priceless moment in the whole history of man, all the people on this earth are truly one; one in their pride in what you have done, and one in our prayers that you will return safely to Earth."

Armstrong: "Thank you Mr. President. It's a great honor and privilege for us to be here representing not only the United States but men of peace of all nations, and with interest and a curiosity and a vision for the future. It's an honor for us to be able to participate here today."

President Nixon: "And thank you very much and I look forward— all of us look forward to seeing you on the Hornet on Thursday."

Aldrin: "I look forward to that very much, sir."[22]

RIGHT:
ASTRONAUT BUZZ ALDRIN SALUTES THE UNITED STATES FLAG ON THE MOON.
Location: Tranquility Base on the moon. Date: 7/20/1969.
© 1996 CORBIS

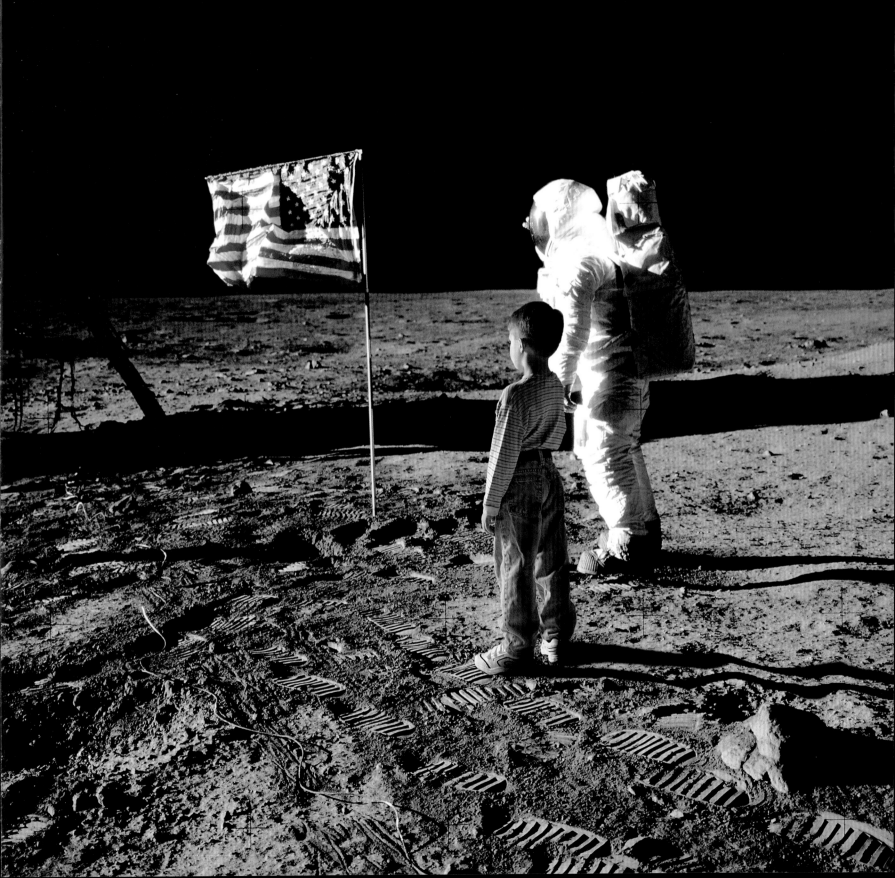

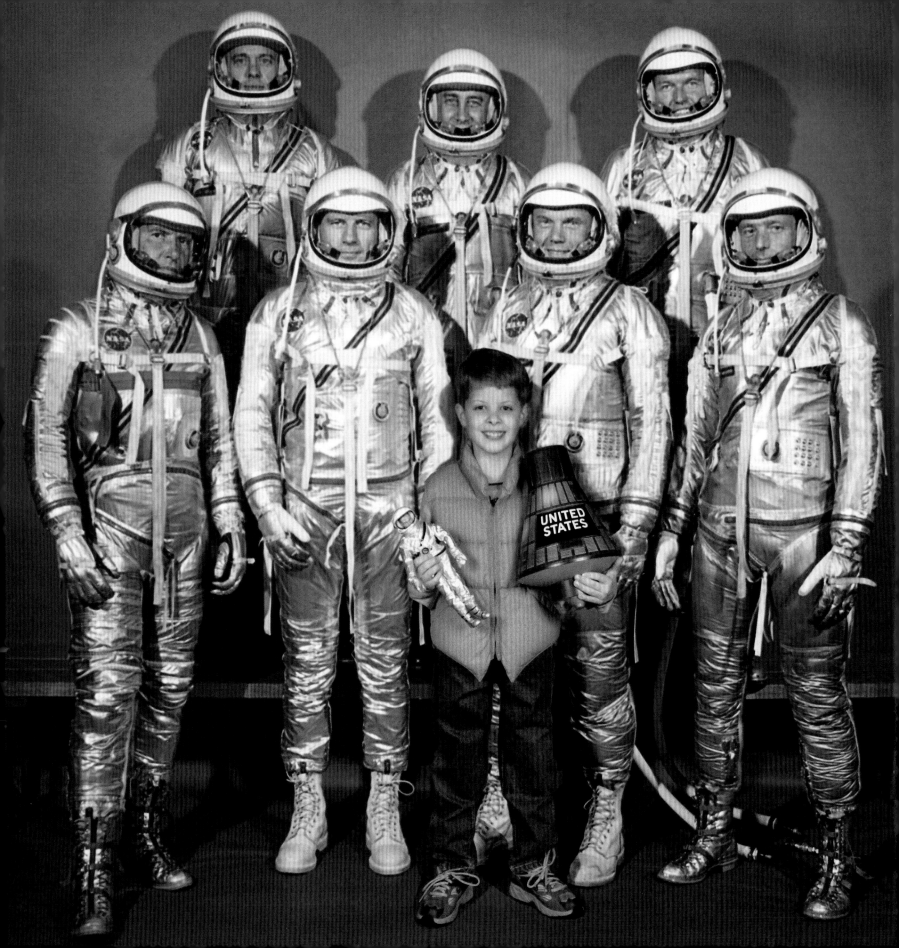

When Alexander Graham Bell spoke the first words through a wire, Thomas Watson was the only one to hear them. But on July 20, 1969, more than six hundred million people, nearly a fifth of the world's population, listened in on the first telephone call to the moon—almost every television and radio on Earth was tuned in! And that meant that for just a few hours, nothing divided humanity—not culture, race, religion, or politics. The entire world put eyes and ears on the same thing, on the actions of three brave men a quarter of a million miles out in space.

After their walk on the moon, the Apollo 11 astronauts returned to Earth as heroes, but they didn't think of themselves as heroes at all. They were, as Neil Armstrong had just told President Nixon, simply honored to participate in what they believed was an enormous team effort. They were simply happy to do their part of the job.

Buzz Aldrin later said: "The footprints at Tranquility Base belong to more than the crew of Apollo 11. They were put there by hundreds of thousands of people across this country, people in Government, industry, and universities, the teams and crews that preceded us, all who strived throughout the years with Mercury, Gemini, and Apollo."[23]

And Michael Collins explained it this way to Americans: "This operation is somewhat like the periscope of a submarine. All you see is the three of us, but beneath the surface are thousands and thousands of others, and to all those, I would like to say, thank you very much."[24]

Of course, the astronauts were right: America's space program was a team effort, and there were many people to thank for the success of Apollo 11. But in the end, three men had to ride the powerful Saturn V rocket and risk their lives to put human footprints on the moon. Neil Armstrong, Buzz Aldrin, and Michael Collins took that risk, and represented the best of America, and all humankind. These three men had the "right stuff."[25]

Neil Armstrong went to Purdue University on a U.S. Navy scholarship, and earned a B.S. in aeronautical engineering in 1955. During the Korean War, he flew seventy-eight combat missions from the aircraft carrier USS *Essex*. After the war, he became an aeronautical research scientist and test pilot for NASA, flying over two hundred different models of aircraft, including jets, rockets, helicopters, and gliders. And while working for NASA, he earned an M.S. in aerospace engineering from the University of Southern California. On March 16, 1966, Neil Armstrong, who was a civilian at the time, commanded the Gemini VIII mission.

Buzz Aldrin earned a B.S. from the U.S. Military Academy at West Point in 1951. He flew sixty-six combat missions for the Air Force during the Korean War. On November 11, 1963, Colonel Aldrin orbited the earth in the Gemini XII spacecraft. Later, he worked out the procedures that NASA would use to dock spacecraft in Earth orbit. Buzz Aldrin earned a Ph.D. in astronautics from the Massachusetts Institute of Technology in 1963.

Astronaut Michael Collins earned a B.S. from the U.S. Military Academy at West Point in 1952. He served as a fighter pilot, and an experimental test pilot, at Edwards Air Force Base in California until 1963. In October 1963, Lieutenant Colonel Michael Collins piloted the Gemini X spacecraft.

....

Speaking of having the "right stuff," I met America's seven original astronauts when the Picture Frame took me to 1959. They had just gone through a tough selection process.

The process began when NASA picked 110 candidates from more than 500 of America's top military test pilots. Interviews and written tests took the list of candidates down to 32. Each of the 32 men went through a series of demanding tests—physical, psychological, and in pressure suits. Finally, 18 men were approved for America's first manned space flights, Project Mercury. From the 18, NASA chose only 7 to go into space. The "Mercury Seven" were: Scott Carpenter, Gordon Cooper, John Glenn, "Gus" Grissom, Walter Schirra, Alan Shepard, and "Deke" Slayton.

The seven astronauts began their formal astronaut training at the NASA Langley Research Center, in Hampton, Virginia. I was there the day that the astronauts took time out for a publicity photo in their cool silver space suits. They invited me to stand with them in the photograph; I grinned from ear to ear![26]

As I posed with the "Mercury Seven" that day in 1959, it occurred to me that from Mercury to Apollo, and to the space shuttle missions in my own time, America's astronauts have always been America's best. And that's a good thing, I figured, because we're not likely to reach Mars with a spaceship full of tourists out for a thrill ride.[27]

....

LEFT:
THE SEVEN ASTRONAUTS SELECTED FOR PROJECT MERCURY. Location: NASA Langley Research Center, Hampton, VA. Date: 1959. Front row, left to right: Walter Schirra, Deke Slayton, John Glenn, and Scott Carpenter. Back row, left to right: Alan Shepard, Gus Grissom, and Gordon Cooper.
© NASA/Roger Ressmeyer/CORBIS

for elk. In their enthusiasm for the view they frequently stumbled on the rocky trails, but when they looked only to their footing, they did not see the elk."[35]

While Neil Armstrong and Buzz Aldrin walked on the moon, and Michael Collins orbited it, everyone in America held their breath. Americans hoped and prayed for the their safe return. The families of the astronauts worried the most, though. The public saw their big, confident smiles, but in private, they feared for the astronauts' safety.

Just before Michael Collins left for the moon, his wife, Patricia, gave him a last minute handwritten note. The note was a poem she'd written for him, entitled: *To a Husband Who Must Seek the Stars*.

I'll be unafraid, undaunted.
Yes, of course! I need not face
Any peril; or be haunted
By the hazards you embrace.

I could have sought by wit or wile
Your bright dream to dim. And yet
If I'd swayed you with a smile
My reward would be regret.

So, for once, you shall not hear
Of the tears, unbidden, welling;
Or the nighttime stabs of fear.
These, this time, are not for telling.

Take my silence, though intended;
Fill it with the joy you feel.
Take my courage, now pretended—
You, my love, will make it real.[36]

When he talked about the risks of space exploration in 1961, President Kennedy said: "If we are to go only half way, or reduce our sights in the face of difficulty, in my judgment it would be better not to go at all."[37]

What Patricia Collins knew, and all of the astronauts' families knew, was that for the astronauts, "not to go at all" was not acceptable. And, as I stood there on the moon, watching Neil Armstrong, Buzz Aldrin, and Michael Collins extend man's reach to the farthest frontier, I think I understood why that was.

To the astronauts, "not to go at all" is . . .

Over the radio, I heard Michael Collins say: "To go places and to do things that have never been done before—that's what living is all about."[38]

. . . not to live.

Aldrin: "Houston. I have the seismic experiment flipped over now, and I'm aligning it, but I'm having a little bit of difficulty getting the B-B in the center. It wants to move around and around on the outside. ***"

Houston: "You're cutting out again, Buzz."

Aldrin: "Roger. I say I'm not having too much success in leveling the PSEP experiment."

Armstrong: "The laser reflector is installed and the bubble is leveled and the alignment appears to be good."

Houston: "Neil, this is Houston. Roger. Out."

Aldrin: "Hey, you want to take a look at this B-B and see what you make of it?"

Armstrong: "I find it pretty hard to get perfectly level, too."[39]

Back on Earth, scientists waited to fire lasers at the moon. They designed the Laser Ranging Retro-Reflector to bounce the laser beams back to the earth, so they could measure the precise distance to the moon. The LR-cubed—that's what they called it sometimes— was a white box, about two feet square by about four inches thick. It was covered on one side by an array of 100 round and shiny mirrors. Neil Armstrong aimed the mirrors toward the earth. He got the Laser Reflector set up without a hitch!

The astronauts also had to set up the Passive Seismic Experiment Package—the PSEP—to measure "moonquakes." Seismic waves through the moon cause the surface to tremble and the PSEP was supposed to transmit the seismic data back to Earth—in real time. Foldout solar panels powered the PSEP, but it had to be level in order to work properly. Buzz Aldrin had a hard time getting it level. I went over to see what the problem was.

The leveling device on the PSEP had a little metal BB that had to be centered within a circular target. It reminded me of those hand-held games in which you have to make a small silver ball fall into a specific hole in order to win; I used to have one in the shape of a baseball diamond—it had four tiny balls that had to be landed on all

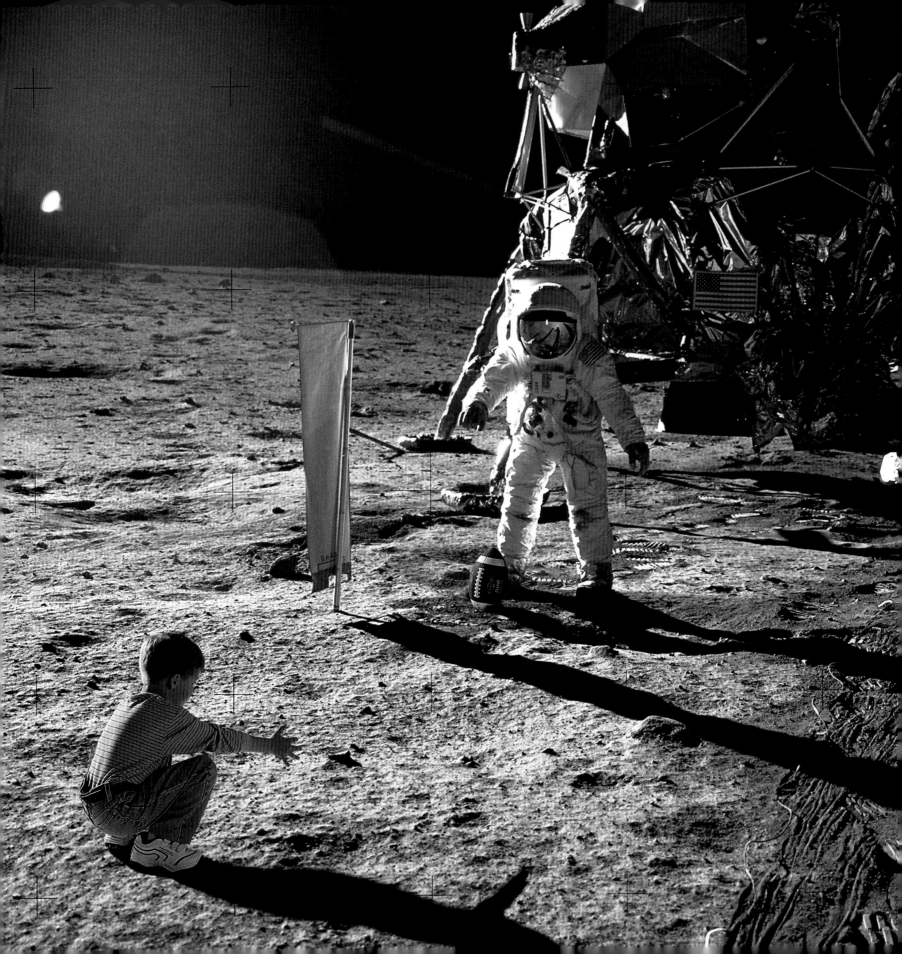

ASTRONAUT NEIL ARMSTRONG AT THE MODULAR EQUIPMENT STORAGE ASSEMBLY (MESA)
OF THE LUNAR MODULE (LM). Location: Tranquility Base on the moon. Date: 7/20/1969.
© CORBIS SYGMA

the bases all at the same time. I never could do it. So I understood the frustration that Neil and Buzz were having as they tried to center the BB on the PSEP. They were just about to give up and level the PSEP by "eyeball," when the BB unexpectedly popped into place. The astronauts quickly deployed the solar panels, and the PSEP began transmitting data to scientists waiting on Earth.

The astronauts also set up the Solar Wind Composition experiment—the SWC. It was a white aluminum foil sheet, about one foot wide, hung from a pole in the sunlight. While the astronauts were on the moon, the SWC collected samples of the electrically charged particles emitted into space by the sun. The particles can't be collected on the surface of the earth, because the earth's magnetic field and atmosphere repels them. But when conditions are just right at the earth's polar regions, the sun's charged particles can sometimes reach down into the upper part of the earth's atmosphere, causing auroras. I saw the aurora borealis once during a camping trip in northern Maine.[40]

Houston: "Buzz, this is Houston. You've got about 10 minutes left now prior to commencing your EVA termination activities. Over."

Aldrin: "Roger. I understand."

Houston: "Tranquility Base, this is Houston. The passive seismic experiment has been uncaged and we're observing short-period oscillations in it. Over."[41]

In my time, space program technology is everywhere, but most people don't know it. They don't know that NASA technology is in the everyday things around them, like cordless drills and smoke detectors, and football helmets and virtual reality games. They never hear about how space technology made laser scalpels possible, or how space technology improved CAT scanners, magnetic resonance imagers, kidney dialysis machines, water filters, freeze-dried food, artificial heart pumps, air purifiers, sunglasses, artificial limbs, satellite radio, aircraft collision avoidance systems, optical sensor thermometers, land mine removal systems, and even golf balls. There are 500 dimples on the longest-flying golf balls because of NASA research and engineering.[42]

In 1962, President Kennedy predicted that the U.S. space program would unleash technical genius and enrich us all. He said: "The growth of our science and education will be enriched by new knowledge of our universe and environment, by new techniques of learning and mapping and observation, by new tools and computers for industry, medicine, the home as well as the school."[43]

President Kennedy's prediction came true—and still, there are people who insist that man should solve all the problems on Earth before venturing further into space. Fix the planet, they say, before leaving it. But, isn't America's space program solving problems on Earth, and not distracting us from them? I think so, anyway.

"We cannot launch our planetary probes from a springboard of poverty, discrimination, or unrest," Astronaut Michael Collins once said. "But neither can we wait until every terrestrial problem has been solved. Such logic 200 years ago would have prevented expansion westward past the Appalachian Mountains, for assuredly the eastern seaboard was beset by problems of great urgency then, as it is today."[44]

While thinking about these things, I threw my football as hard as I could toward the infinite black sky and imagined that it escaped the moon's weak gravity. In my mind, I saw it whiz miles and miles and miles past Mars and Jupiter and the rings of Saturn, past Uranus and Neptune and Pluto, and, like a tiny Voyager spacecraft, leave the solar system entirely.[45]

Voyager, when will man follow you?

It occurred to me that until the Picture Frame brought me to 1969, I had never seen a man stand on the surface of the moon. In my time, more than three decades after Neil Armstrong put his footprints on the lunar surface, manned space exploration of the moon and planets seems almost as improbable as it did when Sputnik crossed the night skies of 1957. I learned in school that it would take sixteen years for America to repeat the feat of Apollo 11, and perhaps twenty years beyond that to put a man on Mars. That's if we ever decide to do it![46]

I noticed that the Apollo 11 astronauts were packing the last pieces of their equipment into the Lunar Module. They would be leaving soon. I approached them to say goodbye, but I was still thinking about the slow pace of space exploration in my own time. Buzz Aldrin seemed to know what I was thinking.

"The Apollo lesson is that national goals can be met where there is a strong enough will to do so," he said.[47]

We shook hands. Then, I watched the two astronauts climb the ladder to the Lunar Module, crawl inside, and close the door.

Aldrin: "Okay. The hatch is closed and latched, and verified secure."[48]

Stepping back from the Lunar Module, I noticed that the astronauts had left some things on the ground, next to the ladder. I think I saw a mission patch, some medals, and a small metal cylinder. I wasn't able to take a closer look, because I had to get to a safe distance before the astronauts fired the Lunar Module's engine to begin their ascent. And I forgot to go back and look after they blasted off, so I have always wondered what it was that they left behind.[49]

Houston: "Columbia, Columbia, this is Houston, Over."
Collins: "Roger, Columbia on Charlie. How do you read?"
Houston: "Roger, Columbia. This is Houston. Reading you loud and clear on OMNI Charlie. The crew of Tranquility Base is back inside their base, repressurized, and they're in the process of doffing the PLSS's. Everything went beautifully. Over."
Collins: "Hallelujah."[50]

"Hallelujah," I repeated.

It was not unusual to hear thanks being given to God by American astronauts in space. When Apollo 8 entered lunar orbit on Christmas Eve, 1968, Frank Borman, Jim Lovell, and William Anders did a live television broadcast during which they took turns reading from the book of Genesis. And shortly after Apollo 11 had touched down on the moon, astronaut Buzz Aldrin set a chalice of wine and some wafers on a fold-down table in the Lunar Module, and said: "This is the LM pilot speaking. I'd like to take this opportunity to ask every person listening in, whoever and wherever they may be, to pause for a moment and contemplate the events of the past few hours, and to give thanks in his or her own way."[51]

In the vacuum of space, the Lunar Module's engine fired without making a sound. I watched as the tiny spacecraft shot up from the surface of the moon and began its long journey back through the heavens, and toward home.[52]

I waved goodbye.

The engine's blast toppled the American flag, so I went over to stand it up. As I was doing that, I glanced over my shoulder and saw that the Picture Frame was no longer displaying my bedroom back home. Instead, a succession of images that I couldn't quite make out, danced wildly within its borders. Somehow, I knew that I would soon be leaving the moon, and that the Picture Frame itself would choose my next destination—and I was okay with that. I took one last look at the planet Earth, shining in the blackness of space above the moon's horizon.

We are meant to see the earth from this vantage point. It's our destiny. It's our purpose. After all, "those who study the stars have God for a teacher." We are meant to someday reach the farthest corner of the infinite universe, and to look back in wonder upon God's magnificent creation. [53]

My father had once read me a passage from a book by astronaut Eugene Cernan, the last man to stand on the surface of the moon. I remembered it: "Too many years have passed for me to still be the last man to have walked on the moon. Somewhere on Earth today is the young girl or boy, the possessor of indomitable will and courage, who will lift that dubious honor from me and take us back where we belong." [54]

After the Apollo 11 mission, astronaut Michael Collins said something similar. He said: "Someday in the not-too-distant future, when I listen to an earthling step out onto the surface of Mars or some other planet, just as I listened to Neil step out onto the surface of the moon, I hope I hear him say: 'I come from the United States of America.'" [55]

I hope to hear the same thing . . . someday.

"Either a man is an American and nothing else, or he is not an American at all."

THEODORE ROOSEVELT (1858–1919),
WRITER, EXPLORER, SOLDIER,
AND 26TH PRESIDENT OF THE UNITED STATES

CHAPTER 3

TO AMERICA I WILL GO ⚓

PART ONE

THE ISLAND OF TEARS

Just before the ship left the port of Naples, Italy, the women passengers tossed balls of yarn over the ship's railing. The women passengers clung tightly to their end of the yarn as the balls unraveled and reached the people on the dock. As the ship pulled out to sea, hundreds of colorful balls of yarn unwound as people cried and shouted goodbyes to family and friends they would never see again. The long, delicate strands of yarn were the last physical connection between the people on the ship and the people on the shore—and the fragile physical connection would last only a few seconds more. The 2,175 people on board the SS *Konig Albert* were bound for America—and a new life.[1]

I was on the SS *Konig Albert*, too. The date was August 23, 1907.

I watched the balls of yarn slowly unravel and then run out. Finally, the people on the dock had to let go. The long strands of yarn were airborne. The women on the ship still gripped their end, but the far ends fluttered in the wind. It seemed to me that the strands of yarn waved final goodbyes from the people on the ship. The ocean breeze responded by carrying the hopeful prayers of the people left behind—prayers that the ancient Italian proverb would be proven true: "Chi esce riesce [He who leaves, succeeds]."

That is the only good memory I have of the fourteen-day voyage by steamship across the Atlantic Ocean in 1907. The rest of the trip was awful. Like most of the immigrants on board the SS *Konig Albert,* I spent a lot of the trip trapped three decks below sea level in the steerage compartment—hungry, thirsty, dirty, tired, seasick, and throwing up.

It was almost impossible to breathe in the steerage compartment: The air was foul—engine fumes and smoke; sweaty, filthy bodies; and the stink of an outhouse. I couldn't sleep much: The beds in steerage were lumpy sacks of straw that poked me. Underneath them were hard and narrow wooden shelves. I was always thirsty. We almost never had fresh water in steerage. When we had water, it was cloudy and had a metallic odor. I just couldn't drink it. And I was always hungry, because I was afraid to eat the food for third-class passengers: The meat, bread, and cheese usually had bits of green mold on them. The pickled fish wasn't rotten, but it tasted terrible.

The only way to escape the miserable environment of the ship's steerage compartment was to go up to the top deck and sit outside. But that's what everyone did, so there wasn't always a lot of room up there. It could get crowded on the top deck. I went topside whenever I could, though, even in pouring rain and freezing cold. I would roll myself up in a ball under an old blanket and put up with the unpleasant weather. At least while I was on the top deck, I could breathe.[2]

As bad as the steerage conditions were, most of the passengers didn't complain. They were too busy worrying that the ship would sink. It was easy to see why they worried. In good weather, the ship rocked from side to side so much that the wood planks in the deck creaked and made popping sounds, and it was hard to walk without falling down or bumping into something. In bad weather, the ship leaned over so far that the deck railings touched the waves, and water washed over the upper decks. During a storm, the only thing you could do was to sit on the crowded and dirty floor in steerage, hold on to the other passengers for balance, and pray that freezing cold ocean water wasn't on it's way down the stairwells to drown you. Of course, drowning would at least have been an end to the torture of traveling in steerage. It was no wonder that the Italians referred to traveling to America by steamship as "via dolorosa [the sorrowful way]."

The Italian immigrants in steerage sang a sad song during the worst times on the ship. The song was about a young girl who asks her mother for a hundred lire [dollars], so she can go to America. Her mother doesn't want her to go to America, because she is afraid of what might happen to her daughter in the strange and distant land. But the girl goes anyway, and then dies when her boat sinks in the Atlantic Ocean and a large fish eats her. The song was called *To America I Will Go,* and it went like this:

Mamma mia dammi cento lire,
che in America voglio andar!
Cento lire io te le do,
ma in America. No! No! No!

[Momma, give me a hundred lire,
And to America I will go!
Daughter, I will give you a hundred lire,
But to America you will go? No! No! No!]

The sad atmosphere on board the SS *Konig Albert* ended on the morning of September 5. That morning, I woke up to the sound of excited voices. It felt like there was electricity in the air!

"L'America!" I heard people say as if it were a magic word. "L'America!"

First, they whispered it, and soon after, they shouted it. Then suddenly, everyone around me got up at once and rushed for the stairs. I was swept up by the mob and carried all the way to the upper deck of the ship—I don't think my feet ever touched the floor!

Topside, it was very foggy. The sun was a pale disk floating above the ship in a spooky gray mist. The fog was so thick that, other than the sun, I couldn't see anything beyond the railing of the ship, not even the water. But I squinted as hard as I could into the fog—in the direction that everyone else was looking—and I waited. And I waited. The fog broke. And then, finally, I saw what everyone had been waiting to see, slowly appear out of the gloom—first, a torch, and then, a crown.

RIGHT:
IMMIGRANTS CATCH THEIR FIRST GLIMPSE OF THE STATUE OF LIBERTY AS THEIR STEAMSHIP ENTERS NEW YORK HARBOR. Date: 1915.
© The Mariners Museum/CORBIS

ARRIVING AT ELLIS ISLAND

LEFT:
IMMIGRANTS ARRIVE AT THE ELLIS ISLAND FEDERAL IMMIGRATION STATION. Date: 1900.
© CORBIS

RIGHT:
A HEALTH OFFICER EXAMINES IMMIGRANT CHILDREN ARRIVING FROM THE ELLIS ISLAND FEDERAL IMMIGRATION STATION. Location: Battery Park, New York. Date: 1911.
© Bettmann/CORBIS

A loud cheer went up among the immigrants on the deck: "L'America! L'America!"

Families hugged and kissed each other as the Statue of Liberty broke through the gray mist and came into view, and the SS *Konig Albert* chugged into New York Harbor. It was a moment of renewed hope, a time to look forward, instead of back. The miserable ocean voyage was finally over. The immigrants had passed the first test. There was just one more trial to endure, and it would come at the next stop: Ellis Island, a place the Italians called "Isola Della Lacrime [The Island of Tears]."³

When I stepped off the ship's gangplank and onto Ellis Island, someone pinned a paper tag on the front of my coat. The tag had a number on it that matched me to the SS *Konig Albert*'s passenger manifest. Then, I had to stand in line with the other tagged passengers, and wait to go inside a large brick building. So, I became the

number on my coat and took my place in line. There were hundreds of people in front of me, and hundreds of people behind me. Men hung on to luggage. Mothers hung on to children. I stood there for a long time—how long, I don't remember—until the line of people finally began inching its way toward the door to America.

Once inside the brick building's front doors, I saw that the line turned to the right and made its way up a flight of concrete stairs. Standing at the top of the stairs, and in the hallways, were men and women who looked like doctors and nurses. They poked and prodded everyone in line, looking at their teeth and hair and eyes. They made all the children being carried prove that they could walk. The doctors had chalk in their hands, and every so often, they would use the chalk to write a letter on a person's clothing. I saw people marked with the letters *H* and *X* and *F* and *L* and *E*.

I don't think that an *X* or an *E* chalk mark was a good thing to get. I saw a mother get an *X* and an *E* drawn on her coat, just before she was pulled from the line. She broke into tears and her children

began to cry—a boy and a girl, each around my age, I guessed. Then the woman's husband wrote something on the paper tags of the two children, hugged them, and stepped out of the line to join his wife. The couple disappeared into a small room with a doctor. I never saw them or their children again, and I have wondered what happened to them.[4]

When I finally reached the top of the stairs, a doctor felt my neck and looked into my ears and my mouth. Then he told me to walk a little farther down the hallway, where another doctor lifted both of my eyelids with a metal buttonhook. That hurt! But I didn't get a chalk mark put on me, and I was told to go down a narrow corridor.[5]

At the end of the hall, I found myself in a huge room with a ceiling that was at least three stories high. The room was packed with tired men and women, crying children, and beat-up luggage. In the center of the room, there were rows of narrow, iron benches that looked uncomfortable. At the edges of the room, there were dozens of winding queues, formed by black railing made from iron pipes. At the end of each queue, there was a uniformed immigration officer asking questions and filling out forms. On the far wall of the room, there was a giant American flag. I noticed that the flag had only forty-five stars.[6]

The gymnasium-sized room was very noisy—it echoed with a cacophony of languages. Hearing so many languages spoken in one room reminded me of the story of the Tower of Babel. I was sure that no one understood anyone else. The immigration officers asked questions, mostly in English, but the new arrivals answered in their own languages. Translators ran around, alternating between speaking English and the languages of the immigrants.

When I concentrated hard, I could pick out some of the questions that the immigration officers were asking: "Do you speak English? What is your name? What is your age? Are you married? What kind of work do you do? Who paid for your passage? Is anyone waiting to meet you? Are you able to read? Are you able to write? How much money is in your possession? Have you ever been in the United States before? Where are you from? What is your destination?"[7]

I wasn't sure what to do next, so I sat down on one of the metal benches in the middle of the room. I sat next to a man who seemed to be traveling with a young woman and two small boys. I decided that I would tag along with them, perhaps even "blend in" and become a part of their group.

Three hours went by, so I thought my adopted immigrant family had been forgotten. But then, an immigration officer came by and motioned them toward one of the queues at the end of the room. I followed them into the queue and stuck close to them as they slowly wound their way toward the head of the line. Finally, they went before a tall immigration officer in a dark blue uniform standing behind a desk. I listened as the officer questioned them.

"C'e qualcuno qui che parla inglese? [Is there anyone here who speaks English?]," the immigration officer asked.

"Si, Yes. I speak English," the man in front of me replied. "I am Liborio Nobile of Vico Equense. This is my son, Lazerio. This is my niece, Maria Savarese. And this is my nephew, Antonio Gaetano."[8]

The hairs on the back of my neck stood up.

Antonio Gaetano? I know that name! Antonio Gaetano is the name of my great-grandfather! Did the Picture Frame put me on the SS Konig Albert so that I would meet my great-grandfather?

I peered around Liborio, and looked closely at the two boys traveling with him. I knew which one was Antonio right away. Antonio was the older boy, and there could be no doubt that he was my great-grandfather. He looked just like me! He was my height, he had my eyes, my hair, my face, my hands—he was my double, in immigrant clothing!

I said hello.

"Buon giorno [Good afternoon]," replied my ten-year-old great-grandfather.

His eyes sparkled, but his mouth formed a crooked, almost mischievous smile. Then he stared straight into my eyes, and gave me a nod. It seemed like a nod of recognition, as if my great-grandfather had said, "I know who you are." I knew that wasn't possible, but even to this day, I have the feeling that he knew who I was from the very start. Sometimes, I think that my great-grandfather was even expecting me.

When the immigration officer finished questioning Liborio, he motioned for all of us to proceed to a staircase behind him. The final test had been passed, and America was waiting, down those stairs.[9]

I was part of Liborio's family, it seemed, so I helped them pick up their few belongings and walked with them down the stairs. We boarded a ferry and took a short ride to the southern tip of Manhattan. No one on the ferry spoke. It seemed that everyone was content to make the final leg of the journey to America in silence. Even the babies were quiet.

But there was a large, noisy crowd of people waiting for us at the dock in Manhattan. And as soon as we stepped off the ferry, a man jumped out of the crowd and ran toward us. He reached Liborio first and shook his hand until I thought it would fall off. Then he kissed

Maria, patted Lazerio on the head, and picked up Antonio and gave him a big hug.

"Welcome to America!" the man shouted. "Come sta [How are you]?"

"Molto bene. Grazie [Very well. Thanks], Francesco," Liborio replied. "E lei [And you]?"

"Bene [Fine]," the man said.

I knew right away that the man was Antonio's father—my great-great-grandfather, Francesco! He had sent for his son in Italy to join him in America.

Liborio, Francesco, Maria, Lazerio, Antonio, and I left the dock, and walked together into the heart of New York City. As we walked those streets in 1907, I realized that what lay ahead was completely unknown to me. I began to appreciate the risk that the immigrants on board the SS *Konig Albert* had taken in their journey to America. Many had sold every earthly possession for their one-way ticket across the Atlantic. Those who were denied entry to the United States would be sent back to their home country to face poverty for sure, and possibly, humiliation. Those who were admitted to the United States faced an uncertain future. In my own time, it would be like going to the moon, with no guarantee that your spacesuit would protect you once you got there, and no fuel for a return trip to Earth if something went wrong.

Why would anyone do this?

"I came to America because I heard that the streets were paved with gold," my great-great-grandfather Francesco suddenly said, as if he were reading my mind. "But when I got here, I found out three things: First, the streets weren't paved with gold; second, they weren't paved at all; and third, I was expected to pave them."[10]

Then Francesco stopped walking, turned, and looked right at me. And with obvious joy, he said, "That third thing? That was the best news of all!"

My great-great-grandfather Francesco had come to America for the same reason that most immigrants had come—to find work.

At the turn of the 20th century, Italy's economy was based mostly on agriculture, with a lot of the land owned by Italian nobility. Millions of Italians were sharecroppers who had to give half of their crops to the landowners. High government taxes took most of the rest. Outside of farming, there were very few jobs, and even fewer that paid well. Francesco knew that because he was born into Italy's lower economic class, if he stayed in Italy he would probably remain poor all his life. So like millions of other Italians, he boarded a steamship and sailed for America. He traded his poverty in Italy for a new kind of poverty in America—"poverty with opportunity."

In America, Francesco found work as a day laborer and as a mechanic, but it wasn't an easy life. The work was backbreaking, the hours were long, and Francesco had to endure terrible discrimination. Francesco was always paid less for his work, just because he was an Italian immigrant. He took the jobs and worked hard, though, even when the people hiring him called him a "Wop" or a "Dago."[11]

Underneath the hardships that Francesco and the other immigrants faced, the forces of freedom and capitalism worked quietly. Slowly, but surely, Francesco and the other immigrants turned opportunity into achievement, and poverty into wealth. I could see it happening. I could feel it happening. I told Antonio I could even "smell it" happening. Antonio laughed and said that all he could smell was the horse manure stuck in New York's cobblestone streets.

Antonio had a point, but sometimes, you couldn't help but notice the wonderful smells, too: warm, fresh bread and pastries at the corner bakery; sweet grapes and ripe tomatoes and crisp apples at the fruit stand; hot roasted chestnuts in the street vendor's pushcart; fresh fish, clams, and crabs at the waterfront market; roses and daffodils at the flower shop. And there was my favorite—the mouth-watering smell of Italian sauces drifting out of neighborhood restaurant windows. They were all the delicious smells of new American businesses.[12]

Francesco's economic situation slowly improved. Each month, he even managed to send some money to his wife—my great-great-grandmother—and family in Italy. His plan was to send them enough money to buy tickets for passage to America. Antonio and I used to walk with him to the Banco di Napoli at 526 Broadway, where he purchased the money orders that he sent to my great-great-grandmother.

Antonio's older sister, Patrizia, was the next to come to America. Francesco sent for her next, because he knew he would need her to take care of the household in the United States. It was August 17, 1910, a really hot and sticky summer day, when Patrizia came off the ferry from Ellis Island. Patrizia was fifteen years old, and she had made the transatlantic trip alone. I remember that it was a hot day, because Antonio, Patrizia, and I slept on the fire escape the first night she was in America. It was too hot to sleep in Francesco's apartment.[13]

Antonio's younger sister, Amelia, arrived in the United States on May 3, 1912. She came with Liborio Nobile, who was returning from

VIEW OF MULBERRY STREET IN THE LITTLE ITALY SECTION OF NEW YORK CITY.
Date: 1900.
© CORBIS

his third trip to Italy. Liborio also brought his wife and children. I remember shuddering in horror at the dock, because Amelia said she had sailed on the same ship Antonio and I had sailed on five years earlier, the SS *Konig Albert*. I knew that it must have been miserable for her.[14]

Antonio's job in America was to go to school, and it was not an easy task. The family lived in "Hell's Kitchen," a rough area of New York City. Hell's Kitchen was a place where America didn't seem to exist at all. Every street seemed to be a different nation, ruled by gangs. An innocent turn down the wrong street could put you in some unfriendly territory. I was certain we were risking our lives every day when Antonio and I walked together to the public elementary school, over on 109th Street and 3rd Avenue. Gang members preyed upon kids walking to school, and sometimes they waited for Antonio. They challenged him to fights, and stole his lunch and any money he had on him. But as Antonio got older, he got tougher, and he learned how to defend himself. Eventually he earned a reputation in the neighborhood for "not taking it." Only then, did the "street toughs" leave Antonio alone. A few even moved to the other side of the street when they saw him coming. But even then, we always had to avoid certain streets.[15]

Life inside the public school was not easy for Antonio, either. He had to study hard. The school's goal was to "Americanize" him as quickly as possible. His teachers expected him to master the language of America, so every subject was taught in English only. His teachers also spent a lot of time teaching American history and civics. They told Antonio how the government of the United States worked, and the duties it would one day expect of him as a citizen. It was at those times in the classroom, that Antonio would lean over to my desk and say, "When I am in school, I am in America. When I am home, I am in Italy. In between there are many countries." It seemed that way, sometimes.

After school, Antonio was always finding ways for us to make money. He knew a baker who would sometimes give us a basket of day-old bread to sell on the street. We used the money we made to buy treats for ourselves. We didn't make much money, usually just enough to share a small pizza from Gennaro Lombardi's store on Spring Street, or a couple of Sfogliatella Napoletana from Caffé A. Ferrara on Grand.[16]

The pizza, by the way, was the best I have ever tasted. It was not at all like the pizza in my own time, which is mostly a saucy mess of cheese and toppings, piled sky-high on doughy, tasteless bread.

No, the pizza back then was much simpler, and yet, far better! I'll never forget the wonderful flavors of fresh tomatoes, fragrant basil, pungent garlic, golden olive oil, and bubbling-hot buffalo mozzarella cheese. Put all that on charcoal-oven crisped bread and it's like heaven in your mouth! The pizza alone was worth the trip through ninety-seven years![17]

Antonio graduated from elementary school on January 31, 1913. I remember the date, because all the kids brought little blue books to school that day, and wrote graduation wishes in them for each other. Some of the things written in Antonio's book were funny. But Antonio insisted that I look at one entry in particular:

January 31, 1913.
To Antonio:
Remember the future; remember the past.
Remember the fun in Mr. Norman's class.
From your classmate,
James Stabile.[18]

Antonio had some money in his pocket that day, so after the graduation ceremony, we spent it on pizza. We sat on the curb outside the restaurant. We were content to watch the street vendors with their pushcarts go by while we ate. I picked up Antonio's graduation wish book, and looked one more time at the entry made by James Stabile.

"But it doesn't make any sense, Antonio." I said. "How can you possibly 'remember the future?'"

Antonio didn't answer me. He just gave me that mischievous smile of his, and continued to chew on his pizza.

PART TWO
THE GREAT WAR

World War I began in Europe in August 1914. Called "The Great War" by people at the time, it involved more than a dozen nations around the world. The war pitted the Central Powers of Germany, Austria-Hungary, Bulgaria, and Turkey, against the Allied Powers of Great Britain, France, Russia, Belgium, Canada, Australia, and others. Italy entered the war on the side of the Allied Powers after signing the Treaty of London on April 26, 1915. The United States entered the war on the side of the Allied Powers two years later on April 4, 1917.

People in Europe thought The Great War would be over in a few months, maybe even by Christmas 1914. Young men rushed to enlist, fearing that the war would be over before they got a chance to fight.

Everyone expected quick victory.

Everyone was wrong.

When the enormous armies clashed on the open fields of Europe, a new invention—the machine gun—mowed down the advancing soldiers. A hundred thousand would die in a single battle, and not an inch of ground would be won. To avoid total destruction, the armies dug trenches and went underground. The Great War soon became a deadly stalemate, with millions of soldiers dug deeply into trenches hundreds of miles long. Often separated by only a few hundred yards, soldiers in opposing trenches could hear their enemies talking, but the "No Man's Land" between the trenches remained an uncrossable killing field.

I saw trench warfare in 1917. I was in the trenches with the Italian Army, near the Isonzo River, on the Austrian front.[19]

October 1917
The Battle of Caporetto

It was 2:00 A.M., on October 24, when the battle began. It began silently in darkness. The soldiers around me suddenly fell to their knees, choking and gasping for breath, and clawing at the muddy earth floor of the trench. They screamed that they were blinded, and that their skin was on fire. The Austrians had launched an attack with poison gas.

Two hours later, word came down the line that every man in the Italian 87th Regiment had been killed by the poison gas. The soldiers near me had experienced only a small bit of the gas—they were the lucky ones who'd survived.

At dawn, the shelling began. It started with a whistling sound in the sky, followed by a thunderous explosion that shook my bones. The earth and sky seemed to blend—to become one. Rocks and dirt rained down on top of me and the soldiers in the trench. One soldier farther down the line was killed and simultaneously buried by falling rock. It was just the beginning of the Austrian artillery assault on the Italian frontline positions along the Isonzo River. When I heard another whistle in the sky, I dove down into the mud. I pressed myself into the earth. I tried to make myself invisible.

"If you hear the whistle you will be all right," a soldier next to me said. "You won't hear the shell with your name on it."

I recognized the voice right away. It was Antonio! The last place I had seen him was in New York City. We had been sharing a pizza.

So, this is why I am here! But why is Antonio here? How did he end up in the Italian Army trenches during World War I?

"The family needed money," Antonio told me, shrugging his shoulders. "I had to drop out of high school to find work. Then my father decided to visit family in Italy and I went with him. In Naples, I joined the Italian Merchant Marines. I always loved the sea. I sailed on the Naples-to-New York route for a year."[20]

But in April 1917, Antonio said, Italy needed more men for its war effort. As Antonio's ship prepared to leave Naples on another run to the United States, the Italian authorities boarded it. They were looking for able-bodied men to draft. Two weeks later, Antonio wore the uniform of the Italian Army.

"I accepted my fate," Antonio said. "But I volunteered for the Reparti d'Assalto. That was my choice."

The Reparti d'Assalto were elite Italian Army "assault troops," trained for the most dangerous assignments. People called the soldiers in the Reparti d'Assalto the "Arditi," meaning the "bold ones." The Arditi moved secretly and fast, and were heavily armed. They were experts in hand-to-hand combat and had a reputation for taking risks, but not for taking prisoners—not alive, anyway. When they were known to be on the front lines, the Arditi struck fear in the hearts of enemy soldiers on the other side of No Man's Land. The Arditi even worried officers in the Italian Army, because they were notoriously difficult to control and manage. Many of the Arditi showed very little respect for authority.[21]

The Arditi led the counterattack against the Austrians and Germans that day. I watched as Antonio and the other Arditi soldiers lined up and prepared for combat. They armed themselves with wire cutters, hand grenades, rifles, and daggers. Their objective was to capture the Austrian trench, two hundred yards on the other side of No Man's Land. It took the Arditi only minutes to get ready, and then they signaled that they were ready to go.

On the signal from the Arditi, the Italian Army artillery units opened fire on the Austrian trench. They fired round after round without stopping. The ground trembled and shook from the exploding shells that fell only two hundred yards away from me. Echoes

RIGHT:
ITALIAN SOLDIERS IN THEIR TRENCH ON THE AUSTRIAN FRONT DURING WORLD WAR I. Date: 1917. Visible: Italian Army standard-issue bolt-action Moschetto Model 1891 rifles, ammunition pouches on the soldiers' belts, and the trademark dagger carried by the Arditi.
© Bettmann/CORBIS

THE 19th REPARTI D'ASSALTO, 1st COMPAGNIA, III ARMATA, AT THEIR TRAINING BASE
IN NORTHERN ITALY. Location: Sdricca di Manzano or Borgnano, Italy. Date: 1917.
Antonio Gaetano is seated in the middle row, third from the right.
© Magic Picture Frame Studio, LLC

of one explosion after another rumbled through the surrounding mountains like thunder. My eardrums ached from the pounding concussion of the big guns behind me. The purpose of it all was to keep the Austrian soldiers pinned down in their trench. Artillery fire rarely killed enemy soldiers because they could hide in underground rooms in their trench. But forcing the Austrians to remain hidden, and to keep their heads down, would make them blind to the coming Arditi attack.

As the Italian artillery shells whistled overhead, I heard Antonio say a prayer and make the sign of the cross. He looked at me and said: "There are no atheists in the trenches." I nodded in agreement. Then Antonio climbed the wall of the trench and waited for the command to go over the top. "I will see you in a couple of hours," he shouted to me over the sounds of the artillery bombardment, ". . . if I am one of the lucky ones to come back."

When the command to attack was given, Antonio and the other Arditi soldiers raised their fists into the air and yelled in unison: "A chi l'onore [Who deserves the glory]? A noi [We do]!" Then, they scrambled over the parapet and into No Man's Land.

"Theirs not to reason why, theirs but to do and die . . ." [22]

I watched as the Arditi crawled on their bellies through No Man's Land. They slithered like snakes underneath tangles of barbed wire, through bomb craters, and past dead bodies and debris. Closer and closer, they crawled to the Austrian trench, moving forward under the cover of the constant artillery fire. When they came within a few yards of the edge of the enemy trench, their own shells were exploding all around them.

Antonio held up his hand, signaling the Italian artillery bombardment to cease. When the bombs stopped falling, the Arditi took hand grenades from their belts and tossed them into the enemy trench, forcing their enemy to stay under cover and to keep their heads down for a few seconds more. Then, the Arditi unsheathed their daggers and slipped into the enemy trench.

The whole area got quiet. It was eerie.

An hour later, I saw Antonio emerge from the Austrian trench. He didn't crawl; he raced back toward the Italian line. He ran through No Man's Land in a zigzag pattern, splashing through mud and puddles, and leaping over coils of barbed wire and debris. When he reached the Italian trench, he dove head first over the parapet, just as Austrian machine gun fire erupted, kicking up bits of rock and earth at his feet. I ducked down.

Antonio picked himself up off the muddy trench floor, clutched his chest, and strained to catch his breath. Many of his friends didn't make it back. Antonio was one of the lucky ones.

"I . . . will . . . survive . . . this," Antonio said, breathing heavily and coughing out his words. "To America . . . I will go." [23]

Christmas Eve 1917
Near the Piave River on the Austrian Front

After a while on the front lines, you don't hear the shelling; you hear the silence when the shelling stops. The shelling stopped on Christmas Eve.

It was a clear night. There was only one wisp of a white cloud in the dark sky. Antonio and I watched the cloud drift across the face of the full moon. The battlefield had been quiet all evening. But then, at about midnight, we heard singing. The singing was low at first, but gradually grew louder. It was the Austrians singing in their trench. Their voices floated on the cold night air, unmistakable even from two hundred yards away, across No Man's Land. I didn't have to understand the words to recognize the song.

Stille Nacht! Heilige Nacht!
Alles schlaft; einsam wacht
Nur das traute heilige Paar.
Holder Knab' im lockigten Haar,
Schlafe in himmlischer Ruh!
Schlafe in himmlischer Ruh!

[Silent Night! Holy Night!
All is calm; all is bright
Round yon Godly tender pair.
Holy infant with curly hair,
Sleep in Heavenly peace!
Sleep in Heavenly peace!]

I sang the carol softly in English, against the background chorus of Austrian voices. Antonio looked at me and asked what the name of the song was. It was the first time he had ever heard the song, *Silent Night.* [24]

May 13, 1918
Near the Piave River on the Austrian Front

Antonio and some other soldiers spent the day playing cards. There wasn't any action on the front. Antonio and his friends weren't playing Poker, their usual game. They played Scopa, I think. I knew when the Arditi soldiers were playing poker, because they would always stick their daggers into the ground in front of them during the game. The daggers reminded them of the price of cheating. I didn't see any daggers at the game.[25]

"Chi tocca [Whose turn]?"
"Tocca me [My turn]?"
"Tocca te [Your turn]."

It was Antonio's turn, but he left the card game and went off by himself. He wrote a postcard to his sister in America.

War Zone, 5-13-18.
From the frontier;
Send you my best Easter Greetings.
Your loving brother,
Antonio.[26]

July 1918
Near the Piave River on the Austrian Front

The U.S. Army's 332nd Infantry Regiment, 83rd Division, arrived at the front with medicine and supplies. They mostly came to train in the harsh mountain conditions of northeastern Italy, but their presence was also meant to create the impression that the Italians and Americans planned a joint offensive into Austrian territory. The trick kept the Austrians laying low.[27]

Antonio spent the month serving as a translator for the American troops, because he spoke excellent English and Italian. He had

LEFT:
BERSAGLIERI CAPORALE ANTONIO GAETANO OF THE 19th REPARTI D'ASSALTO, 1st COMPAGNIA, III ARMATA. Location: A portrait studio in a town near the Austrian Front. Date: 1918. Visible: The Italian Ribbon of Valor above the left breast pocket, the Italian Army five-pointed silver stars on the uniform collars, the crimson flame patches that signify the Arditi unit was composed of soldiers from the Bersaglieri [light infantry regiments], and the Italian Army standard-issue gray-green puttees [leggings]. The plume of cockerel feathers on the right side of the steel helmet is the trademark of the Bersaglieri; the feathers represent bravery. Antonio Gaetano's left hand rests on the handle of his trademark Arditi dagger.
© Magic Picture Frame Studio, LLC

learned English in school in the United States. Antonio also accompanied the Americans on reconnaissance missions into enemy territory. For me, speaking English was a blessing; I hadn't heard English spoken in such a long time that it almost seemed strange to me.

November 11, 1918
The Great War Ends

The day the war ended, Antonio lay in a hospital bed, nearly unconscious from fever. He had contracted malaria from the mosquitoes that swarmed in the wet trenches and on the riverbanks during the late summer and early autumn. I was with Antonio in the Italian army hospital in Treviso, Italy, near the Piave River and the Austrian Front. The medics had carried him out of heavy fighting during the Vittorio-Veneto offensive that began on October 24. In the hospital, Antonio was being treated for his malaria with quinine.[28]

I was glad that the war was over. The horrible, bloody war was waged for nothing more than territory and power and pride. The Great War wasted a generation of young men.[29]

I told Antonio that the war was over, but because of his high fever, I wasn't sure that he had heard me. He had been delirious for hours. But then he looked up at me and whispered: "I . . . will . . . survive . . . this. To America . . . I will go."

PART THREE
THE GREAT DEPRESSION

My great-grandfather returned to the United States on December 2, 1920. It was the second time that he walked through the doors of the Ellis Island Federal Immigration Station, but it was the first time that he did so by his own choice. He moved in with his older sister, Patrizia, and her husband, Girdamo Pellegrino, who were living at 322 East 116th Street in Harlem. I caught up with my great-grandfather about a month after his return to America, in mid-January 1921.[30]

"I need to find a job," my twenty-three-year-old great-grandfather said to me.

I heard him, but I wasn't paying much attention. I was too busy putting nickels into slots, and turning knobs to get a hot plate of baked macaroni and cheese, a glass of chocolate milk, an apple, and some oatmeal cookies. We were having lunch at the Automat in Times Square.[31]

dinner afterward. We ate the most amazing Italian food. Everyone was happy, and everyone danced. It was a great celebration. But Antonio got that worried look on his face again toward the end of the evening.

"I need to find a better job," Antonio told me, before he and Mary left the reception. "I want to make more money so I can raise a family and buy a house."

A few months later, Antonio landed a job as a salesman for Consolidated Edison, the electric company in New York. He was given a small office in the corner of the Consolidated Edison showroom in the Bronx. Antonio's job was to demonstrate and sell lamps, toasters, and other electric household appliances. He offered special low prices to Con Ed's customers because the appliances would increase their consumption of electricity.

I remember the excitement of my great-grandfather's first day on the job at Con Edison. My great-grandfather wore a brand new suit of clothes and a straw hat. He bought me a straw hat for the occasion, too. Mary, my great-grandmother, took our photograph.

In 1927, everything was going great and the future looked bright. No one expected that the good times would end just two years later.

....

1929

The good times ended abruptly on Thursday afternoon, October 24, 1929. My great-grandfather came home from work early and tossed a newspaper on the kitchen table.

"The whole world changed today," he said.

I looked at the front page of the newspaper. The headline screamed: "PRICES OF STOCKS CRASH IN HEAVY LIQUIDATION, TOTAL DROP OF BILLIONS: PAPER LOSS $4,000,000,000. MANY ACCOUNTS WIPED OUT . . ."[37]

In a single day, the rich had become poor, and the poor had become destitute.

1930

Money was hard to come by. People stopped buying things and neighborhood stores closed. Factories cut back on production and fired workers. People who used to have jobs stood on street corners selling apples for five cents apiece. The newspapers said that one out of every ten Americans was out of work.

Antonio still had his job at Con Edison, but the pressures of providing for the family were mounting. His first child, Frank, was two years old and another mouth to feed. Antonio's father, Francesco, and his younger sister, Amelia, lived in the house, too. Francesco still had his job as a mechanic, but there were rumors that the factory where he worked would close soon. Amelia had a job at the embroidery shop, but business had slowed to almost nothing. Mary didn't work outside the home. She was busy taking care of Frank and doing housework and laundry and making meals.[38]

1931

Francesco lost his job in March. He looked for work for several months but couldn't find anyone who would hire him. The newspapers said that the unemployment rate had risen to 15 percent.

We heard stories of "food riots" going on in other cities. People said that angry mobs would throw bricks through the glass windows of grocery stores and then steal the food. I never saw anything like that happen, but the stories were on my mind because Francesco opened a small bakery in September. He hoped to make some money by selling fresh bread to people in the neighborhood.

We also watched the Empire State Building get taller every day. It was sadly ironic to see 3,000 construction workers on the project race toward unemployment at the rate of two floors a week, but that's what they were doing. When the building was completed on May 1, Antonio and I went to the dedication. New York Governor Franklin Delano Roosevelt was there, giving a speech. Antonio and I rode the elevator to the top of the building and looked out over the city. It was a spectacular view. The hard times below were invisible from the observation deck of the tallest building in the world.[39]

1932

No one thought the stock market could go any lower, but it did. Many stocks became worthless. No one thought the unemployment rate could get any higher, but it did. One out of every four Americans

ANTONIO GAETANO: ITALIAN IMMIGRANT, WORLD WAR I
VETERAN, AND AMERICAN BUSINESSMAN IN BROOKLYN,
NEW YORK. Date: 1927.
© Magic Picture Frame Studio, LLC

was out of work. The family's embroidery shop closed. I don't know if 1932 was the worst year of the Great Depression or not, but it sure felt like it.

In July, 20,000 World War I veterans marched on the capitol in Washington, D.C., demanding that their pensions and bonuses be paid early. The veterans said that they had lost all of their savings in the stock market crash of 1929. Congress deliberated, but then refused to pay the bonuses early. It got ugly when the U.S. Army forced the protestors out of town at gunpoint. The soldiers even burned down the ramshackle "Hooverville" that the veterans and their families were living in, on the outskirts of town. [40]

On the radio, Bing Crosby sang: *Brother Can You Spare a Dime?* It was the question everyone was asking.

When my great-grandfather and I walked past the Automat in Times Square, we always peered through the windows to see who was inside. The Automat was never empty, but even dining on nickels had become a luxury. "Now, the rich eat here," my great-grandfather would say.

Down the street from the Automat, there was usually a breadline—one of many in the city. Hundreds of hungry people stood in the long, winding line, waiting for a free piece of bread, a free cup of coffee, or a free a bowl of soup.

We weren't hungry because my great-grandfather still had his job at Con Edison. But money was tight, and my great-grandmother Mary had to make cheap meals. She would feed the whole family with a soup made from just green leafy escarole and dried cannellini beans. Along with a loaf of bread from Francesco's bakery, we considered the soup to be a complete dinner. It filled me up pretty well. Breakfast was usually simple and cheap, too, just a bowl of hot wheat farina with a raw egg mixed in and a slice of toast.

Sunday was the only day my great-grandfather splurged on food. Every Sunday after church, he invited the entire family to his house and served them a late afternoon dinner. It was a simple meal, usually just spaghetti and meatballs and sausage, but there was a lot of it! And in the summer months, my great-grandfather would sometimes add fresh Maryland Blue Crabs to the sauce. Mmm, mmm, that was my favorite!

1933

On the evening of March 12, my great-grandfather and I were in the living room, listening to music on the radio. An announcement said that the President of the United States wanted to talk to the American people. We got the rest of the family together and listened to the President's speech.

"I want to talk for a few minutes with the people of the United States about banking," President Franklin Delano Roosevelt said. "I want to tell you what has been done in the last few days, why it was done, and what the next steps are going to be." [41]

The president explained that he had closed all the banks in the country. He did it because, in a panic, bank depositors had rushed to their local banks and demanded all of their money; the people were afraid that the banks would fail, and that all of their money would be lost. But the rush on the banks, the president said, had just made things worse. Banks loan depositors' money to businesses and to other people, so the money is not really just sitting in a vault waiting to be withdrawn. When too many people suddenly demand their money back, the president explained, banks can run out of money to give them, and be forced to sell their assets at rock-bottom prices to meet the demand. To stop the potential destruction of the U.S. banking system, the president had temporarily closed the banks by declaring a national "bank holiday." Then he had asked Congress to find a way to reopen the banks with an assurance that depositor's money would be there if they still wanted it. Some banks, the president said, were already starting to reopen. The rest just needed more time.

"People will again be glad to have their money where it will be safely taken care of and where they can use it conveniently at any time," President Roosevelt promised. "I can assure you that it is safer to keep your money in a reopened bank than under the mattress." [42]

President Roosevelt had a way of talking to people and explaining things that always inspired optimism. But still, the best medicine for the hard times was temporary escape. The next night, my great-grandfather and I went to the movies to see King Kong climb the Empire State Building. [43]

1934

Surprising everyone, my great-grandfather's younger brother, Roland, showed up for dinner on August 4, 1934. No one was expecting Roland for dinner because the last anyone had heard, Roland was living in Italy. Roland said he had to leave Italy because the Great Depression was worse in Europe than in the United States.

1935

My father's father was born, my father's mother was born, and Boulder Dam was completed. Other than that, it was a terrible year.[44]

1936

My great-great-grandfather Francesco returned to Italy, and Antonio and Roland took over the bakery. The two brothers decided to expand their father's business by converting the bakery into an Italian and American grocery store. The excitement of starting the new business was a bright spot during the hard times.

I saw the faces of the hard times when the newspapers published some photographs of migrant workers on the west coast. I remember one photo particularly. It was a photograph of a migrant woman with her hand on her chin, while her two children clutched her, but looked away from the camera. The mother's eyes seemed to say: "I am suffering, but I persevere."[45]

1937

One Tuesday morning, a woman spent more than half an hour shopping in my great-grandfather's grocery store, but when she came to the cash register all she put on the counter was a can of beans and two pears.

"Is that all you want, Maria?" my great-grandfather asked.

But the woman didn't say anything. She just took what looked like the last bits of change out of her purse and offered it to my great-grandfather.

"You know," my great-grandfather said, turning toward the shelf behind him as though he were suddenly looking for something, "a salesman came in here a few days ago and he gave me some sample packages of pasta. I think he left a box of oatmeal, too. Ah . . . here they are."

Then, turning back toward the woman, my great-grandfather continued, "Maria, why don't you take these? No charge. But do me a favor. After you and your husband try these products, let me know how you liked them. I might decide to carry these items in the store if customers like them. And for doing this favor for me, please just take the beans and the pears."

"Molte grazie [Thank you very much], Antonio," the woman said, hurrying out of the store. She was crying.

My great-grandfather turned to me and winked. Then he said: "The bad times are almost over. I believe that. Have faith."

....

I met my other great-grandfather in the winter of 1934. A man was holding a gun to his head at the time.

The Picture Frame placed me in a narrow alley, next to a door that appeared to be a side entrance to a large factory. It was early afternoon, maybe around one o'clock or so. I was there only a minute when, from the sidewalk along the street, a man turned into the alley and walked toward me. He was wearing a long black overcoat with the collar turned up against the cold February wind, and a gray hat with the brim turned up. He seemed not to see me at all. He walked right by me and toward the factory door. When he reached the door, two men jumped out from behind a stack of wooden crates and grabbed him. I saw that one of the men had a gun.

"Where is the vault?" asked the man holding the gun.

"On the second floor, in the cashier's office," answered the man in the overcoat.

"Take us there now!" commanded the gunman's accomplice.

The man in the overcoat took a key out of his pocket and unlocked and opened the factory door. Then his two abductors forced him inside the building, following him closely. I stuck my foot in the door just before it closed and relocked behind the three men. Then, I slipped inside the building. When I got inside, the three men were only about ten feet ahead of me, climbing a flight of wooden stairs to the second floor. The stairs let out a loud creak just as the men reached the top step.

"Who is there?" shouted someone from beyond the top of the stairs. "Salvatore, is that you?"

ROSINA DI NOME AND SALVATORE VINCENZO POSE
FOR A WEDDING PORTRAIT. Location: New York City.
Date: 9/7/1930.
© Magic Picture Frame Studio, LLC

The man with the gun raised it to the head of the man in the overcoat. No one said anything. No one moved. I froze about halfway up the stairs. I held my breath wondering what would happen next.

Then a security guard appeared at the top of the stairs with his gun drawn. The two would-be robbers suddenly turned and ran down the stairs, slamming me into the stairway railing as they raced past me and out the door.

"Are you alright?" asked the security guard. "That was awfully close!"

"I'm fine," answered the man in the overcoat. "Desperate times, I guess. I'm glad you were up here."

And that's how I met my great-grandfather, Salvatore Vincenzo, during an attempted robbery in the middle of the Great Depression. He was returning from lunch to his office on the second floor of the Breyers Ice Cream Plant in Long Island City, New York. He was the head cashier, in charge of payroll and bookkeeping.[46]

That night, I had dinner with my great-grandfather at his apartment on 33rd Street, in Long Island City. I met my great-grandmother Rosina, who was expecting their first child in April. I knew the child would grow up to be my father's father, but I didn't say anything. My great-grandmother made us a dinner of Pasta e Fagioli [Pasta and Bean Soup]. My great-grandfather called it Italian "poverty food," but I thought it was delicious. After dinner, my great-grandfather told me his story.[47]

"I was born in Italy, in a town called Santa Maria Capua Vetere. My father was a cobbler—a shoemaker. We were poor and there were no prospects that the family's circumstances would get any better in Italy. So, my father left for America when I was only one year old. That was 1907. He came back to get me in 1912, when I was almost seven years old. I remember we went through Ellis Island and entered the United States in November or early December of that year, because I was an altar boy in the church and I was disappointed that I would miss serving during the Christmas Mass. It was usually a pretty big celebration in town. The necessity of going to America was not something I understood at the time, I guess.[48]

"My two sisters, Rachela and Teresa, were brought to America in 1920. I was in high school at the time. But with the whole family in America and living under one roof, I had to drop out of high school the next year and go to work. Because I was only fifteen, my father signed child-worker papers from the State of New York that allowed me to work eight hours a day, six days a week.[49]

"At the time, my father was an assistant foreman in a musical instrument factory. He got me a job making saxophones. I never learned to play one, though. What I really wanted to do was to finish high school. So, I went to high school classes at night, even after putting in an eight-hour day in the factory.

"When I graduated from high school, the company promoted me to the accounting department. I was good at math. I wrote invoices, tallied receipts, and did some bookkeeping.

"But after the stock market crashed, people pretty much stopped buying musical instruments. They stopped buying almost everything, really. The instrument factory reduced its payroll and I was out of a job. My father went back to shoe repair and opened a small store. But having a high school education and being good at math was my salvation. I got the job at Breyers in 1930.

"My job at Breyers helped save the family, too. In 1930, there were ten of us living under one roof. There was my father, myself, my sisters Teresa, Rachela, and Dorothy, and my brothers Patsy, Vincent, Henry, Alfred, and Joseph. My mother died the year before, in 1929. Rachela was a sales clerk in a department store, so that helped. And Patsy was an errand boy for a local flower shop, so that helped, too. But my father's shoe repair business went bankrupt and I had to loan him money to reopen it. It's struggling again now, and it probably won't make it."[50]

My great-grandfather paused his narrative while my great-grandmother served hot tea and some Italian cookies—I liked the pignoli cookies the best. I noticed that my great-grandmother had a bandage around the fingers of her right hand.

"How did you meet my great-grandmother?" I asked.

"We met at a dance in 1928," my great-grandfather answered. "She was a flapper."[51]

"Oh, I was not!" my great-grandmother interjected.

My great-grandfather laughed. "Well, let's just say that she dressed very stylishly. She was a rarity, you know. She was a woman with a job and pocket money. I couldn't turn that down!"

"Oh, stop being silly," admonished my great-grandmother. Then she looked at me and said, "I was a cashier at Orbach's department store. I still am. That's where I work now. At least until the baby is born."

She poured some more tea in my great-grandfather's cup. Then she continued, "And we got married at St. Anne's Church on September 7, 1930. The church is on 110th Street. We had a small reception at a restaurant about a block away from the church. It was very nice."

I looked again at the bandage on my great-grandmother's hand.

"Oh, that's nothing," my great-grandmother said, noticing my stare the second time. "I got my fingers caught in the Comptometer

ROSINA DI NOME STANDS NEXT TO THE 1931 MODEL A FORD PURCHASED BY HER
HUSBAND, SALVATORE VINCENZO. Location: The Pocono Mountains in Pennsylvania.
Date: 1933.
© Magic Picture Frame Studio, LLC

last week. My boss took me to the hospital to get it stitched up. It will be OK."[52]

The scene started to fade around me, and I knew that the Picture Frame was taking me to a different time and place. But, I heard my great-grandfather say: "Yes, times are hard. But, no matter what the obstacles are, we keep moving forward. Life is a one-way road, after all. There is no way to stop or slow down or turn back. Only if we take a step forward each day, do our best each day, and stay optimistic, will things get better. We believe that. We have to believe that."

My great-grandfathers kept up a strong show of optimism, even in the most difficult years of the Great Depression. They managed to smile, even when the air of hopelessness was all around them. My great-grandfathers were resolved to do whatever was necessary to support their families and survive the hard times.

In a small way, my two great-grandfathers were lucky—they had jobs through the Great Depression when many of the people around them didn't. But even so, the decade of economic hardship stung my great-grandfathers in a way that they never forgot. My father told me that my great-grandfather Antonio lived the rest of his life fixing even the littlest things that broke, because he was unwilling to spend money to buy something new unless he absolutely had to. My great-grandfather Salvatore never regained his trust in the stock market, and he kept some emergency money under his mattress for decades after the Great Depression ended. He also held on to his job at the Breyers Ice Cream Company for forty-two years.

....

PART FOUR
AN AMERICAN IN AMERICA

The last time I saw my great-grandfather Antonio was in the summer of 1938. It was a Saturday morning and we had just opened the grocery store for another day of business. A few early morning customers were inside the store, buying fresh fruit, fresh bread, and fresh coffee for breakfast. Mrs. Cassotto was in the store with her baby; she came in from time to time to buy fresh eggs and milk. My great-uncle Roland was inside the store, too, assisting a customer at the coffee-grinder. My great-grandfather and I were outside the store, setting up a sidewalk display.[53]

As I helped my great-grandfather stack cans of tomatoes and olive oil, I thought about everything the Picture Frame had shown me about his life. As a child, he was dragged across the Atlantic Ocean, in the foul belly of an overcrowded steamship, for the opportunity to live in a rundown tenement building in Hell's Kitchen. Growing up, he had to fight, or deftly avoid, street thugs on his way to school. As a young man, he was tossed by cruel chance into the bloody frontline trenches of World War I. After the war, his hopes for the "good life" in America turned into a sour decade of hard times.

I had to ask: "Do you ever regret your decision to come to America?"

"No, I have never regretted my decision to come to America," my great-grandfather answered, without hesitation. Then he stopped stocking the display, and turned toward me. "Why do you ask? Do you think that life can't be hard in America?"

My great-grandfather took two fresh peaches out of the pocket of his grocer's apron, and tossed one to me. Then he sat down on an empty crate by the curb. I sat down next to him and took a bite of my peach. For a few minutes we just sat side by side, eating our peaches and watching the early morning traffic go by.

"Life can be hard anywhere," my great-grandfather said, suddenly breaking the silence and continuing his earlier thought. "But America is a place where, even in the hard times, every morning brings new hope and a new opportunity for a fresh start. You see, in America, today is not tomorrow, and the past is not the future."

"I'm not sure I understand," I said.

"I mean that in America, my past is not my future—if I don't want it to be," my great-grandfather explained. "My father was poor, but in America, I can become wealthy. My father was uneducated, but in America, I can become a scholar. My father was a laborer, but in America, I can become a business owner. America is the only place I know where I can choose not to let my past, or my circumstances, define who I am—or who I will become. People say that America is the land of the free. Well, isn't choice the ultimate freedom?"

I nodded agreement.

"No, I have never regretted my decision to come to America," my great-grandfather said once again. "But you have asked me the wrong question, I think. What you really want to know is do I regret becoming an American?"

I remember the day that you became an American . . .

....

My great-grandfather became an American on June 19, 1931. I was there, watching from the gallery of a New York City courtroom, as my great-grandfather and seventeen other people raised their right hands and took the Oath of Allegiance to the United States.

"I hereby declare, on oath," my great-grandfather swore in front of the judge, "that I absolutely and entirely renounce and abjure all allegiance and fidelity to any foreign prince, potentate, state, or sovereignty, and particularly to the Crown of Italy, of whom or which I have heretofore been a subject or citizen; that I will support and defend the Constitution and laws of the United States of America against all enemies, foreign and domestic; that I will bear true faith and allegiance to the same; and that I take this obligation freely without any mental reservation or purpose of evasion; so help me God."[54]

In addition to taking the oath that day, my great-grandfather was required to pass a test on American history and civics. He passed it with flying colors. He had prepared for the test by taking some American citizenship classes that were offered in the evenings at the public school in his neighborhood. I would usually meet him there after his class had ended. For some reason, he thought it was funny to quiz me from his citizenship study guide as we walked home together. He was always trying to find a question that would stump me.

ROSINA DI NOME AND SALVATORE VINCENZO WITH
BABY VINCENT. Location: New York City.
Date: 3/30/1936.
© Magic Picture Frame Studio, LLC

"Who was the main writer of the Declaration of Independence?" my great-grandfather would ask.

"That's an easy one," I would say. "Thomas Jefferson, of course."

"Hmmm. But what is the basic premise of the Declaration of Independence?"

"That all men are created equal."

"Where do our rights to life and liberty come from?"

"From God."

"What did the Emancipation Proclamation do?"

"It freed the slaves."

"Why did the Pilgrims come to America?"

"For religious freedom."

"What is the United States Constitution?"

"It's the supreme law of the land."

"What is the Bill of Rights?"

"The first ten amendments to the Constitution."

"OK, smarty-pants," my great-grandfather would say, when he got frustrated that he couldn't stump me. "Can you name three rights or freedoms guaranteed by the Bill of Rights?"

"The freedom of speech, the freedom of the press, and the freedom of religion," I'd answer. Then I'd think for a moment and throw something back at him that I thought he wouldn't know—and to prove that I really was a smarty-pants. Something like: "The Bill of Rights says that any right not described by the Constitution is a right reserved for the states or the people. So we may have more rights than the Constitution says."

"Good one," my great-grandfather would say when he had to admit he was impressed. Then he would try to find a harder question in his book. "Okay, here's a harder question. In what year was the Constitution written?"

"That's harder?" I would ask, wrinkling my brow in a funny way. "1787."

"What kind of government does the United States have?"

"You're trying to trick me again. You want me to say that we have a democratic government, but we don't. We have a republican government. There's a difference."

"Right. How many stars are there on the flag?"

"Fifty."

"Wrong!" my great-grandfather would shout, followed by a loud laugh. "But you get that one wrong every time!"

After my great-grandfather took the Oath of Allegiance, we went home to celebrate. When we got there, family and friends were already gathered on the front porch, waiting to shake the hand of the new American citizen.

"Congratulations, Antonio!" they shouted as we climbed the front steps.

My great-grandfather smiled and shook hands with everyone. Then he kissed my great-grandmother.

"Yesterday, I was an Italian. Today, I am an American," my great-grandfather told everyone, proudly. "E Pluribus Unum! Yesterday, I was part of the many. Today, I am part of the one!"[55]

A tiny bit of Italy was added to the landscape of America that day in June 1931. But a whole lot of America took root in its newest citizen.

....

"Anthony . . . Anthony . . ."

A man came up to the storefront display and took a can of tomatoes from the stack. He said good morning, tipped his hat, and then went into the store. The sudden appearance of the man surprised me and got me out my daydream-like recollection of the past. I realized that my great-grandfather was trying to get my attention. He had been trying to ask me a question.

"Anthony . . . Anthony . . . Did your teachers make you read the Declaration of Independence and the Constitution of the United States?" my great-grandfather asked, probably for the second or third time.

"Yes," I said.

"Mine did, too. But I didn't understand what the words meant until I was older—until I had seen more of the rest of the world . . ."

My great-grandfather's voice trailed off; he seemed to suddenly get lost in a new thought. So, for the next few minutes, we just sat quietly on the crate and took the last bites of our peaches. They were the last peaches of the summer, sweet and fleshy and full of juice. I don't think I have ever had a peach that tasted as good.

My great-grandfather stood up and tossed his peach pit into an empty coffee can by the curb. Then he said: "Being an American is not about heredity, or blood, or ancestry. America was designed such that it wouldn't be about that. That's what my teachers were trying to tell me—and that's what your teachers were trying to tell you. Being an American is about believing in the ideas in those documents your teachers wanted you to read."

I nodded, but I wasn't sure what my great-grandfather was getting at. I wasn't sure I understood.

"You see," my great-grandfather continued, "you could go to Italy and live there all your life—you could even become a citizen—but you could never become an Italian. Yet, I became an American overnight. I became an American because I believe in America, and it's my belief in America that makes me an American. Capisce [Do you understand]?"

Those were the last words that my great-grandfather ever said to me. I thought about them for a long time; long after the Picture Frame took me to other times and places. And finally, I realized that my great-grandfather was right. America is an idea as much as it is a place. I was born in the United States, so no one would ever question whether I am an American. But in truth, even though I was born in the United States, I am no different than my great-grandfather and all the immigrants who came to this land: I can only be an American by choice.

Capisco [*I understand*].

ABOVE:
THE *SPIRIT OF ST. LOUIS* TAKES OFF FOR PARIS. Location: Roosevelt Airfield,
New York. Date: 5/20/1927.
© Underwood & Underwood/CORBIS

RIGHT:
CHARLES LINDBERGH IN THE PILOT'S SEAT OF THE *SPIRIT OF ST. LOUIS*.
Location: Roosevelt Airfield, New York. Date: May 1927.
© CORBIS

the Atlantic would bring that future closer. I'm jumping ahead of my story, but after the transatlantic flight, when asked why he did it, Charles Lindbergh said: "Gentlemen, 132 years ago Benjamin Franklin was asked: 'What good is your balloon? What will it accomplish?' He replied: 'What good is a new born child?' Less than twenty years ago when I was not far advanced from infancy M. Bleriot flew across the English Channel and was asked, 'What good is your aeroplane? What will it accomplish?' Today those same skeptics might ask me what good has been my flight from New York to Paris. My answer is that I believe it is the forerunner of a great air service from America to France, America to Europe, to bring our peoples nearer together in understanding and in friendship than they have ever been."[10]

Although he didn't mention it, Lindbergh had one other reason for making the transatlantic trip. It was a reason so intensely personal and important to him that it overshadowed everything else, even the possibility of winning the Orteig Prize. The reason was simply this: Lindbergh wanted to be the first person to fly nonstop across the Atlantic Ocean. In fact, Lindbergh wanted to be first so badly that he was taking off for Paris before his application to the Orteig Prize committee was officially accepted. That's right, on the morning of May 20, 1927, Lindbergh was officially ineligible for the Orteig Prize—and he knew it. But he just couldn't wait any longer and take the chance that another pilot might beat him to Paris.[11]

Hour 13

Our altitude is 800 feet. Our air speed is 90 mph. Visibility is five miles . . . fog below us. We're over the Atlantic Ocean, but I can't see the water. We're flying into the night . . .

The last of North America was behind us and we would not see land again until we reached the European continent. We had flown 1,200 miles, but there were still 2,400 miles left to go.

The long night over the Atlantic Ocean had begun, and it brought with it a new adversary for Lindbergh: Sleep. Sleep meant death. Sleep promised an ice-cold grave in the depths of the Atlantic Ocean. The lone pilot of the *Spirit of St. Louis* couldn't allow himself to sleep.

Don't sleep . . .

Hour 19

Our altitude is 9,000 feet. Our air speed is 87 mph. Visibility is good, but there are thick clouds ahead. We're over the Atlantic Ocean. Lindbergh is tired . . . so tired . . .

Lindbergh stomped his feet on the floor of the plane. Then, he ran in place while sitting in his cockpit chair. He was trying to shake the numbness from his legs and feet, and quicken his heartbeat and respiration. He was trying to stay awake and in control of the *Spirit of St. Louis*. But it had been more than a day since Lindbergh had slept, and his body's urgent cry for sleep began to transform itself into physical pain.

"My back is stiff; my shoulders ache; my face burns; my eyes smart. It seems impossible to go on longer. All I want in life is to throw myself down flat, stretch out—and sleep."[14]

Lindbergh tried everything he could think of to stay awake. A few times, he took the *Spirit of St. Louis* to just a few feet above the ocean's surface, and let the cold salty spray of the whitecaps splash through the open cockpit window and slap his face. Other times, he let freezing rain drive through the open window and drench the entire cockpit. After the soaking, Lindbergh shivered in his nearly frozen flight suit, but his trembling succeeded in keeping him awake for a few minutes more. All night long, Lindbergh waged his battle with sleep minute by painful minute.

Lindbergh even starved himself in his battle to remain conscious and in control of his body and his plane. He said it was easier to stay awake if he was hungry, so the five sandwiches he had packed remained wrapped and unopened in a brown paper bag. He barely

sipped the single quart of drinking water he had brought with him. Even so, with each passing hour, Lindbergh's eyelids got heavier, and his brain demanded more firmly to shut down and rest. Lindbergh's mind wanted to wander through the land of dreams, not remain in the real world of air and sky and ocean—and cockpit controls and gauges and maps. Lindbergh's mental sharpness came under attack, and I heard him struggle with course corrections in the long, black night.

"Eight degrees right rudder. Swing the nose back south. I'm twenty degrees off-course! Now, right rudder twelve degrees. Level out. I'm five degrees off course again, I've got to be more careful."[15]

In addition to his battle with sleep, Lindbergh silently fought fear. He was always listening intently to the monotonous drone of the plane's engine—listening for the slightest change in pitch, the slightest cough or sputter. He knew the terrible fate that awaited him if the plane's single propeller stopped turning over the cold Atlantic water.

Hour 20

Am I sleeping? Am I dreaming? The plane is spinning . . . diving . . . crashing . . .

Although I had been sleeping, it was not a dream—the plane really was falling from the sky! Lindbergh, with his eyes wide open, had fallen asleep, too, and he had allowed the *Spirit of St. Louis* to wander in the sky, completely out of control. How long the plane had been spinning and diving was impossible to say, but it was the sensation of falling that snapped Lindbergh back to consciousness. He seized the plane's controls just in time to stop it from tumbling into the black ocean water below. Lindbergh leveled the *Spirit of St. Louis* and pointed it once again toward Paris.

That was close!

"Maybe you should turn back!" I said to Lindbergh. "You have regained control of the airplane . . . maybe you should turn back! Are you past the Point of No Return?"

I said it, but I knew that Lindbergh would not turn back. I also knew that the Point of No Return never really held much meaning for Charles Lindbergh, beyond the pencil mark on his flight map. I knew this because I had already realized that reaching Paris was more than just a dream for Lindbergh, it was a decision. Nothing was going to stop Lindbergh from following through on his decision.

Charles Lindbergh decided to be the first person to fly nonstop across the Atlantic Ocean one night back in September 1926. He was flying his mail plane in the night sky over Peoria, Illinois, headed for Chicago. Alone in his cockpit, beneath a crisp and clear fall sky filled with bright twinkling stars, Lindbergh dreamed of the Orteig Prize and what it might be like to cross the Atlantic Ocean in an airplane. He wondered what it might really take to fly from New York to Paris. He wondered why other pilots had failed in their attempts. He compared his own flight experience and piloting skills to theirs. And he thought: "What makes them different from me? Why can't I do it? Who is to stop me from trying, but me?"

And then, Lindbergh stopped dreaming beneath the stars and made a decision: to be the first person to fly nonstop from New York to Paris. He said to himself: "But if I'm really going to fly to Paris, I must be willing to put everything I've got into the project—time, energy, money, even my position as chief pilot on the air-mail line."[16]

And that is the difference between a dream and a decision: Dreams are followed by nothing but a smile, but decisions are followed by action. And Lindbergh followed his decision with several actions: He gave up his job delivering airmail. He developed a plan for his project. He won financing from business executives. He had a plane built to his own specifications. He charted his course across the ocean.

Lindbergh's plan was unique and daring—it called for an airplane with only one wing, only one engine, and only one pilot. Unlike all the pilots who had attempted the transatlantic flight before him, Lindbergh would fly alone. He reasoned: "That will cut out the need for any selection of crew, or quarreling. If there's upholstery in the cabin, I'll tear it out for the flight. I'll take only the food I need to eat, and a few concentrated rations. I'll carry a rubber boat for emergency, and a little extra water."[17]

Lindbergh believed in himself and his radical plan so much, that he convinced others to believe, too. Lindbergh convinced businessmen in St. Louis to finance his transatlantic flight, promising them publicity, honor, and a place in aviation history. Then, he convinced executives at the Ryan Airplane Company in San Diego, California, of his need for a specially designed plane. Lindbergh collaborated mostly with Ryan engineer Donald Hall on the design of the *Spirit of St. Louis*, but it didn't take long for Lindbergh's passion and enthusiasm to infect almost everyone involved in the construction of the unique plane. Claude Ryan, who owned the company, said: "We talked it over with our people, a pretty compact group of people; almost every workman in the plant was taken into the decision. Of course, Lindbergh added a lot to morale because it got to be a challenge to everybody. He went around the plant all the time. He

had such a nice personality, was just such a young boyish fellow. They all fell for him. They liked him very much."[18]

And while the *Spirit of St. Louis* was being built, Lindbergh planned his route, read and reread his navigational charts, and visualized the transatlantic flight in his mind. In Lindbergh's mind, I think, a successful flight had already become a reality.

From plan to plane to Paris, Lindbergh's project was a gigantic, complicated undertaking. The New-York-to-Paris project involved thousands of details, each one demanding Lindbergh's full attention. A mistake on any one detail could mean the difference between success and failure—life and death. The complexity of the project would have made an easy excuse for Lindbergh to leave it in his dreams, or to quit the project at the first sign of trouble. Lindbergh didn't quit, though, he stuck to his plan no matter what obstacle he encountered and kept moving forward. He said: "The important thing is to start; to lay a plan, and then follow it step by step no matter how small or large each one by itself may seem."[19]

So, as Lindbergh cruised through the night, just a few hundred feet above a cold, ocean death and surrounded by flammable fabric and explosive gasoline—fighting sleep and cut off from the whole world—it was clear to me why there was no turning back for him. To Lindbergh, every second of his transatlantic journey followed naturally from the decision he had made months before, when he was flying his mail plane over Peoria. Lindbergh had decided to fly nonstop to Paris, and he had developed a plan to do it. Now, Lindbergh was following his plan, and he was going to keep on following it all the way to Paris. Step by step.

Hour 27

It's afternoon. We are flying low . . . only about fifty feet above the water . . . we're circling some fishing boats! We must be near Europe . . .

There were several small fishing boats in the water below us. We were still pretty far out at sea, but the boats meant we were nearing the coastline of Europe. Lindbergh took the *Spirit of St. Louis* down for a closer look and circled above the boats. I think we were both excited to see another human being.

A fisherman poked his head out of the porthole of one boat and looked up at us, but no one else appeared. We circled several times, but the fisherman never moved and no one else ever came out on deck. It was strange that no one came out onto the decks of the other boats. The plane's engine was easy enough to hear and I thought for sure that it would arouse curiosity.

Why doesn't the fisherman in the porthole at least wave to us? And where is everyone?

Later, with the boats far behind us, I began to think I hadn't really seen even the one fisherman in the porthole. Maybe it was my imagination, I thought, or a ghost.

Hour 33

Am I sleeping? Am I awake? Are we circling? It feels like we're circling. We're not level, the wing is tipped low to one side . . . but at least the altimeter reads 4,000 feet . . . that's strange, there are lights below us . . .

I had fallen asleep again—and again I woke up to the odd sensation that we were flying in circles. I jumped up toward the cockpit window, certain that we were lost over the Atlantic Ocean, or crashing. But there were city lights below us! We were circling the Eiffel Tower!

"You've done it!" I shouted when I saw the city below. "We're going to make it!" We were just a few minutes from landing in Paris. All I wanted was solid ground underneath my feet.

Lindbergh didn't respond right away. He was leaning out the cockpit window, getting his final bearings so he could head the *Spirit of St. Louis* in the direction of the Paris airport. When he popped his head back inside the cockpit, he made a quick notation in his flight log, checked his gauges, and then adjusted our route in a northeasterly direction. Then he turned to me and said something, well, shocking: "I almost wish Paris were a few more hours away. It's a shame to land with the night so clear and so much fuel in my tanks."[20]

"Not land? You can't be serious!" I said. "A few hours ago you were in agony, just trying to stay awake! Now you want to bore holes in the sky for a few more hours? Why? You've done it!"

Lindbergh never answered me. I'll never know what he was really thinking at that moment, when he circled the Eiffel Tower and was only minutes from achieving his goal. I've been told that achieving a goal can sometimes be a bittersweet moment in life—a moment when all the energy that drove you to success morphs into a nagging whisper in the back of your mind: "Yes, you've done it. Now, what will you do next?"

LEFT:
CHARLES LINDBERGH INSPECTS THE ENGINE CYLINDERS ON THE *SPIRIT OF ST. LOUIS*.
Date: 1927.
© CORBIS

Hour 34

Paris! The airport! Le Bourget Aerodrome!

As we approached the airport, Lindbergh said that the runway lights didn't look right to him, so we didn't land. We circled and approached again. I looked out of the window as we made our second approach. The lights ahead of us did seem strange and confusing; they were lined up in a long row, but only on one side of us, and not on the other. It didn't appear to be a runway at all.

What are those lights?

As we descended, shapes slowly began to appear out of the gloom of the moonless night. I was able to make out the faint outlines of buildings on both sides of the plane. They could have been hangers, but I don't really know. Then, up ahead, I saw the strange lights again. But this time, because our second approach was lower, I saw that the strange lights were actually car headlights! There were hundreds of cars, with their headlights on, lined up on one side of the runway! There was also a huge traffic jam outside the airport!

What's going on down there?

Lindbergh put the *Spirit of St. Louis* down firmly. He didn't know if the ground was wet or dry, and he didn't want to take any chances. We came to a stop, and Lindbergh switched off the engine. It was 10:22 P.M., Paris time. Lindbergh and I had been in the air for 33 hours, 30 minutes, and 29.8 seconds. It felt great to be on solid ground.

When Lindbergh switched off the engine, I expected silence, but instead, heard a loud roar. At first, I thought the roar was the residual effect of listening to the constant drone of the engine for so many hours. I thought my ears had been damaged. No, it was something else. The roar came from outside of the plane.

I looked out the window and I couldn't believe my eyes: Thousands of people were running toward us. They were tearing down fences and barricades, running past soldiers and police—desperately trying to get to the plane. As the crowd got closer, the roar became a deafening mixture of shouts and cheers. People in the mob chanted: "Lindbergh! Lindbergh! Lindbergh!"

Lindbergh seemed oblivious to the advancing mob. His mind was still on his plane. He stuck his head out the window and shouted: "Are there any mechanics here? Does anyone here speak English?"

Lindbergh never got an answer. The mob attacked the plane and invaded the cockpit! Dozens of hands came through the cockpit door and pulled Lindbergh from the plane. Then, the frenzied people hoisted Lindbergh up over their heads and carried him away. They were still chanting: "Lindbergh! Lindbergh! Lindbergh!"

THE *SPIRIT OF ST. LOUIS* FLIES OVER PARIS.
Location: The Eiffel Tower by the River
Seine in Paris, France. Date: Unknown.
© Underwood & Underwood/CORBIS

I was left alone in the cockpit of the *Spirit of St. Louis*. I never saw Charles Lindbergh again.

I found out later that there were was another twelve-year-old American boy who saw Charles Lindbergh land in Paris that night. His name was Tudor Richards, and he was standing in the crowd, holding the hands of his mother, Julia, and his father, Dicky. His younger sister, Anne, was there, too. Tudor's family was vacationing in Paris when they decided to follow the crowds to Le Bourget Aerodrome and try to catch a glimpse of Charles Lindbergh. Tudor's mother described Lindbergh's landing in a letter she wrote to her brother the next day: "It must have been about a quarter past ten when the roar of an aeroplane overhead was distinctly heard above the answering roar of the mob below. It passed, but people all about us had distinctly seen the outline of a plane. A few minutes more and we heard it again; it grew in volume, and then suddenly, out of the black darkness, there flew a great silver moth—it seemed to me—which glided down the path of light in the middle of the field and was as suddenly swallowed up again in the seething, howling mass of humanity that surged towards it from every direction of the compass."[21]

....

The world's response to Lindbergh's achievement was swift and dramatic. First, kings and queens of Europe showered him with ribbons and medals. The people of Europe cheered him everywhere he went. Then, in June, President Calvin Coolidge sent the USS *Memphis* to bring the American flyer home. The cruiser, with Lindbergh standing on her deck, steamed into Chesapeake Bay on its way to Washington, D.C., accompanied by a convoy of four destroyers, two army blimps, and forty airplanes in the sky. Two million congratulatory letters, and hundreds of thousands of telegrams, waited back home for Lindbergh. Later, a parade for Lindbergh in New York City had so much ticker tape and confetti pouring down from the surrounding buildings that it looked like a snowstorm had hit New York in the middle of June! Thousands of poems and hundreds of songs about Lindbergh's flight played on the radio all over the United States. And Charles Lindbergh was overwhelmed by it all: "I was astonished at the effect my successful landing in France had on the nations of the world. To me, it was like a match lighting a bonfire."[22]

Lindbergh had never given much thought to what he would do, or what would happen, after he landed in Paris. He had simply imagined that he would just spend some private and quiet weeks touring Europe in his plane. Lindbergh had not packed the new clothes of celebrity in his suitcase, and the soft-spoken man didn't wear them comfortably. The world called him a hero, but Lindbergh felt that he had simply done what he had set out to do.

In my time, the world still remembers Charles Lindbergh as a hero, and as a man of daring and courage—and there is no doubt that he was all of that. But because of the Picture Frame, I know that it was a lot more than heroism and daring and courage that carried Lindbergh over the thousands of miles of cold ocean water in 1927. I know that it was the power of his decision, and his steady determination to follow his plan, that led him to his destiny.

"Step by step," Charles Lindbergh had said.

Step by step.

EDISON'S GREATEST MARVEL

THE VITASCOPE

"Wonderful is The Vitascope. Pictures life size and full of color. Makes a thrilling show."
NEW YORK HERALD, April 24, '96.

PRINT ADVERTISEMENT FOR THOMAS EDISON'S VITASCOPE MOTION PICTURE PROJECTOR. Date: 1896. Movies were silent in 1896; notice the orchestra depicted below the screen.
© CORBIS

"Anything that won't sell, I don't want to invent, because anything that won't sell hasn't reached the acme of success, its sale is proof of its utility, and utility is success," Edison said. [34]

And once Thomas Edison decided what he wanted to invent, he poured all his energy into inventing it—and he never slept again until he invented it! Well, at least it seemed that way. Time and again, I saw Edison get completely lost in his work, often going for days without a full night's sleep. When he got so tired that he had to sleep, he still didn't go home—he just took short naps in his laboratory and then continued to work "round the clock."

It was funny to see Edison's assistants struggle to stay awake with him. Sometimes they would walk around the lab with their arms out in front of them like zombies, calling themselves "Edison's Insomnia Squad." Edison would laugh.

"The man who keeps at one thing and never minds the clock is always sure to do something. He may miss many social engagements, of course, but his success is assured," Edison told his tired assistants. [35]

Hunger was a certain thing, too! Edison got so involved in his work that he often forgot to eat until his stomach growled so loudly

THOMAS EDISON DABBLES WITH HIS MOTION PICTURE PROJECTOR.
Location: Probably Edison's West Orange, NJ, laboratory. Date: 1905.
© Bettmann/CORBIS

that we all heard it! We ate our meals at the oddest times. Dinner at midnight in the laboratory was typical. I can tell you that I was never more tired and hungry than during the time I spent with Thomas Edison and his Insomnia Squad, living on catnaps and eating dinner in the middle of the night!

But don't get the wrong impression, because it wasn't all work and no play. I had a lot of fun in Edison's laboratory, too. Edison had a great sense of humor. His assistants thought so, too. One of Edison's assistants, Robert Halgrim, said: "He was always playing practical jokes on everyone in the lab. You could pull one on him if you were good enough. It was his wonderful personality that kept one working for him, to realize that he was working harder than anyone else."[36]

There is no doubt that Edison demanded hard work from his team, but I think he appreciated them too. In 1929, I attended a celebration dinner held on the fiftieth anniversary of the invention of the light bulb. After Edison was honored and given awards, he made a short speech in which he thanked the people who had worked for him.

"I would be embarrassed at the honors that are being heaped on me on this unforgettable night were it not for the fact that in honoring me you are also honoring that vast army of thinkers and workers of the past without whom my work would have gone for nothing," Edison said.[37]

I was invited to Thomas Edison's birthday in 1920; he was 73 years old. I asked him what was on his mind, considering all the things he had achieved over the years.

"Today, I am wondering what would have happened to me by now, if, fifty years ago, some fluent talker had converted me to the theory of the eight-hour day and convinced me that it was not fair to my fellow workers to put forth my best efforts in my work? I am glad that the eight-hour day had not been invented when I was a young man. If my life had been made up of eight-hour days, I don't believe I could have accomplished a great deal," Edison said.[38]

I smiled. It was impossible to argue the point. You can't achieve success by watching the clock, or by complaining about the hours. It takes hard work.

Edison's hard work resulted in 389 patents for the electric light and electric power, 195 patents for the phonograph, 150 patents for the telegraph, 141 patents for storage batteries, and 34 patents for the telephone. Thomas Edison had created numerous companies, invented whole industries, employed thousands of people directly and indirectly, and created wealth for himself, his family, his investors, and the people who worked for him.[39]

Looking back, I think that hard work was really only one of the reasons for Edison's incredible success, though. I think that there were two other reasons: God-given talent, and incredible focus. Thomas Edison, it seems to me, amplified the talents that God gave him through hard work, and then focused his talents on the opportunities he saw.

Thomas Edison saw opportunity all around him, and he was often frustrated that other people couldn't see it—or chose not to see it. "Opportunity is missed by most people," Edison often said, "because it is dressed in overalls and looks like work."[40]

It's a lesson I won't soon forget.

Thomas Edison died on Sunday, October 18, 1931, at the age of eighty-four. The newspapers reported that his estate was worth over $12 million, so he died a rich man.

But I think that the greatest wealth Mr. Edison attained was the love of the American people. On October 20, while his body lay in state in the library of his New Jersey laboratory, more than fifty thousand people came to say goodbye to the "Wizard of Menlo Park." Then, the next day, on October 21, President Herbert Hoover asked the American people to turn off all of their electric lights for one full minute, in remembrance of Thomas Edison's greatest gift.

And all across America, at 10:00 P.M. Eastern time, they did.

RIGHT:
THOMAS EDISON AND HIS INSOMNIA SQUAD SHARE A MEAL IN THE LABORATORY.
Location: Edison's West Orange, NJ, laboratory. Date: 1912. Standing, left to right: Ed McGlynn, Bob Spahle, and Archie Hoff. Seated, left to right: Johnny LaMonte, Billy Fulton, Sam Moore, Thomas Edison, and Anthony.
© CORBIS

"The only thing necessary for the triumph of evil is for good men to do nothing."

EDMUND BURKE (1729–1797),
BRITISH STATESMAN AND PHILOSOPHER

CHAPTER 6

FOR YOUR TOMORROW ⚔

PART ONE

THE WAR IN EUROPE

At first, I thought the Picture Frame had dropped me into the front car of a roller coaster that was cresting a hill and ready to plunge at high speed. I had that nauseating feeling that comes when the floor suddenly drops away, and your stomach is in your mouth. But I realized it wasn't a roller coaster when the sensation repeated: I rose and fell, rose and fell, over and over again. Then, I heard the rumbling of a powerful engine, combined with a strange gurgling sound—as if the engine's tailpipe was submerged in water. I smelled the sea, but the ocean air was mixed with the sharp smell of gasoline fumes and thick engine exhaust. With every breath of the polluted air, I got sicker. I doubled over and threw up.

When I lifted my head, I found myself staring at big rusty rivets in a dull gray steel wall. The wall was just an inch in front of my face, and I couldn't move backward or away from it. A crowd of people that had suddenly appeared around me pressed me into the wall. They were soldiers, and there were a lot of them.

AMERICAN SOLDIERS IN LANDING CRAFT APPROACH THE FIGHTING ON D-DAY.
Location: Normandy, France. Date: 6/6/1944.
© Hulton-Deutsch/CORBIS

All of a sudden, the metal wall in front of me fell away with a loud crash. Waves splashed over the wall as it transformed itself into a ramp. The soldiers ran past me, hurrying down the ramp and wading into the choppy water. In the distance, I saw a hazy, smoky beach. I could see that there was a fierce battle going on. Thunder crackled over my head, and then I heard loud explosions on the cliffs above the beach. There was a rattling, "ting-ting-ting" sound on the metal ramp at my feet.

I froze.

A soldier grabbed me and pulled me down the ramp. We zigzagged through the bullets striking the ramp—"ting-ting-ting." The soldier dragged me through the water to the beach. Then we ran. More bullets whizzed by my head, buzzing like bees, before they slammed into the sand with a zipper-like sound.

We reached a broken seawall halfway up the beach and threw ourselves down behind it. There were a lot of soldiers crouching behind the wall, trying to stay out of the line of fire. I tried to catch my breath, but I was breathing so fast that I couldn't get enough air into my lungs, and I got dizzy. My heart pounded hard in my chest. It made my head hurt.

"Where am I now?" I yelled, but no one could hear me over the noise of the battle.

There was a look of terror on the faces of the soldiers around me. It was a look that came from knowing that no matter what choice you make, or no matter what you do, the outcome will be bad. I was sure that the same expression was on my face, too.

I looked back toward the water. There were thousands of boats, battleships, and troop carriers as far as I could see—all the way to the horizon, and maybe even farther. Hundreds of landing craft were chugging to the shore to pour more soldiers onto the beach. I recognized the scene from a movie I had once seen, and I knew where—and when—I was.

I was on Omaha Beach, probably in Dog Green or Dog White sector. It was D-Day, June 6, 1944, just after dawn. Operation Overlord, the Allied Invasion of Normandy, was underway. I was witnessing 175,000 men from the United States, Great Britain, and Canada storm the beaches of France to join the fighting of World War II, and punch their way toward Berlin. These brave men were the vanguard of a larger army, destined to free Europe from Adolph Hitler's evil Nazi regime. On the cliffs above me, and opposing the Allied soldiers, was the front line of the German Army. Beyond the cliffs, lay Nazi-occupied France.[1]

Fortified emplacements on the bluff in front of me, and on the surrounding high cliffs, gave the Germans a commanding position over the Allied soldiers storming the shore. The Germans took full advantage of that position by training their machine guns on the approaching landing craft. All they had to do then was wait patiently for the transport doors to drop open. They cut down the emerging soldiers faster than they could leave the boats. The Germans also raked their gunfire up and down the beach, looking especially for clusters of soldiers shielding themselves behind low embankments and debris. It rained bullets and bombs on Omaha Beach.[2]

This is horrible. I don't want to look. There are dead bodies everywhere. No place is safe. How do you dodge raindrops in a monsoon?

There were so many helmets and packs and bodies bobbing in the rough channel water, I couldn't tell who was alive and who was dead—but the water was turning red. A soldier near me said: "They wiped out almost the entire 116th Infantry Regiment; they just murdered them. They were floating all over the place, there was blood in the water—it was just dark."[3]

The scene on the beach horrified me even more than the scene in the water, because there was no deep water to hide what the machine guns did to human bodies. I saw people cut in half. I watched soldiers trip over the bodies of their friends who had fallen just two steps in front of them. I watched until I just couldn't watch any more.

More soldiers arrived at the seawall. They thought they had found shelter, but they were wrong. The bullets came straight down on them from the cliffs. The soldiers at the seawall were pinned down, and the German gunners picked them off one by one. I covered my eyes. I had seen enough. I wanted to go home.

And then I saw the most amazing examples of bravery and courage.

Farther down the beach, General Norman Cota stepped out into the open, waved his .45 in the air, and yelled: "Rangers, lead the way!" The sight of their commander out in the open, defying the enemy's non-stop fire, lifted the soldiers out of their fright. The General's four words electrified the soldiers who heard it, and they passed the command down the line.[4]

Then, Colonel George Taylor, of the 16th Infantry Regiment, came running up to the soldiers who were hunkered down behind the seawall. He found his officers, pointed to the top of the bluff, and said: "If we're going to die, let's die up there."[5]

Like General Cota, Colonel Taylor knew that retreat was impossible, and standing still meant death. The only way off the beach

AMERICAN SOLDIERS LAND AT NORMANDY BEACH. Location: Normandy, France.
Date: 6/7/1944, the day after D-Day.
© Hulton-Deutsch/CORBIS

was forward. Turning to the rest of his men, Colonel Taylor yelled: "There are only two kinds of people on this beach: The dead, and those about to die. So let's get the hell out of here!"[6]

A mortar exploded near the seawall, spraying shrapnel over the area. Private Raymond Howell, an engineer attached to D Company, was hit in his helmet and his hand. But he said: ". . . if I'm going to die, to hell with it I'm not going to die here. The next bunch of guys that go over that goddamn wall, I'm going with them."[7]

And the soldiers went over the wall. They cut and blasted their way through rows of concertina wire that the Germans had laid to thwart their advance. They marked paths through minefields with tape, so others could follow. They worked out in the open—so brave, so determined—as German machine-gun fire zeroed in on them. When soldiers were killed, others jumped over the wall without hesitating to push on. When the soldiers finally made it to the base of the bluff, they found paths to the top, and began a direct assault on the German emplacements above. In some places along the beach where the cliffs were almost vertical, the soldiers built ladders and climbed straight up into the waiting German guns.

I remained behind the seawall, as I watched the ferocious battle progress. A soldier ran up to the wall and threw himself down in the sand. He had a radio with him. I heard orders being given, and soldiers talking about the fighting and the locations of the enemy. Then, after a while, I heard the words: "Praise the Lord!" The words meant that the Army Rangers had made it to the top of the cliff. A few hours later, the shooting stopped. The Germans had been driven back, or killed, and the Allies owned the road to Nazi-occupied France.

There was little rest for the soldiers when the fighting was over: Right away, they had to locate their regiments and prepare for the march into France. But the soldiers did take a few moments to look for their friends, and to wonder who had made it and who hadn't.

John Raaen, an officer in the 5th Ranger Battalion, looked for his friend, Father Lacy. Lacy was the last man to step off the landing craft that had brought Raaen to the beach. John Raaen said: "He stayed down there in the water's edge pulling the wounded forward ahead of the advancing tide. He comforted the dying. Calmly said prayers for the dead. He led terrified soldiers to relative safety behind debris and wreckage, half-carrying them, half-dragging them, binding up their wounds. Never once did he think of his own safety. Always helping those that needed his help to survive that awful inferno."[8]

The fighting had resulted in more than five thousand casualties, and the beach was littered with bodies. A medical detail had already been formed to evacuate the wounded and collect the dead. I hoped that Father Lacy was okay. With tears in my eyes, I knelt in the sand and said a prayer for him, and all the fallen heroes on the beach. I asked God to watch over the brave men who were getting ready to march inland and take on the enemy.

....

The next morning, I met a journalist who came ashore with the second wave of G.I.s. He was sitting on the beach, surrounded by the remains of the previous day's chaos—crumpled machinery, dead bodies, and spent artillery. His name was Ernie Pyle and he was writing his latest dispatch to the newspapers in the United States.[9]

"Due to a last minute alteration in the arrangements, I didn't arrive on the beachhead until the morning after D-Day, after our first wave of assault troops had hit the shore," Pyle wrote in his notebook. "Now that it is over it seems to me a pure miracle that we ever took the beach at all. . . . In this column I want to tell you what the opening of the second front in this one sector entailed, so that you can know and appreciate and forever be humbly grateful to those both dead and alive who did it for you."[10]

Why are there no reporters like Ernie Pyle in my time?[11]

I was glad that somebody would tell the story of what happened on the beaches of Normandy. I was glad that somebody would describe the heroism that I'd seen. I remember something that Sergeant John Ellery, who had landed at Normandy with the 16th Infantry Regiment, once said: "It is good to be reminded that there are such men, that there always have been and always will be. We sometimes forget, I think, that you can manufacture weapons, and you can purchase ammunition, but you can't buy valor and you can't pull heroes off an assembly line."[12]

I walked up the path to the top of the cliffs, and then I looked out over the English Channel. It was still an amazing sight: An armada of four thousand ships that had brought an army of liberation to Europe—an army of hundreds of thousands of human shields against Hitler's evil regime.[13]

In the months that followed, I marched through Europe with the American soldiers. I saw bloody battles as the Allies drove the German Army back toward Germany and liberated towns, one after the other.

In every town they liberated, people came out of the rubble to greet the American soldiers. The people were so happy that they often cried. They hugged and kissed the soldiers. They were thankful that their Nazi oppressors were gone. If the people had any food at all, they offered it to the American soldiers—sometimes only bread,

ABOVE:
FRENCH CIVILIANS ERECTED THIS TRIBUTE TO AN AMERICAN SOLDIER WHO DIED
WHILE LIBERATING FRANCE FROM NAZI OPPRESSION. Location: Near Caranten, France.
Date: 6/17/1944.
© CORBIS

RIGHT:
AMERICAN SOLDIER OFFERS CANDY TO LITTLE GIRL IN FRENCH TOWN LIBERATED
AFTER D-DAY. Location: Near Normandy, France. Date: 6/13/1944.
© Bettmann/CORBIS

sometimes some wine, sometimes a little more. The American soldiers offered small gifts in return, usually American candy bars and chewing gum.

One day, as we marched through a small town in France, I noticed a little girl and her mother watching us from the side of the road. A soldier marching next to me noticed the mother and daughter, too, and he stopped to give the little girl some candy. The little girl giggled with delight as she ate the candy, but her mother cried.

When this little girl grows up, will she remember how her freedom was won? Will she know the price that was paid? Will she honor the memory of the men who paid it? The men who died on Normandy Beach were strangers to this little girl, yet they laid down their lives as though she was family. Will she ever understand that? [14]

I thought about that little French girl for a long time. I think about her still. It must have been terrible for her to live in fear, to not be free. I didn't know that I was about to discover something even more terrible.

....

PART TWO
THE HOLOCAUST

"Was that once a factory?" I asked.

It was a bright and sunny morning in the spring of 1945, and I was with a small patrol of American soldiers on the outskirts of Oswiecim, Poland, near Krakow. The two cities had already been liberated by Soviet troops, so there was no fighting going on in the area. We had been marching through a forest for a couple of hours. The ground was covered by a few inches of new wet snow. When we came out of the forest, we were standing before a gigantic complex of burned-out and empty buildings, smokestacks that had fallen over, torn barbed-wire fences, broken gates, and pitted gravel roads. [15]

"It was once a factory, all right," one soldier in the patrol said. "It was a Nazi factory of death."

The civilians in the area called the place Konzentrationslager Auschwitz, but the American soldier called it Auschwitz-Birkenau, for the two towns that the huge facility occupied.

The soldier explained that the Nazis brought people to Auschwitz-Birkenau by train from all over Europe. When they got there, the Nazis murdered them one after another, as if that was their job on an assembly line. The Nazis packed men, women, and children into cold cattle cars, starved them, and shipped them as animals to Auschwitz-Birkenau. When the prisoners arrived, the Nazis forced

most of them into large concrete rooms that they locked shut and filled with poison gas. After the people died, the Nazis burned the bodies in huge ovens. Sickening smoke had filled the sky day and night, the soldier said, because the Nazis had to work overtime to incinerate the bodies—more than one million men, women, and children were murdered at Auschwitz-Birkenau.

"No! It's not possible," I said. "I don't believe it."

"There is evidence," the soldier assured me, "and there are witnesses."

The soldier told me about Ruth Webber, who was my age when she was liberated from Auschwitz-Birkenau by Soviet troops. She was a witness to Nazi crimes. She said: "A transport would come in with a lot of people and they would move in a certain direction, and then they would disappear. They would never come out. So you realized that something is happening to them, and seeing the, the chimneys smoking continuously, especially after a transport—even at my age you kind of put two and two together and realize that yes, this is where you go, behind those, that fence that has the, uh, the blankets on it and the trees covering something that goes on behind there, that you go in and you don't come out anymore. Exactly what was happening I don't know, all I knew is that you come out the chimney."[16]

"But why?" I asked, as if a reason even mattered—as if any reason could justify such evil.

"Because they were Jews," the soldier said. "Because they were Jews."

It was Hitler's plan, the soldier explained, to murder every Jewish man, woman, and child living in Europe—for no reason other than that they were Jewish. Auschwitz-Birkenau was the centerpiece of an elaborate system of camps that Hitler's henchmen built to exterminate them. The soldier told me that Allied forces were finding and liberating camps like this all over Europe. American forces, the soldier said, had recently liberated camps with names like Dachau, Mauthausen, Dora-Mittelbau, and Buchenwald. But Hitler's death factories were so efficiently run, he said, that the Nazis had already succeeded in killing nearly six million people—mostly Jews, but also some Christians and others whom Hitler considered inferior and had sent to the camps.

The soldier warned me not to enter the Auschwitz-Birkenau camp. He said I wouldn't like what I would see, but I walked through the gate anyway. I had to know the truth. Words above the front gate said, "Arbeit Macht Frei [Work Shall Set You Free]." The words

were part of a deception, the soldier said, because 70 percent of the people arriving at Auschwitz-Birkenau were killed immediately. The rest were put to work, but there was never any intention to set them free. The Nazis meant to force the prisoners to work as slaves and starve them until they died.

I entered what was left of a long one-story concrete building. I shut its incredibly heavy metal door behind me. There were no windows in the room, but sunlight filtered in through broken areas of the walls and ceiling. The air in the room was cold—much colder, I thought, than the weather on that winter day could possibly have made it. Out of the corner of my eye, I thought I saw odd shadows in the room, and I thought I saw them moving, too. Then, over a broken wall, I saw the oven.

"It's true," I said, as I felt the tears start to come, and I slumped to the gas chamber's floor. "My God, it's true."

As I cried, I saw the shadows move again, and I heard the voices of a million ghosts calling out to me. They echoed my words. "Yes, it's true," they said. "We were here. Please don't forget us."

I promised I would never forget.

Later, as I walked through the ruins of the Auschwitz-Birkenau camp, I realized that it had not been destroyed by bombs or by fighting. The buildings looked like they had been dynamited and burned deliberately, some from the inside. It was the Nazis, I realized, who had destroyed the camp when they tried to hide their crimes. They didn't want the world to know what they had done. They didn't want any evidence.

The Nazis didn't want any witnesses, either. When they learned that Soviet troops were advancing on the camp, the Nazis sped up the pace of their murder. But they ran out of time to kill everyone, so they decided to evacuate the rest of the prisoners by making them march hundreds of miles to other camps deeper inside Germany. The prisoners called the relocation a "Death March."

Lilly Malnik was a teenager who was forced to march from Auschwitz-Birkenau to a camp named Bergen-Belsen inside Germany. She was a witness to Nazi crimes. She said: "Word came to us that we were going to evacuate Auschwitz. Why were we evacuating Auschwitz? It is because the Russians were coming close by. And so we . . . we all walked out of Auschwitz and we started walking. We walked for days. I'll never forget it. I don't know how many days we walked. We walked and then took cattle cars and then we walked again. And as we walked, we heard gunshots and they told us to keep on marching. We heard gunshots and they were shooting people in

GAS CHAMBER AND CREMATORIUM AT AUSCHWITZ-BIRKENAU. Location: Auschwitz-Birkenau Memorial, Oswiecim, Poland. Date: 1996. The crematorium (left) operated from August 1940 until July 1943. The large room (right) was initially a morgue, but it was adapted to become a gas chamber in 1941. When the camp was expanded in 1942, the Nazis shifted the mass murder of the Jews to newer Auschwitz facilities and gradually stopped using this gas chamber and crematorium; the furnaces and chimney were demolished, the openings in the roof through which the Nazis had poured poison Zyklon-B gas were plastered, and the building became a storage facility and air raid shelter.
© Michael St. Maur Sheil/CORBIS

the back who couldn't keep up with the walking. It ended up being called the death march because the ravines and the gutters, they were all red from blood."[17]

Battle-hardened soldiers were shocked by what they found in the Nazi death camps, and prisoners could not believe that they were being saved. On April 15, 1945, the British 11th Armoured Division liberated the Bergen-Belsen camp. Inside the camp, the British soldiers found more than sixty thousand sick and wasted prisoners, and more than thirteen thousand unburied corpses. Alan Zimm was one of the prisoners freed from the Bergen-Belsen camp. He was a witness to Nazi crimes. He said: "Uh, exactly at nine o'clock the gate of the camp which was, uh, two blocks away. You could see far away, the gate, opened up and a jeep with four military police, the English dressed up in the white belts and the white gloves and the red hats. They sit in the front of the jeep, four of them with machine-guns like that. And a truck with loudspeakers behind them, and he said, 'My dear friends . . .' in every language. In German, in Polish, in Yiddish, you name it. 'From now on you are free. You are liberated by the Allied forces. And the Germans have nothing to do to you anymore. You are free people.' Everybody was crying. It was, uh, such an emotional experience. It's hard to describe it. The people were jumping and hugging and kissing. And everybody was running to the jeep. They . . . the MP went down and they lifted up the MPs on their shoulders and carried him all the way around the block. And still people did not believe. There were a lot of people still afraid."[18]

The people around Alan Zimm were still afraid because they were not used to being helped. They were used to a world that had ignored their misery. The people in the Nazi death camps were there because their friends and neighbors had looked the other way as the Nazis rounded them up and forced them into cattle cars.

After the war, people would tell Alan Zimm, Lilly Malnik, Ruth Weber, and the other victims of Hitler's holocaust, that they just didn't know what Hitler was up to. People would claim that the truth about the Nazis had been hidden from them. People would lie. The

LEFT:
U.S. MARINES RAISE THE AMERICAN FLAG ON THE ISLAND OF IWO JIMA. Location: Mount Suribachi on Iwo Jima. Date: 2/23/1945, the fifth day of battle. Pictured: Private First Class Ira Hayes is the figure on the far left, Private First Class Franklin Sousley (later killed in action on Iwo Jima) is to the right front of Hayes, Sergeant Mike Strank (later killed in action on Iwo Jima) is on Sousley's left, U.S. Navy Corpsman John Bradley is in front of Sousley, Private First Class Rene Gagnon is in front of Strank, and Corporal Harlon Block is closest to the bottom of the flagpole.
© CORBIS

truth is that Hitler's evil was never hidden at all—it was always out in the open for everyone to see. Hitler succeeded because people closed their eyes to his evil. Hitler succeeded because people did nothing as long as his evil stayed away from their backyards. Hitler succeeded because people were too afraid to stop him. "Every sin is the result of a collaboration," after all.[19]

In my own time, evil is visible again—and I have seen it. I've seen the evil in the eyes of Islamic terrorists. Their ski masks don't hide it. I've seen the evil tucked behind the belts of suicide bombers. They show it off like a badge of honor on videotaped messages to their families. I've seen the evil in the desert palaces of dictators who are rich because they steal their country's wealth and resources. It's in the torture chambers dug beneath their ornate palace floors. I've seen evil in all the places where people are denied equal rights, denied freedom of religion, and denied freedom of speech.

In my time, evil is the cause of a new World War. And once again, it's a war in which some people fight, some people surrender, and some people sit by and do nothing—praying that evil visits others, but not them.[20]

History repeats, I guess.

....

PART THREE
THE WAR IN THE PACIFIC

Seventy-five feet below the surface of a small island in the South Pacific, inside an intricate network of tunnels, caves, bunkers, and tiny rooms, I saw a notice on a wall. It said: "We are here to defend this island to the limit of our strength. Each of your shots must kill many Americans. We cannot allow ourselves to be captured by the enemy. If our positions are overrun, we will take bombs and grenades and throw ourselves under the tanks to destroy them. We will infiltrate the enemy's lines to exterminate him. No man must die until he has killed at least ten Americans. We will harass the enemy with guerilla actions until the last of us has perished. Long live the Emperor!" The notice bore the signature of Lieutenant General Tadamichi Kuribayashi, the commander of Japanese forces on the island of Iwo Jima.[21]

I had to remind myself that it was February 23, 1945, because the words in the notice sounded so familiar to me. In my time, Islamic terrorists use the same words when they command their followers to kill Americans by turning themselves into "human bombs." But they issue their orders on videotape, and they instruct their soldiers to die not for an emperor, but a God.[22]

I climbed out of the maze of tunnels and onto the surface of the island. I was just in time to see six marines raise the American flag in the rocky ground of the island's dormant volcano, Mount Suribachi. When the flag went up, the marines on the mountainside and the beach below gave a loud cheer, the U.S. Navy ships anchored offshore blasted their horns, and a coded message crackled on the radio of a marine standing near me: "Ni-he da-na-ah-taj ihla [Our flag waves]." Then, a news photographer snapped a picture of the six marines with the American flag flying proudly over their heads.[23]

To the people back in the United States who would see the photograph in a newspaper, it would probably seem like the moment of victory had been captured on film. But the battle wasn't over. The brutal fighting raged for nearly a month more, as the Japanese soldiers followed the orders posted on the cave wall. One by one, and sometimes in groups, the Japanese soldiers surfaced from their underground hideout to attack—or to die by blowing themselves up in the middle of the Americans.

This was a contrast I'll never forget: American soldiers on the sunny surface of the island, and Japanese soldiers below them in the dark caves—the American soldiers fighting to survive, and the Japanese soldiers following orders to die.

The American marines struggled to understand the enemy that would not surrender, the enemy that left no choice except to be wiped out. I overheard a young marine talking about it: ". . . and all of a sudden these rocks parted, and out comes a Japanese soldier just reeking with smoke. His uniform was on fire. Tears were coming out of his eyes. I could even see that, I was so close to him. He had one of those Japanese grenades in his hand. He was in the process of throwing that as a last resort right amongst us. He got it away, but we dodged it, and we proceeded to mow him down. We quickly searched him because lots of times they were booby-trapped. I took his helmet off and found a picture in the top of his helmet of his family back in Tokyo or somewhere in Japan. He was standing erect with his helmet under his arm, wife and six children—cute-looking little children. Even after all we went through, all these tough Marines started to tear up a little bit . . . they choked up seeing that."[24]

On March 16, 1945, the battle for the island of Iwo Jima ended in victory for the Americans, but the price was extraordinarily high: twenty-four thousand American casualties, and more than six thousand Americans dead. The Japanese did worse: They willingly sacrificed the lives of twenty thousand of the twenty-one thousand soldiers they had on the island.

I heard a Marine Corps general sum up the fighting on Iwo Jima during the dedication of a cemetery on the island. He said: "Victory was never in doubt. . . . What was in doubt, in all our minds, was whether there would be any of us left to dedicate this cemetery."[25]

On August 6, 1945, at 9:15 A.M., plus 17 seconds, I saw the bomb bay doors open. I saw Little Boy, the product of top-secret atomic research in the desert of New Mexico, drop from the B-29 Superfortress, *Enola Gay*. I saw it fall toward the Japanese city of Hiroshima six miles below.[26]

I felt it, too. First, the plane jumped violently upward in the sky, because it was instantly nine thousand pounds lighter. Then, the plane lost 1,700 feet of altitude almost as quickly, as the pilot put the plane into a crushing 155-degree diving turn to the right, with a 60-degree bank at full engine power. The pilot had to get the plane out of the way of the blast that was coming.

I was in the bombardier's position in the nose of the plane, with Major Thomas W. Ferebee. I was looking through the bombsight as the plane made its gut-wrenching escape maneuver. I turned the knobs of the bombsight, tracking Little Boy's free fall to the city below.

In those brief seconds before the blast, even as I watched the bomb fall, I thought about the plane and not the bomb. I had built a scale model of the *Enola Gay* with my dad, so I knew the plane inside and out. I had held the parts in my own hands, painted them, and glued them together. But now, the parts were alive and all around me. The four 2,200 horsepower 18-cylinder engines and their superchargers screamed loudly in my ears. Like gigantic spinning eggbeaters, the plane's 16-foot-long propellers chopped through the thick morning air and sent waves of vibration through the plane that I could feel deep in the pit of my stomach.[27]

I remembered facts about the plane from the assembly instructions for the model. The B-29 was one of the first aircraft to have a fully pressurized crew compartment. It's four gun turrets were remote-controlled, operated from "glass-bubble" sighting stations

RIGHT:
COLONEL PAUL W. TIBBETS STANDS IN FRONT OF THE ENOLA GAY. Location: Island of Tinian, North Mariana Islands. Date: 8/6/1945, after the Hiroshima mission.
© Bettmann/CORBIS

along the fuselage. The plane was usually armed with ten .50-calibre machine guns and one 20-millimeter cannon, earning it the moniker "Superfortress." The heavy armaments made the B-29 particularly lethal to attacking enemy aircraft. When flying in formation, B-29s could place their attackers in deadly machine gun crossfire. For the secret mission to Hiroshima, though, the *Enola Gay*'s gun turrets had been removed, and its bomb bay had been specially adapted to hold the uranium-based atomic bomb, Little Boy.[28]

Little Boy detonated 1,890 feet above the city of Hiroshima. A blinding light was the first evidence of the bomb's power. It was as if the sun had somehow managed to appear right underneath the plane. The light was so intense that the shadows it cast on the walls of the plane's interior seemed to be frozen in position for several seconds. I moved, but my shadow didn't. Time seemed to stop. The bright flash temporarily blinded Major Ferebee, who had forgotten to put on his dark goggles.

I rushed through the two-foot diameter tunnel that led to the rear of the plane. I wanted to reach the tail gunner's position and get a better look at what was going on below. While I was inside the tunnel, the nuclear blast's shock wave struck and rattled the plane. I was tossed around inside the tunnel. I lost my bearings, and for a few moments, I panicked. I was sure that the plane was upside down and going to crash. Then the flight smoothed out.

When I reached the rear of the plane, I came upon the tail gunner, Staff Sergeant George R. Caron. He took off his dark goggles. The look on his face was deep shock. Because of his position in the plane's tail, I knew that he had witnessed the explosion, but I don't think it was the explosion that had shocked him. I think it was the result.

Outside the tail gunner's window, a thick black cloud boiled up from the city of Hiroshima. The cloud rose high into the sky. Its dark, bubbling top was already several miles above the plane and I had to crane my neck to see it. The cloud towered over us like a wicked giant set free from a cage, and it seemed to be laughing at us for having set it free. Far below us, and underneath the cloud, there was a huge black smudge on the surface of the earth where the city of Hiroshima used to be. I saw bright fires in places, but no matter how hard I looked, I could not see a single sign of life.[29]

The scene outside the tail gunner's window was horrifying, but the level of destruction was anything but new. Recent B-29 firebombing missions over Tokyo, Nagoya, Kobe, Yokohama, Osaka, Kawasaki, and Hitachi, had wreaked the same level of death and destruction. Bombing missions over Europe had done the same there. What was new—and frightening—was that this level of death and destruction

could now be accomplished with a single plane carrying a single weapon.[30]

I crawled back through the narrow tunnel to the front of the plane and entered the cockpit. The pilot, Colonel Tibbets, and the copilot, Captain Lewis, were staring at the monstrous dark cloud outside their window.

"I think this is the end of the war," Colonel Tibbets said to Captain Lewis.[31]

Then Colonel Tibbets turned toward me and noticed the shock on my face. He said that he was also painfully aware that thousands of people were dying on the streets of Hiroshima. He said that he felt shame for humanity as a whole.

"It is not easy for a soldier to be detached from the misery he has created," Colonel Tibbets said. "Every fighting man with normal sensitivity, even if he has simply pulled a rifle trigger and slain a fellow soldier of another nationality, is painfully aware that he has brought tragedy to some household."[32]

I asked Colonel Tibbets if he thought the bombing of Hiroshima had been necessary. He said the answer to my question was really all around me.

"The real answers lay in thousands of graves from Pearl Harbor around the world to Normandy, and back again," Colonel Tibbets said. "The actual use of the weapons as ordered by the President of the United States was believed to be the quickest and least costly way to stop the killing. . . . We had a mission. Quite simply, bring about the end of World War II."[33]

As the *Enola Gay* flew back toward its base on the island of Tinian, I thought about what Colonel Tibbets had said, and what I had seen. The evil unleashed by Adolph Hitler, and the aggression of the Japanese warlords, had plunged the world into a war that had already claimed more than thirty-six million lives: Thirty-six million men, women, and children had perished, before the *Enola Gay* had even lifted off the runway for Hiroshima.

Thirty-six million people. . . . How long will it take to recite the names of the dead? How long will it take to weep for them? This evil must be defeated. This war must end.[34]

But a single atomic bomb would not end World War II—it would take another one. And the second atomic bomb almost didn't end the war, either.

The day after we landed on Tinian, American warplanes once again took to the skies over the cities of Japan. But the planes dropped leaflets, not bombs. The leaflets said: "TO THE JAPANESE PEOPLE: America asks that you take immediate heed of what we say

THE *ENOLA GAY* STANDS ON THE RUNWAY ON TINIAN. Location: Island of Tinian,
North Mariana Islands. Date: 8/6/1945, after the Hiroshima mission.
© Bettmann/CORBIS

on this leaflet. We are in possession of the most destructive bomb
ever devised by man. We have just begun to use this weapon against
your homeland. If you still have any doubt, make inquiry as to what
happened to Hiroshima when just one atomic bomb fell on that city.
We urge that you begin the work of building a new, better and peace-
loving Japan. You should take steps now to cease military resistance.
Otherwise, we shall resolutely employ this bomb and all of our other
superior weapons to promptly and forcefully end the war. EVACUATE
YOUR CITIES."[35]

But the Japanese did not heed the warnings. The Japanese did not
surrender.

On August 9, 1945, a second atomic bomb was dropped on the
Japanese city of Nagasaki. After the blast, the governor of Nagasaki
cheerfully reported to his superiors in Tokyo that no senior officials
had been killed. He erroneously reported that the number of dead in
the city was small.

The day after the bomb was dropped on Nagasaki, on August 10,
Japanese military commanders renewed their call to fight to the last
man. The Japanese Minister of War, General Korechika Anami, said:
"Even though we may have to eat grass, swallow dirt, and lie in the
fields, we shall fight on to the bitter end, ever firm in our faith that

we shall find life in death." The Emperor of Japan, Emperor Hirohito, initially agreed: Japan would fight on.[36]

But then, three days later, Emperor Hirohito changed his mind. He made plans to surrender to the Americans during a radio broadcast to the Japanese people on August 15. Some Japanese military commanders on General Anami's staff decided they couldn't let that happen. They plotted to stop the emperor from surrendering. They sent soldiers into the emperor's palace in the darkness before dawn on the day of the broadcast, and searched for the emperor and his pre-recorded surrender announcement. At the same time, some American B-29s flew over Tokyo, on their way to bomb an oil refinery. Japanese air defense officials, who feared that a third atomic bomb would be dropped, ordered a complete blackout of Tokyo. In the darkness of the blackout, the soldiers could not find the emperor or his recording, and the attempted coup failed.

When he learned that the coup had failed, General Anami, who had thought all along that the emperor's order to surrender should be obeyed, committed suicide. He gave the reason for taking his own life in a handwritten note: ". . . the broadcast of the Emperor's recording will be made at noon tomorrow—I could not bear to hear it."[37]

Colonel Tibbets had once asked: "Do you have any idea how many American lives would have been lost had we launched a ground invasion of Japan, instead of dropping the bomb? And how many Japanese lives?"[38]

I think I do.

An American invasion of Japan would have been extremely costly to both sides. The monthlong battle on Iwo Jima had claimed six thousand American lives, and nearly all of the twenty-one thousand Japanese defenders. Victory on the island of Okinawa had cost twelve thousand American lives, and more than one hundred thousand Japanese defenders. Japanese soldiers were under orders to fight until no one was left alive. They were trained from a young age to prefer death to surrender. In Japan, military leaders were prepared to sacrifice the lives of hundreds of thousands, maybe even millions, of civilians if Americans invaded their homeland. They told the people of Japan to prepare for hand-to-hand combat in the streets with American soldiers, and they taught mothers and children how to survive in the hills by eating berries and nuts.

I cried for the people of Hiroshima, and I prayed that nuclear weapons would never be used again. Like Colonel Tibbets, I felt a deep shame for humanity as a whole. But I couldn't help thinking that all the horrors I had seen during this war were somehow connected—that the thirty-six million dead, the Death Camps in Europe, and the dropping of two atomic bombs were all part of the shameful price for not stopping evil early enough. It's been said that "every evil in the bud is easily crushed; as it grows older, it becomes stronger."[39]

But it's a lesson that still hasn't been learned in my own time. Nearly a million bodies floated down the rivers of Rwanda, while the whole world watched and did nothing. Four hundred thousand men, women, and children were murdered and then buried in the sands of Iraq, while the United Nations mailed neatly typed letters to Saddam. Entire villages were wiped out in Sudan, while the world's leaders calmly debated the definition of genocide. In Israel, suicide bombers detonated themselves on school buses, in grocery stores, and at wedding celebrations, while nations argued about a fence.[40]

Colonel Tibbets once said: "Our crew did not do the bombing in anger. We did it because we were determined to stop the killing. I would have done anything to get to Japan and stop the killing."[41]

Yes. Thirty-six million lives are enough.

....

PART FOUR
SACRIFICE

At 3:30 P.M., on April 30, 1945, inside a fortified bunker beneath the city of Berlin, Adolph Hitler bit into a thin glass vial of cyanide as he put a bullet into his head with a 7.65 mm Walther pistol. Because Allied troops were closing in on the Nazi capital, Hitler's henchmen emerged from the underground hiding place only long enough to douse their leader's dead body with gasoline and burn it in a bomb crater. Adolph Hitler would never stand trial before the people of the free world. He would never be held publicly accountable for his crimes. The Allied troops would discover only the charred remains of Satan's man on Earth.

The war in Europe officially ended at midnight on May 8, 1945. At 9:00 A.M., President Truman announced the news of the unconditional surrender of Germany in a radio address to the American people. He said: "The western world has been freed of the evil forces which for five years and longer have imprisoned the bodies and broken the lives of millions upon millions of free-born men. They have violated their churches, destroyed their homes, corrupted their children, and murdered their loved ones. Our Armies of Liberation have restored freedom to these suffering peoples, whose spirit and will the oppressors could never enslave. Much remains to be done. The victory in the West must now be won in the East. The whole world must be cleansed of the evil from which half the world has been freed."[42]

The war in the Pacific ended four months later, on September 9, 1945, with the unconditional surrender of Japan. Addressing the American people, President Truman said: "We think of those whom death in this war has hurt, taking from them fathers, husbands, sons, brothers, and sisters whom they loved. No victory can bring back the faces they longed to see. Only the knowledge that the victory, which these sacrifices have made possible, will be wisely used, can give them any comfort. It is our responsibility—ours, the living—to see that this victory shall be a monument worthy of the dead who died to win it."[43]

The Picture Frame transported me back to the beach in France, where I had witnessed the Allied invasion a year before. The beach was quiet, except for the rhythm of the waves crashing on the empty shore. There was no thunder in the sky, and there were no explosions in the sand. The water was blue, not red. The pillboxes on the bluff were silent and empty. Bullets did not rain down from above. There was nothing disturbing the small birds that hopped along the shore, looking for food.

In the warm late afternoon sun, I walked up a dusty trail from the beach to the top of the bluff—a path that Allied soldiers had walked on D-Day. It was hard to believe that what I had seen on the beach just a year before had actually happened. The fields of tall grass above the beach carried the evidence that it had, though: Row after row of wooden crosses lined the countryside as far as I could see. Like the beads on a giant abacus that had been laid down on its side, the crosses were the final tally of the high price of freedom and the cost of fighting evil.

I knelt in the tall grass and prayed for the souls that the crosses represented. I could hear their voices in the gentle ocean breeze: "When you go home, tell them of us, and say: For your tomorrow, we gave our today."[44]

Standing among some crosses farther down the shoreline, I saw a young American soldier. I walked over to him. His uniform was covered with medals. He wore the Medal of Honor, the Distinguished Service Cross, the Silver Star, the Bronze Star, the Purple Heart, the French Croix de Guerre, the Medal of Liberated France, and more than a dozen others. He told me that his name was Audie Murphy, that he was a 2nd Lieutenant, and that he was returning soon to his home in Texas. He was twenty-one years old, he said, but a tired look in his eyes made him seem older to me.[45]

I told Lieutenant Murphy what the Picture Frame had shown me— what I had seen of the war. I told him how different real war was from "playing army" with my friends back home. Lieutenant Murphy said that war was not at all the way he had imagined it, either, when he was a boy.

He said: "I was on a faraway battlefield, where bugles blew, banners streamed, and men charged gallantly across flaming hills; where the temperature always stood at eighty and our side was always victorious; where the dying were but impersonal shadows and the wounded never cried; where enemy bullets always miraculously missed me, and my trusty rifle forever hit home."[46]

Lieutenant Murphy turned away and looked out over the channel. The late afternoon sun looked like a bright orange disc burning just above the water at the horizon. It sent streaks of light across the darkening sky.

"I have seen war as it actually is," Lieutenant Murphy said, "and I do not like it."[47]

Lieutenant Murphy and I walked together on the bluff, following the contours of the rugged coastline. We stopped every now and then to look out at the point where the sun was disappearing from the sky. We didn't talk very much. I broke one of the long silences between us when I asked Lieutenant Murphy if the war had changed him. I asked him whether fighting monsters had made him into a monster himself.

He replied: "When I was a child, I was told that men were branded by war. Has the brand been put on me? Have years of blood and ruin stripped me of all decency? Of all belief?

"Not of all belief. I believe in the force of a hand grenade, the power of artillery, the accuracy of a Garand. I believe in hitting before you get hit, and that dead men do not look noble.

"But I also believe in . . . all the men who stood up against the enemy, taking their beatings without whimper and their triumphs without boasting. The men who went and would go again to hell and back to preserve what our country thinks right and decent."[48]

I thought that Lieutenant Murphy's words were remarkable because, in his time, it was never obvious that the forces of good would triumph over the forces of evil. Satan had arranged a nearly even match. In my time, things are different: The forces of good clearly have the power to prevail over the forces of evil—it's only the will to do what is necessary to win that is in doubt. People demand endless negotiation with the Hitlers of my time, limited responses to brutal attacks, and quick exits from the fields of battle. They whimper that the smallest sacrifices are too much to bear, too expensive, and too inconvenient. They seem to be angry that their daily routine has been disrupted, not that the foes of freedom are on the march. In my time, the men and women who risk the supreme sacrifice to fight for what is right seem fewer and farther between. Their character seems more rare, less appreciated, and even mocked.

As the last bit of the sun dipped below the horizon, and the final streaks of red light faded from the sky, I wondered what Lieutenant Murphy would do with the rest of his life, now that the war was over. I wondered what the future held for him.

"What will you do now?" I asked.

"I will go back. I will find the kind of girl of whom I once dreamed. I will learn to look at life through uncynical eyes, to have faith, to know love. I will learn to work in peace as in war. And finally—finally, like countless others, I will learn to live again."[49]

AUDIE MURPHY HOLDS HIS SON AS HIS WIFE LOOKS ON. Location: Yakima, WA, on the movie set of Audie Murphy's autobiographical film, *To Hell and Back*. Date: 10/4/1954. Terry Michael Murphy is two and a half years old; Pamela Murphy, Audie's wife, brought Terry to watch his father work.
© Bettmann/CORBIS

EARL COMBS AND MARK KOENIG SCORE ON LOU GEHRIG'S TRIPLE, AS GEHRIG ROUNDS
THIRD. Location: Yankee Stadium in New York. Date: 10/7/1927, during the third game
of the World Series.
© Bettmann/CORBIS

Lou Gehrig—Henry Louis Gehrig—was born June 19, 1903 in Manhattan. He was named after his father, Heinrich, but he never used his first name. He preferred Lou. His mother, Christina, gave birth to four children after marrying Heinrich, but only Lou survived. The other three children died shortly after birth.

Heinrich and Christina had both immigrated to the United States from Germany—Heinrich in 1888, and Christina in 1899. Heinrich first settled in Chicago, but then moved to New York City, where he met and married Christina. The newlyweds started out poor and struggled to make ends meet. Heinrich got a job as a sheet metal worker. Christina took jobs doing laundry and cleaning apartments for people in the wealthy parts of town. Even after Lou was born, Christina worked because she wanted to provide the very best that she could for Lou.

"I don't pretend Lou was born with a silver spoon in his mouth," she said. "But he never left the table hungry, and I can say he had a terrible appetite from the first time he saw daylight. Maybe his clothes were torn, dirty, and rumpled after playing baseball and football, but he was always clean and neatly dressed when I sent him off to school."[2]

Lou graduated from Public School Number 132 in Manhattan, and then entered the New York High School of Commerce, with firm plans to go to college. Lou's mother expected him to become an engineer. It had always been her dream that her son would get a good education and a good job in America. In 1920, when Lou accepted an athletic scholarship from New York's Columbia University, he followed his mother's mandate and began his engineering studies. Lou longed to be a baseball player, but he didn't want to disappoint his mother or destroy her dream. Lou settled in at Columbia and resigned himself to becoming an engineering student who just happened to play great baseball.

But on a spring day in April 1923, fate caught up with Lou. Pitching for the Columbia University Lions, Lou struck out more than a dozen Williams College hitters. At bat, Lou slammed in home run after home run for Columbia. Paul Krichell, a New York Yankees scout, was in the stands that day, and he saw the whole thing.

"I think I've just seen another Babe Ruth!" Paul Krichell reported to New York Yankees owner Ed Barrow.[3]

The New York Yankees approached Lou and offered him a slot on the team. Lou was torn: He wanted to play baseball, but he didn't want to defy his mother's plan for his future. It was a tough decision for Lou, and he might have turned down the Yankees' offer, if it wasn't for the fact that his father was ill and the family needed money to pay hospital bills. Lou knew that a New York Yankees paycheck would go a long way in paying those bills. So on June 23, Lou signed the contract to play baseball in the Major Leagues. He put on a New York Yankees uniform and left his engineering studies at Columbia University behind.

Lou's father was pleased with his son's decision. For a long time, he'd hidden from his wife that he supported Lou's desire to play baseball. The decision disappointed Lou's mother, though. She was convinced that her son was throwing away a valuable education and a chance for a respectable career. According to Lou's mother, engineering was an honorable and serious profession, but there was nothing admirable or serious about playing baseball. Playing baseball was for children, Mrs. Gehrig thought, not for grown men.[4]

It took a while, but Lou's mother eventually got over his decision to make baseball his career. By the time I arrived in 1927, Lou's mom was one of the most enthusiastic supporters of the New York Yankees. After home games, she regularly opened her kitchen to Yankees players that Lou brought home for dinner. The practice became a ritual, and to top it all off, she was a great cook, too. Some players enjoyed Mrs. Gehrig's cooking so much, and ate dinner at the Gehrig house so often, that they became known as "Mom's Boys."[5]

Maybe Lou's mom just needed to see baseball played really well, by one of the best teams of all time, before she understood what Lou saw in the game—and why he wanted to play it. I don't know. But as I watched the game from the front-row seat Lou Gehrig gave me in the Yankees dugout that day in October 1927, I saw near perfection! Yankees pitcher Herb Pennock was on the mound, and he put down the Pirates batters one-by-one, not giving up a single hit to them until the eighth inning of the game. The poor Pirates batters looked more beaten each time it was their turn to step into the batter's box. And when the Yankee sluggers of "Murderer's Row" got up to bat, the Pirates pitcher looked nervous, and his fielders all took several steps back. They all looked like they were preparing themselves for the cover to be knocked off the ball!

Step back! It's Murderer's Row!

Murderer's Row was the name the newspapers had given to the home-run hitters in the powerful Yankees batting lineup. The members of Murderer's Row were Babe Ruth, Lou Gehrig, Tony Lazzeri, Bob Meusel, and Earle Combs—and they were feared for good reason. In 1927, right fielder Babe Ruth had a .356 batting average and slammed 60 home runs. First baseman Lou Gehrig hit 47 home runs in 1927, with a .373 average and 175 runs batted in. Second baseman Tony Lazzeri had a .309 average, and his 18 home runs ranked him third in the American League in 1927. Fielder Bob Meusel had a batting average of .337 in 1927, and he slammed in 103 runs. Center fielder Earle Combs slugged his way to a .356 average and 231 hits in 1927. In a single game in 1927, Combs hit 3 triples in a row.

The New York Yankees completely dominated the game that day, pitching and slugging their way to an 8–1 victory over the Pittsburgh Pirates. Pennock had allowed the Pirates only one run and three hits. In the Pirates dugout after the game, a player even told a newspaper reporter: "If the two teams had played a hundred games, I honestly think the Yankees would have won them all. That's how intimidated we were."[6]

After the game, Lou Gehrig took Babe Ruth, Tony Lazzeri, and me to his parents' house for a celebration dinner. It was my turn to become one of Mom's Boys! What a feast she had prepared, too! There was more food than anyone could possibly eat, and all of it was delicious. I ate something called Rouladen, with potato dumplings on the side. For dessert, I had a huge slice of German apple cake. Mmm, it was good! I skipped the pickled eels, though. I just watched in horror, as Babe Ruth ate a whole plateful of them. There's no accounting for taste, I guess.[7]

During dinner, I noticed that Lou's mother really liked Babe Ruth. I think the Babe was her favorite Yankee, next to her son, of course. Ruth told jokes to Mrs. Gehrig all through dinner, and she laughed and laughed. By contrast, Lou's father was the quietest person at the table. He was content just to be surrounded by the happy chaos. But his broad smile, and the twinkle in his eye, made it clear that he enjoyed himself, and that he was as proud as he could be of his son, the New York Yankee.

I had a great time that evening, too. I enjoyed watching everyone eat and be happy.

But why did the Picture Frame bring me here? What am I supposed to learn from baseball players in 1927?

....

The year 1927 stretched into 1928, and I still didn't have the answers to my questions, but I knew they would come eventually. In the meantime, I figured, I might as well have fun. I asked Lou if he'd take me down to the ballpark the next time he practiced, and if he would give me some pointers on hitting and fielding. Lou said that he loved to go to the ballpark and practice every chance he could, and yes, I could come along. You can't get too much practice, Lou insisted. Practice reduces errors, he said.

"I worked real hard to learn to play first base. In the beginning, I used to make one terrible play a game. Then I got so I'd make one a week, and finally, I'd pull a real bad one maybe once a month. At the end, I was trying to keep it down to one a season."[8]

On the first sunny day in the spring, Lou kept his promise and took me down to Yankee Stadium. We had the entire stadium to ourselves because the season hadn't started yet. I went out to first base and Lou hit some balls to me.

"Learn from the start to get your body in front of the ball whenever possible. Sometimes, of course, you can't do it—you'll be tearing at top speed and will be lucky to get near it. When you can, though, plant yourself squarely in its path. Then, if you misjudge a hop of the ball, or it makes a freak bound, it's likely to hit your body and fall dead, and you can still make a play."[9]

I followed Lou's advice and found that he was right. When I got in front of the ball, I could always stop it and make the play, even when the ball came so hard and fast that it popped out of my glove. The more difficult thing was predicting where the ball was going, so that I would have enough time to get in front of it in the first place. Lou said being able to predict where the ball is going is an essential skill, especially for first basemen and the other infield players.

"Remember always to keep your eye on the ball. That can't be overstressed. From the moment the bat starts it on its way, until it socks into your mitt, don't take your eye off it. You'll avoid a lot of muffs and fumbles if you follow this rule."[10]

I had a great time that afternoon, and I learned a lot. I even got some batting practice in. Now, how many people do you know who got to hit balls to Lou Gehrig in Yankee Stadium in 1928? Not many, I'd bet!

As we walked home from the ballpark that day, I asked Lou if there was any one thing that contributed most to his success in the game. I wanted to know his secret.

"My success came from one word—hustle," he explained. "There is no excuse for a player not hustling. Every player owes it to himself, his club, and to the public to hustle every minute he is on the ball field. And that goes for the star as much as for the kid who is fighting to get a regular job."[11]

"I'll remember that!" I said.

RIGHT:
THE MEMBERS OF MURDERERS' ROW POSE FOR A PHOTOGRAPH. Location: Yankee Stadium in New York. Date: 4/16/1931. Left to right: Lou Gehrig, Earl Combs, Tony Lazzeri, Babe Ruth, and Anthony.
© Bettmann/CORBIS

NEW YORK YANKEE FIRST BASEMAN LOU GEHRIG SWINGS HIS BAT.
Location: Probably Yankee Stadium in New York. Date: 1927.
© Bettmann/CORBIS

But it wasn't until 1933 that I realized just how much "hustle" Lou gave his teammates and his fans. Lou Gehrig and I had just finished having breakfast in a Washington, D.C., hotel, when Dan Daniel, a sportswriter for the *New York World Telegram,* cornered Lou in the lobby. Daniel asked Lou if he had any idea how many baseball games he had played in.

"No, I don't," Lou said, in all sincerity. "I do know that I started in 1925, and this is 1933. So I guess I've played somewhere in the hundreds."[12]

"It's much more than that," suggested Daniel.[13]

Daniel informed Lou that he had played in 1,250 games in a row! An astonishing record, Daniel said, but it didn't seem to faze Lou at all! When Daniel published the number, and people began to make a big deal about it, Lou was puzzled by the public's interest in the number, too. Lou just thought it was his job to show up every day and play ball.

In August 1933, Lou's record of consecutive games played reached 1,308. In 1936, his record topped 1,800 straight games. On May 31, 1938, with the Red Sox in New York, Lou's wife, Eleanor, suggested that Lou take a break from baseball and not play that day. She thought he needed some rest. Lou was determined to face the Red Sox that afternoon, though, and he completed his 2,000th game! It was just another day at the office for Lou!

People started calling Lou Gehrig the "Iron Horse" of baseball. They speculated that he had some unique physical makeup that enabled him to play so many games and not run out of steam. Believe it or not, the New York Yankees team manager took Lou to Columbia University's Medical Clinic, and asked the doctors to examine him—to see if the doctor's could discover what gave Lou his stamina! The results of the physical showed Lou to be in good shape, but quite an ordinary man.

Lou's medical examination did reveal one curious thing. The X-rays showed that at one time or another, every one of Lou's fingers had been broken, and his hands had been fractured seventeen times. Even more incredible, the doctors determined that all the bone damage had healed naturally, because Lou had never gotten medical attention. Lou had never let a broken hand stop him from playing ball! In hundreds of the games he played, Lou had just ignored the pain. Lou believed that he had a job to do on the baseball field, and he did it no matter what. Lou didn't want to let anyone down. He didn't want to complain. To Lou, playing in every game, no matter what, was just part of the "hustle" that he felt he owed his teammates and his fans.

When the results of Lou's medical tests were made public, New York sportswriter Ed Farrell wrote: "A fractured finger is an injury serious enough to force any ballplayer out of action. That is, any ballplayer whose name is not Lou Gehrig. It is going to take more than a thumb fracture to produce the unusual sight of the Yankees starting a ball game without Gehrig at first base."[14]

During my travels with the New York Yankees each season, I discovered other things besides "hustle" that contributed to Lou's success as a ballplayer. Maybe Lou didn't mention these other things to me because they were just part of his nature, but they were easy for me to see. There were obvious and striking differences between Lou Gehrig's behavior and the behavior of the other ballplayers on the team.

After a home game, for example, Lou would go back to his parents' house and eat a home-cooked dinner. Then he'd take a walk, and go to bed early. After an away game, Lou's routine was similar. He would eat a good meal, take a brisk walk, and then retire early in the evening to his hotel room. The other players would go out drinking and "clubbing" until all hours of the night. Not Lou. Lou had a code that he lived by.

"Ten hours of sleep a night, a lot of water, a sensible choice of food, and you'll never have a day's worry in your life," Lou would say.[15]

And I wasn't the only one to notice that Lou Gehrig always set the best example both on and off the field. A sportswriter named Stanley Frank wrote: "Polishing the Yankee's public image was Lou's full-time job. This may seem a trivial point, but he never appeared in a restaurant, hotel lobby, or any other public place without a coat and tie."[16]

It was so true! Lou always spoke, and behaved, and dressed like a gentleman—and he demanded that his teammates do so, too. A Yankee who showed up to a restaurant without a coat and tie when Lou was around, wouldn't make that mistake twice. "You're a big-leaguer," Lou would tell him sharply. "Look like one!"[17]

Some of the players ribbed Lou about what they called his "Boy Scout" behavior, but they all respected him. They also tried to emulate him. Whenever Lou was around, his teammates seemed to act better than they normally would. Lou had class, and some of it rubbed off on the other players, whether they wanted to admit it or not. Sportswriter Stanley Frank wrote: "It is significant that the Yankees never were involved in nightclub brawls or drew adverse publicity from clashes between managers and players until DiMaggio and Henrich, the last men who had been exposed to Lou's influence, had left the club."[18]

Now, I know why I am here . . .

I finally knew why the Picture Frame had dropped me into Yankee Stadium on that October day in 1927! It was Lou Gehrig's character that I was intended to see! It was Lou Gehrig's quiet strength that I was supposed to notice! Unlike some of the professional athletes in my own time—with their foul mouths, arrest records, drug-habits, tattoos, and nipple rings—Lou Gehrig was an athlete to be admired. Lou Gehrig was a positive role model for his teammates and his fans.[19]

"When the last great scorer comes to mark against your name, it's not whether you won or lost, but how you played the game."[20]

....

On May 2, 1939, thousands of New York Yankees fans saw the impossible happen. I was there, and I saw it happen, too. On that day, the New York Yankees started a baseball game without Lou Gehrig on first base.

"It is going to take more than a thumb fracture to produce the unusual sight of the Yankees starting a ball game without Gehrig at first base."[21]

News reporters ran from their press boxes and rushed to the Yankees dugout, demanding to know why the Iron Horse of Baseball was not at his post. Joe McCarthy, the Yankees team manager, tried to tell the reporters that Lou Gehrig had voluntarily taken himself out of the lineup, but the reporters couldn't believe it. Why on Earth, the reporters demanded to know, would Lou Gehrig take himself out of the lineup after playing 2,130 consecutive games?[22]

Finally, Lou stepped forward to explain: "I decided last Sunday on this move. I haven't been a bit of good to the team since the season

034.jpeg   f4.0   1/125   11:15pm   09.11.2004

Anthony

ABOVE:
BABE RUTH AND LOU GEHRIG. Location: Shibe Park in Philadelphia, PA. Date: Anthony took this photograph on 4/12/1932, but his digital camera recorded the time as 11:15 P.M. and the date as 9/11/2004.
© Photofest

LEFT:
ANTHONY SNAPS A PICTURE OF BABE RUTH SNAPPING A PICTURE OF LOU GEHRIG. Location: Shibe Park in Philadelphia, PA. Date: 4/12/1932, before the start of the New York Yankees vs. Philadelphia Athletics game. Shibe Park was renamed Connie Mack Stadium in 1953; Connie Mack Stadium was demolished in 1976, and home plate was moved to Veterans Stadium in 1971.
© Bettmann/CORBIS

started. It wouldn't be fair to the boys or Joe, or to the baseball public for me to try going on. In fact, it wouldn't be fair to myself, and I'm the last consideration."[23]

Lou's simple statement shocked everyone who heard it, and everyone who read about it in the papers later that day. Yes, it was true that Lou had been in a hitting "slump" for a while, and that his batting average had mysteriously dropped—but to take himself out of the game? That made no sense at all. Excellent players like Lou can recover from a slump, the reporters insisted, it just takes time.

Only a handful of people close to Lou suspected that there was something else going on with him, something that might be more than just a hitting slump. They knew that Lou was just a little bit slower on the field. They knew that he sometimes said his back hurt, and that he said he couldn't get a tight grip on the ball. They knew that he said he felt tired more often than he used to. And they knew about the time Lou lost his balance and fell down in the Yankees locker room, and then found it difficult to get back up.

Something was wrong, but the reason for Lou's slump was a mystery, even to Lou. Lou had tried to compensate for his performance slump by doing what he had always done: working harder and practicing more often. He even stayed on the field after official practice was over to do extra exercises and routines. But, no matter what he did, Lou just couldn't shake the feeling that he was getting weaker and weaker.

"I just don't know," said Lou. "I can't figure what's the matter with me. I just know I can't go on this way."[24]

I was with Lou Gehrig on his thirty-sixth birthday. It was June 19, 1939. We were at the Mayo Clinic in Rochester, Minnesota. Lou's birthday present was a letter from his doctors that said he was suffering from Amyotrophic Lateral Sclerosis, or ALS. The letter explained: "This type of illness involves the motor pathways and cells of the central nervous system and in lay terms is known as a form of chronic poliomyelitis (infantile paralysis). The nature of this trouble makes it such that Mr. Gehrig will be unable to continue his active participation as a baseball player, inasmuch as it is advisable that he conserve his muscular energy."[25]

The mystery of Lou Gehrig's progressing weakness was finally solved, but the letter was a half-truth. The whole truth was that the ALS diagnosis was a death sentence for Lou. I overheard Dr. Mayo talking on the telephone with Lou's wife, who was back in New York. He told her that Lou probably only had two or three years left to live. Mrs. Gehrig asked Dr. Mayo not to tell that to Lou. She would tell him later.[26]

Lou knew the truth without anyone telling him. Once, when a small crowd of admirers gathered around him outside the stadium, he turned to a writer companion and whispered, "These people are yelling 'Good luck, Lou' and are wishing me well, and I'm dying."[27]

Everyone, everywhere, always wished Lou well, because everyone loved Lou. Sportswriter Fred Lieb even said: "There was absolutely no reason to dislike him, and nobody did."[28]

New York Yankees fans chose July 4, 1939, to officially show Lou Gehrig how much they loved him. It was "Lou Gehrig Appreciation Day" at Yankee Stadium, and I was there. The capacity crowd of sixty-one thousand people stood up in the bleachers and chanted: "We want Lou! We want Lou! We want Lou!" The team manager, Joe McCarthy, had to go back into the locker room and coax a very reluctant Lou Gehrig out onto the field to address his noisy friends in the stands. The crowd did not quiet down until Lou finally appeared and stood before the microphone in the middle of the field.

"Fans," Lou Gehrig said into the microphone, his voice reverberating throughout the stadium, "for the past two weeks you have been reading about a bad break I got. Yet today, I consider myself the luckiest man on the face of the earth. I have been in ballparks for seventeen years and I have never received anything but kindness and encouragement from you fans."[29]

Lou paused for a moment to look at his Yankee teammates, who had lined up behind him on the ball field. Then he continued: "Look at these grand men. Which of you wouldn't consider it the highlight of his career just to associate with them for even one day?"[30]

Lou praised his teammates and his managers, and then focused his final remarks on his family and his life: "Sure, I'm lucky. When you have a father and mother, who work all their lives so that you can have an education and build your body, it's a blessing! When you have a wife who has been a tower of strength, and shown more courage than you dreamed existed, that's the finest I know. So I close

in saying that I might have had a bad break, but I have an awful lot to live for!"[31]

Lou's words seemed a contradiction to me. Lou Gehrig never let his teammates down. He showed up to play thousands of games, sometimes even with broken fingers. Lou Gehrig never disappointed his fans. He always gave them "hustle" on the field, and a good example to follow off the field. Lou Gehrig loved and supported his wife and family. Lou Gehrig was a person who gave and gave and gave. Yet, Lou said "thank you" to all of them.

It took me a while to understand completely, but I finally realized that Lou Gehrig was saying that he was thankful for the time God had given him. He was thankful for his loving family and his courageous wife. He was thankful for his teammates and his friends. And he was thankful for having had the opportunity to play baseball.

When Lou Gehrig finished speaking, and his last words had finished echoing through the stands, the stadium fell completely silent. Lou slowly backed away from the microphone. There were tears in his eyes. In front of thousands of his friends, the Iron Horse of Baseball was melting.

Then, Babe Ruth ran up to Lou and hugged him. Every person in the stadium stood up and cheered in a volcanic eruption of respect and love. It felt like Yankee Stadium would crumble to the ground from the vibration and noise.[32]

....

Lou Gehrig said "thank you" and "goodbye" on July 4, 1939, but what many people may not know, is that Lou Gehrig never quit. Although he couldn't play baseball, he attended every Yankee game to the end of the 1939 season. Then, he accepted a job as a New York City parole officer, and worked serving the public and helping some people who were "down on their luck." When ALS made it impossible for him to work at all, Lou finally went home. And at home, he continued to battle the disease in his own quiet and courageous way.[33]

Lou Gehrig died at home on June 2, 1941, surrounded by his wife and family. I wasn't there, but I visited Mrs. Gehrig a few weeks later. I'll never forget what she said: ". . . I knew the precise moment he had gone. His expression of peace was beyond description. A thing of ecstatic beauty, and seeing it we were awestricken and even

RIGHT:
LOU GEHRIG IN TEARS AFTER THUNDEROUS OVATION GIVEN HIM BY FANS IN YANKEE STADIUM. Location: Yankee Stadium in New York. Date: 7/4/1939.
© Bettmann/CORBIS

DON'T QUIT

reassured. We didn't cry. We seemed stronger, and not one of us left that room without feeling: There is a better place than this."[34]

God bless you, Lou Gehrig.[35]

....

"The known facts were these: It was the fall of 1933, the country was mired in the Depression, signs were appearing in store windows with the initials 'N.R.A.' for Roosevelt's National Recovery Act, some of the young ones in the army of out-of-work were going to work in the Civilian Conservation Corps camps, Hitler was consolidating his power moves inside Germany. All of that, though, seemed safely in the background as my man—my 'Luke' is what I called him—and I settled into the apartment at 5 Circuit Road in New Rochelle, at the corner of the Boston Post Road, sort of around the corner from his parents' place at 9 Meadow Lane."[35]

Mrs. Gehrig paused for a moment. I think she pictured in her mind that other time and place. I was visiting her in July 1941, a little more than a month after Lou had died. Then she continued: "They were the happiest days of my life, and that was one of the known facts, too. The unknown fact was that they would last just six years."[36]

Henry Louis Gehrig was introduced to Eleanor Twitchell at a Yankees vs. White Sox game in Chicago in 1928. They met for the second time in 1931 in Chicago at a party. It was love at second sight.

For the next two years, Lou never failed to take Eleanor to lunch or dinner when he was in Chicago. When he was on the road, Lou called her, no matter how late he arrived at his hotel. This introverted and reserved man even wrote her love letters.

I was there when Eleanor and Lou were married on September 29, 1933, in their new apartment at 5 Circuit Road. It was an unexpected affair, really, because the wedding was supposed to be held later on Long Island. It had all been well planned. But Lou's mom didn't approve of the marriage, and she threatened not to attend the wedding. Frustrated with the stubbornness of his mother, Lou telephoned the mayor of New Rochelle and asked him to come right over to the apartment. An hour later, Mayor Otto and a bunch of motorcycle cops pulled up outside the apartment building.

The mayor married Lou and Eleanor right there in the apartment. The couple took their vows in a room full of carpenters, wallpaper hangers, carpet installers, plumbers, and painters. Then, everyone sipped champagne out of plastic cups as the giggling newlyweds hurried out the front door. They were in a hurry because Lou Gehrig had a baseball game to play in that afternoon! I watched as a parade of motorcycle cops, with their sirens blaring, escorted the new Mr. and Mrs. Gehrig directly to Yankee Stadium.

Eleanor and Lou had such different personalities that many people found it hard to believe that they were together. Lou was a quiet man who liked cowboy movies, home-cooked meals, and, of course, baseball. Lou was a man of simple tastes. Eleanor was a sophisticated city woman who liked novels, fine restaurants, and music. I think they complemented each other perfectly!

Eleanor introduced Lou to opera, and he got hooked on it. Lou often sat on the living room floor, listening to opera records with a tear in his eye. On Saturday afternoons, he listened to live radio broadcasts from the Metropolitan Opera House. Whenever he could, he bought tickets and took Eleanor to the opera.

"That's the way he was," Eleanor said. "Anything he loved, he embraced to the point of tears, and it was that way in every direction he turned."[37]

Before the Picture Frame took me away from Mrs. Gehrig, I asked her about the two hardest years—the years that Lou battled ALS. It was a tough question for me to ask, but she didn't hesitate in answering.

"Do I have an 'answer' to those six years of towering joy followed by those two years of ruin? Would I trade it all for forty years of lesser joy and lesser tragedy? Not ever."[38]

And then Mrs. Gehrig said: "I would not have traded two minutes of the joy and the grief with that man for two decades of anything with another. Happy or sad, filled with great expectations or great frustrations, we had attained it for whatever brief instant that fate had decided. The most in life, the unattainable, and we were not star-crossed by it. We were blessed with it, my Luke and I."[39]

LEFT:
LOU GEHRIG PUTS HIS ARM AROUND HIS WIFE, ELEANOR, ON OPENING DAY AT YANKEE STADIUM. Location: Yankee Stadium in New York. Date: 4/20/1937.
© Bettmann/CORBIS

Some polio victims never got out of their iron lungs. They depended on the huge metal cylinders for the rest of their lives. They installed iron lungs in their homes. Portable respirators and wheelchairs gave them some mobility, but they were always tethered to a breathing machine.

It was ironic that modern technology kept so many polio victims alive, because it was modern technology that turned polio into a world epidemic. For centuries, children commonly encountered poliovirus during their first year of life. They survived the infection because of temporary immunity passed on from their mothers, and they developed their own lifelong immunity to the disease. But in the more sanitary environments of the modern world, children often were not exposed to poliovirus until they were older and immunity had already faded from their bodies. They were suddenly vulnerable to the virus. Clean cities and indoor plumbing actually caused polio to spread.

Polio epidemics claimed victims every summer of the first decades of the twentieth century, but it was in the 1940s and early 1950s when polio in America was at its worst: twelve thousand new cases of polio in 1943 grew to twenty-seven thousand new cases by 1948, and in 1952, an all-time high of fifty-nine thousand new cases were reported. Five decades of polio epidemics left hundreds of thousands of people in America crippled for life—and millions of people in panic.

Probably the most well known victim of polio was Franklin Delano Roosevelt. He was diagnosed with polio in August 1921 when he was thirty-nine years old, during a vacation at his family's summer home on Campobello Island in New Brunswick, Canada. FDR survived polio and went on to become the thirty-second President of the United States in 1932, and the only president to be reelected three times, but he never got the full use of his legs back. He relied on a wheelchair for the rest of his life. In striking FDR, polio set in motion the events that would ultimately bring about a cure for the disease. Roosevelt began the nationwide campaign to defeat it.

PRESIDENT ROOSEVELT TALKS TO CHILDREN AT THE MERIWETHER INN IN WARM SPRINGS, GA. Date: 4/2/1938.
© Bettmann/CORBIS

In 1924, Franklin Delano Roosevelt visited the Meriwether Inn in Warm Springs, Georgia, because he heard that the warm water of the natural springs would have a therapeutic effect on his paralyzed legs. Roosevelt swam in the spring water, and had his legs massaged by doctors at the inn's spa. His leg muscles didn't improve, but Roosevelt felt better and more energetic. He also came to believe that the exercise and massage regimen stopped progression of his paralysis. He returned to Warm Springs often.

In 1926, Roosevelt decided that other polio victims would benefit from the warm water and massage treatment, so he purchased the Meriwether Inn and surrounding property. Then, in 1927, with the help of his friend and former law partner, Basil O'Connor, Roosevelt established the Georgia Warm Springs Polio Foundation. The foundation opened the doors of the Meriwether Inn to anyone stricken with polio, regardless of their ability to pay for treatment.

To pay for doctors and nurses at the inn, the foundation's management came up with an innovative way to raise money: They held dances nationwide. "Dance So That Others May Walk," was the official motto of the fundraising program, and the dances were held on anniversaries of FDR's birthday.

The first dances were held on FDR's fifty-second birthday, January 30, 1934. That day, they raised more than a million dollars for the treatment of polio victims at Warm Springs. President Roosevelt was so moved by the support that people across the country gave to his cause that he decided to address the nation on the radio that same night. I heard the President's broadcast.

"Tonight I am very deeply moved by the choice of my birthday anniversary for the holding of Birthday Balls in so many communities, great and small, throughout the country," President Roosevelt began. "I send you my greetings and my heartfelt thanks; but at the same time I feel that I have the right to speak to you more as the representative on this occasion of the hundreds of thousands of crippled children in our country. It is only in recent years that we have come to realize the true significance of the problem of our crippled children. There are so many more of them than we had any idea of."[6]

"Warm Springs," President Roosevelt continued, "is only one of the many places where kindness and patience and skill are given to handicapped people. There are hundreds of other places, hospitals and clinics, where surgeons, doctors and nurses of the country gladly work day in and out throughout the years, often without compensation."[7]

President Roosevelt thanked the American people for their charitable spirit, and doctors and nurses for their sacrifices. He also believed that helping in the fight against polio was more than just charity. He believed that it was important work for the nation, and that everyone benefited from it.

"Let us well remember," President Roosevelt said, "that every child and indeed every person who is restored to useful citizenship is an asset to the country and is enabled 'to pull his own weight in the boat.' In the long run, by helping this work we are contributing not to charity but to the building up of a sound Nation."[8]

I couldn't see President Roosevelt. I could only hear his words. But I knew that he was addressing the nation from his wheelchair behind his desk in the Oval Office of the White House. President Roosevelt spoke with unique authority. He was a man who had achieved great things despite his disability, and he reminded us that other disabled persons could do the same, but sometimes they needed a little help.

"It is with a humble and thankful heart," President Roosevelt said in closing that night, "that I accept this tribute through me to the stricken ones of our great national family. I thank you but lack the words to tell you how deeply I appreciate what you have done and I bid you good night on what is to me the happiest birthday I ever have known."[9]

Happy birthday, Mr. President!

....

In 1935, two attempts at developing a vaccine for polio were made. Both failed horribly.

The word "vaccine" comes from the Latin word "vacca," which means cow. In 1796, Dr. Edward Jenner noticed that people who had milked cows infected with "cowpox," seemed immune to the deadly human disease called "smallpox." Dr. Jenner speculated that cowpox was really a weaker version of smallpox. He had a theory that when the human body is exposed to a weak form of a disease, it somehow learns to protect itself against the stronger version. Dr. Jenner tested his theory on an eight-year-old boy named James Phipps. He scratched the boy's arm with a knife and placed tissue from a cowpox-infected cow into the wound. James became very ill, but survived. A few weeks later, Dr. Jenner exposed James to infectious smallpox. James never contracted the disease.

In 1885, the French chemist, Louis Pasteur, conducted a similar experiment on a small boy who had been bitten by rabid dogs. Rabies germs take several weeks to travel from the site of infection to the brain, where they cause seizures, paralysis, and then death. Pasteur thought he could teach the boy's body to fight the disease before the rabies germs reached the boy's brain and killed him. Pasteur took live rabies germs from infected dogs and weakened them by drying them on glass slides. Then he injected the weakened germs into the boy in a series of small doses over several days. The boy did not contract rabies and survived.

In 1935, Dr. John Kolmer incubated poliovirus in monkeys and then ground up their infected spinal cords. He weakened the poliovirus in the resulting mixture by passing it through several healthy monkeys and by treating it with chemicals. Dr. Kolmer injected the final vaccine into himself, his family, and about twelve thousand children. At about the same time, Dr. Maurice Brodie and Dr. William Park, working for the New York Health Department, took things a step further. The doctors treated their polio-infected monkey spinal cord material with formaldehyde to kill the poliovirus. They thought that a "killed-virus" vaccine could still teach the human body to fight polio, and it would be safer than Dr. Kolmer's weakened "live-virus" vaccine. Injecting a person with even a weakened version of poliovirus, the doctors argued, ran the risk of actually causing the disease to occur. The two doctors injected several thousand children.[10]

The results of the 1935 polio vaccine experiments were tragic. Neither vaccine worked. Some children died, and others actually contracted polio from the injections. The vaccinations were stopped quickly, but no one really knew why the vaccines didn't work.

What went wrong? What don't we understand about poliovirus? Now, people not only fear polio, they fear vaccines . . .

....

After the vaccine failures in 1935, many people lost hope that polio would ever be beaten, but not FDR. President Roosevelt believed that the American people could solve any problem if they worked together. So, in September 1937, President Roosevelt and Basil O'Connor announced that the Georgia Warm Springs Polio Foundation would take on a broader mission. Going forward, they said, the foundation would fund polio research nationwide, so that the next vaccine would be safe and effective. And they changed the foundation's name to the National Foundation for Infantile Paralysis.

On the radio, a popular comedian named Eddie Cantor asked his listeners to send a dime apiece to the White House to support President Roosevelt's new "War on Polio." The campaign became known as the "March of Dimes," and the American people responded to it

PRESIDENT ROOSEVELT RECEIVES A MARCH OF DIMES CAMPAIGN CHECK FOR ONE MILLION
DOLLARS FROM BASIL O'CONNOR. Location: The White House, Washington, D.C. Date: 1938.
© Bettmann/CORBIS

with a lot of enthusiasm. Soon, there was so much mail going to the White House that the postal service had to hire extra workers to handle it all. Official government letters and packages got permanently lost in the unexpected flood of mail from citizens all over the country. On January 29, 1938, President Roosevelt addressed the nation about the incredible success of the March of Dimes campaign. I was there, in the Oval Office, when the president took the microphone.[11]

"During the past few days," the President said, "bags of mail have been coming, literally by the truckload, to the White House. Yesterday between forty and fifty thousand letters came to the mailroom of the White House. Today an even greater number—how many I cannot tell you, for we can only estimate the actual count by counting the mail bags. In all the envelopes are dimes and quarters and even dollar bills—gifts from grown-ups and children—mostly from children who want to help other children get well."[12]

I ran to the mailroom of the White House and I couldn't believe what I saw! There were hundreds of mailbags, piled up to the ceiling—mountains of mailbags! When all the mailbags were opened, and all the money was counted, there was more than $1.5 million to begin the War on Polio. And nearly $300,000 of it was in shiny new dimes![13]

The battle lines were drawn, and the War on Polio had officially begun. President Roosevelt promised: "Not until we have removed the shadow of the Crippler from the future of every child can we furl the flags of battle and still the trumpets of attack. The fight against infantile paralysis is a fight to the finish, and the terms are unconditional surrender."[14]

But polio would not surrender easily. It ruined summers and claimed lives for many more years. What had to happen next was for the National Foundation for Infantile Paralysis and its war chest to find the person who would invent the polio vaccine.

The man who would deal polio its final blow and end the Summers of Fear forever was only seven years old when FDR got polio in 1921. I met him in a college classroom in 1936, when he was twenty-two. He was studying to be a doctor. His name was Jonas Salk.

....

March 1936
A Question Is Asked

I was sitting in the tenth row of a big lecture hall on the campus of the New York University School of Medicine when I first saw Jonas Salk. The packed room held about a hundred medical students. The subject of the class was printed in white chalk on a blackboard in the front of the room: "Bacteriology and Immunology." Two adjacent blackboards were covered with chalk diagrams of bacteria cells, medical terms, and mathematical equations. From behind a podium, a professor lectured in a monotone about things I didn't fully understand. He'd been droning on for almost an hour. Most of the students in the room had their heads down and looked like they were busy taking notes, but I could see that a few of them were asleep. I was just about to get up and leave, when a student in the second row raised his hand and asked a question.

"Why do you say that it is not possible to immunize against a viral infection by using a killed version of the virus in the vaccine?" the student asked.

The professor looked up from his lecture notes to see who had asked the question. He stared at the student in the second row. The professor seemed a little disturbed that he had been interrupted and that his point had not been clearly understood.

"Because the only way that cells in the human body can learn to fight a viral infection," the professor said with some sharpness, "is for the cells to actually experience the infection. Cells learn to fight infection by becoming infected. So only a vaccine with live virus in it can possibly work."

"But, doesn't a virus actually destroy the cells it infects?" the student asked. "And how do the remaining uninfected cells learn to fight the virus, if they don't experience the infection at all?"

Just then, a bell rang, indicating the end of the class. "We'll take it up next time, Mr. Salk," the professor said.[15]

But Jonas Salk never got a satisfactory answer to his question. He graduated from medical school convinced that the biological mechanisms behind the human body's immune system were still a mystery—still part of an unsolved puzzle.

Solving puzzles appealed to Jonas Salk. That's why he was in medical school—not to become a doctor, but to become a medical researcher. Jonas Salk wanted to solve some of the big puzzles challenging humanity. By becoming a medical researcher, he believed that he'd be able to solve bigger problems and help more people than a physician treating patients one at a time. Salk's wife, Donna, once said: "Jonas had the idea, from a time when he was quite young, that he wanted to do something that would make a difference to humanity."[16]

Winter 1943
A Question Is Tested

One by one, college students came into the first floor lab of the University of Michigan's School of Public Health. They were volunteers. I watched as each student got a single injection. Half of the students received an experimental flu vaccine, and half of the students got a placebo. At a nearby U.S. Army base, the same procedure was being followed. About twenty-five hundred soldiers received injections as part of the trial. Dr. Thomas Francis, a leading virologist and former professor at the New York University School of Medicine, ran the vaccine trial.

The U.S. Army paid for the trial. War planners worried that an outbreak of flu overseas could hinder the army's ability to fight and win the battles of World War II. They also worried that infected soldiers might bring flu virus back to the United States and start an epidemic. The Army officials had good reason for their fears. In 1918, at the end of World War I, a flu epidemic broke out and killed nearly 20 million people, including 850,000 Americans. Cities in the United States ran out of coffins and cemetery space, and public health workers had to burn bodies by the thousands, or bury them in mass graves. To prevent a replay of the 1918 epidemic, the U.S. Army wanted a flu vaccine.

When Dr. Francis assembled his team of researchers for the Army project, he chose his former student, Jonas Salk. Dr. Francis was taking a killed-virus approach to the vaccine formulation, so the project offered Jonas Salk an opportunity to test the question he had asked years before in medical school. Dr. Francis believed that the key to success was to formulate the vaccine in such a way that it tricked the human body into responding as though a live virus were infecting it. But to do that, his team would have to find a way to measure the body's response to infection—the number of "antibodies" in the blood. The human body produces antibodies to attack and kill invading germs and viruses. When doctors say that the body can "learn" to become immune to a disease, they mean that the body can learn to produce the specific type of antibody needed to destroy the invading germ or virus.

Dr. Salk found a way to calculate the level of antibodies in the blood. Thanks to his work, the research team could judge the relative effectiveness of different vaccine formulations. The vaccine that produced the highest level of antibodies in the blood made it into the winter trial.

By the end of the winter flu season, it was clear that the killed-fluvirus vaccine had worked. The students and soldiers who'd been injected with the experimental vaccine had a 75 percent lower incidence of flu than the people who'd received a shot of plain sugar water.

But . . . why didn't the killed-poliovirus vaccine work in 1935?

Winter 1947
Joining the Fight

I was there when Basil O'Connor and Dr. Harry Weaver, from the National Foundation for Infantile Paralysis, visited Dr. Salk's new Virus Research Laboratory at the University of Pittsburgh. It was about ten o'clock in the morning when they arrived.

Dr. Weaver said that he had reviewed all of the research on polio to date, and that he had concluded that there was more than one strain of poliovirus. He didn't know for sure exactly how many strains, though. There would be no further progress in the fight against polio, Dr. Weaver said, until all of the poliovirus strains were known.

Aha! The 1935 vaccines failed because there was more than one kind of poliovirus!

Basil O'Connor asked Dr. Salk if he would lead the project to identify all of the strains of poliovirus. He said it would probably take two or three years of detailed work, but the National Foundation for Infantile Paralysis would supply all of the money, equipment, and monkeys that Dr. Salk would need.

Monkeys? Oh, yeah. The only way to grow poliovirus is in the spinal cords of monkeys.

Dr. Salk said: "Yes."

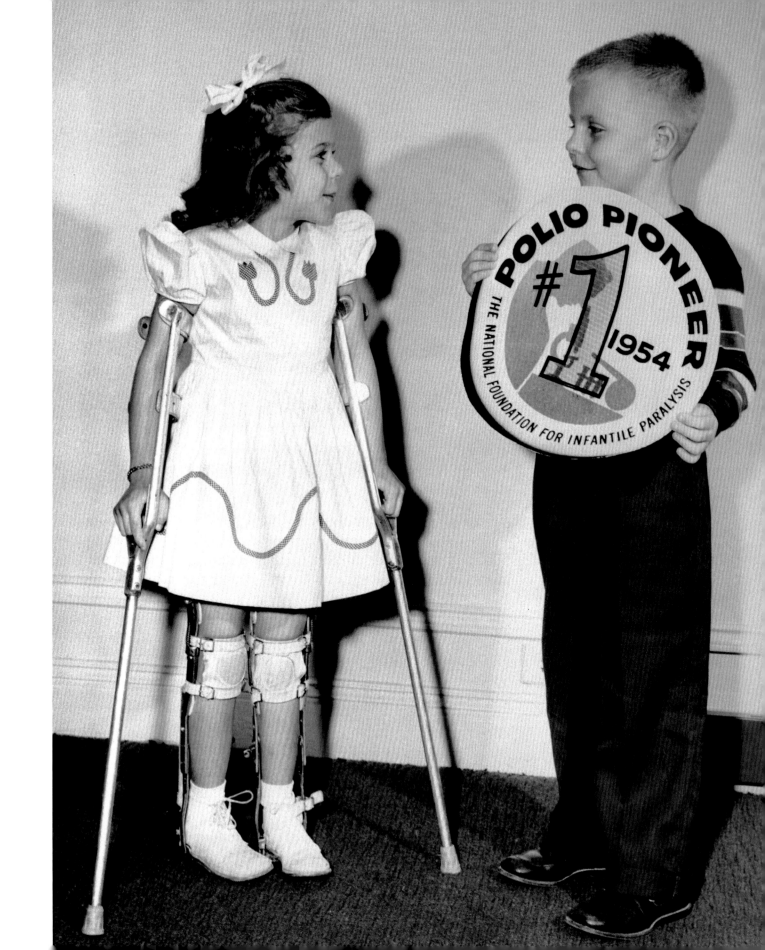

POLIO PIONEER
#1 1954
THE NATIONAL FOUNDATION FOR INFANTILE PARALYSIS

trending lines on his graphs and extrapolated from his data—he decided to "cook" the viruses in the formaldehyde bath a little bit longer, just to be sure.

Finally, Dr. Salk and his team formulated a few precious milliliters of a clear, pink liquid—the vaccine. They injected the experimental polio vaccine into monkeys and measured the antibody levels in their blood. The antibody levels rose. Dr. Salk added mineral oil to the formula and found that the antibody levels rose even higher.

Does this mean that the vaccine works? Will this magic pink liquid work in humans, too?

Dr. Salk reported his findings to the National Foundation for Infantile Paralysis. Again, he was ready to take the next step. It would be the biggest step yet. Dr. Salk asked permission to test children.

Spring 1952
The Secret Tests

Scientists at the National Foundation for Infantile Paralysis said that the safest thing to do was to test Dr. Salk's vaccine on children who already had polio. Dr. Salk totally agreed. He didn't want to risk giving polio to a healthy child. He only wanted to measure the antibody response that the vaccine produced in humans.

I went with Dr. Salk to the D.T. Watson Home for Crippled Children, in Leetsdale, Pennsylvania. There, I watched him inject seventy-nine children with his experimental pink liquid. I also watched him pace the floors at night, as he worried about the children's safety.

I am worried, too.

The doctors and nurses at the D.T. Watson Home were sworn to secrecy. They promised not to discuss the tests with anyone, especially not newspaper reporters. No one said a word.

1953
Hope, Fear, and Controversy

In January 1953, Dr. Salk presented the results of the secret test to a panel of scientists and researchers from the National Foundation for Infantile Paralysis. He told them that the experimental vaccine had significantly raised antibody levels in the tested children, and that the vaccine had caused no bad effects. There was a real possibility, Dr. Salk said, that the vaccine would produce a strong immune response in healthy children.[20]

Dr. Salk's report caused wild controversy. The scientists knew that the next step would be to test the vaccine on healthy, non-infected children. Dr. Sabin immediately repeated his argument that a killed-virus vaccine could not work. He said that Dr. Salk's vaccine promised only temporary protection against polio, and that it would ultimately leave vaccinated children susceptible to reinfection later. He also warned that the vaccine might not be safe. It was just too dangerous, he said, to take the next step. He asked the National Foundation for Infantile Paralysis to wait until his live-virus vaccine was ready. He went before Congress and testified against proceeding with Dr. Salk's vaccine.

The scientific controversy raged, and it confused the public. People were torn between hope and fear. On February 9, 1953, *Time* magazine wrote an article about Dr. Salk. The article suggested that a polio vaccine might be close at hand. Basil O'Connor worried that people expected too much too soon, so he convinced Dr. Salk to speak to the American people on a national radio program. On March 26, 1953, Dr. Salk went on the air, explaining in simple terms the progress that had been made in the fight against polio, and why a vaccine might still be more than a year away. Patience and caution were needed, Dr. Salk said, but there was reason for hope.

Ironically, Basil O'Connor decided not to wait any longer. He just couldn't bear to see another summer come and go without the vaccine—another Summer of Fear. In October 1953, Basil O'Connor announced that the National Foundation for Infantile Paralysis would take the next step: a national trial of Dr. Salk's experimental polio vaccine. And Dr. Thomas Francis would run the trial, he said.

Not everyone appreciated Basil O'Connor's decision. On his national radio program, Walter Winchell alerted the American people that a dangerous experimental polio vaccine was going to be injected into millions of healthy children without adequate testing. He said that the National Foundation for Infantile Paralysis was stockpiling little coffins for the children who would probably die from the hazardous vaccine.[21]

Dr. Salk had already injected himself and his family.

MARY KOSLOSKI, 1955 MARCH OF DIMES POSTER GIRL, AND RANDY KERR, POLIO PIONEER, POSE FOR PUBLICITY PHOTOS. Date: 11/15/1954. Mary is five years old; seven-year-old Randy was the first child to receive the Salk polio vaccine during the nationwide field trial.
© Bettmann/CORBIS

Murrow: "Who owns the patent on this vaccine?"

Salk: "Well, the people, I would say. There is no patent. Could you patent the sun?"[25]

April 22, 1955
A Grateful Nation

I was there, at the White House, when President Dwight D. Eisenhower gave Dr. Jonas Salk a medal and a citation from the thankful people of the United States.

"Dr. Salk," the president said, "before I hand you this citation, I should like to say to you that when I think of the countless thousands of American parents and grandparents who are hereafter to be spared the agonizing fears of the annual epidemic of poliomyelitis—when I think of all the agony that these people will be spared seeing their loved ones suffering in bed—I must say to you I have no words to adequately express the thanks of myself and all the people I know, all 164 million Americans, to say nothing of all the people in the world who will profit from your discovery. I am very, very happy to hand this to you."[26]

Dr. Salk shook the president's hand. He told the president that he was happy to accept the award on behalf of all the people in all the laboratories of the world who had worked so hard to defeat polio.

Then, Basil O'Connor was brought to the podium and President Eisenhower gave him a medal, too. Basil O'Connor accepted the medal on behalf of all the men and women of the National Foundation for Infantile Paralysis. And then the president told him: "And there, of course, remains the great problem of rapid production, distribution on the fairest possible basis, and to that problem . . . you and many others are working and contributing to carry the thing forward until there is no more poliomyelitis remaining in the United States. And I thank you and all of the Foundation of which you are President."[27]

There was still a lot of work to do, but the worldwide polio vaccination program had begun!

Summer 1955
A Terrible Mistake

It was a race against the clock to save lives, a race to inject as many children as possible with Dr. Salk's magic pink liquid before polio could strike again. Pharmaceutical companies ran their plants at high speed to make the tens of millions of doses of polio vaccine that people demanded in the United States and around the world.

Millions of bottles of Salk's vaccine rode down conveyor belts and into boxes marked "POLIO VACCINE: RUSH." Day and night, the boxes were loaded onto trucks and driven to airports, and then flown on special planes to cities where doctors waited, and children lined up.

But then something horrible happened. Some of the first children to receive the Salk vaccine got polio—and it looked liked they got the disease from the vaccine itself.

But that's impossible! It's a killed-virus vaccine. It's supposed to be safe . . .

The mass vaccination program was temporarily halted. Some people wanted to halt the program permanently. No one knew what was wrong with the vaccine, but there was one clue. All of the children who got polio had been given vaccine manufactured in one laboratory: the Cutter Pharmaceuticals Laboratory in California. Dr. Salk and his team investigated.

Dr. Salk determined that the vaccine produced by the Cutter lab still had some live poliovirus in it. The Cutter lab had not properly followed procedures in manufacturing the vaccine. It wasn't "cooked" in the formaldehyde long enough, and it wasn't properly agitated while in the chemical bath. The problem was corrected immediately, and the vaccination program was restarted. And from that day on, polio vaccine production at all the laboratories was inspected more closely.

Because of the Cutter lab mistake, two hundred children contracted polio, fifty were paralyzed, and eleven died. Still other children contracted polio because the vaccination program was temporarily stopped. Six-year-old Mark O'Brien was one of those children: "I couldn't get the vaccine because there had been a bad batch of Salk vaccine released in Southern California. A lot of people got polio out of that. The governor of Massachusetts suspended the distribution of the Salk vaccine during September of 1955. And the rate of polio infection went way up, so near the end of the month the governor revoked that order. So I just had this little window of opportunity. That's why I got polio."[28]

Dr. Salk was devastated by the Cutter incident. Though he was not at fault, he never wanted to see anyone come to harm, especially from a vaccine so strongly associated with his name—and after so many people had placed their trust in him. I think the incident weighed heavily on his soul.

1962
Victory Is in Sight

"The fight against infantile paralysis is a fight to the finish, and the terms are unconditional surrender," President Franklin Delano Roosevelt said in 1944. And by 1962, after more than thirty-five years, the War on Polio was almost over. Polio was slowly surrendering. Only 910 cases of polio were reported in the United States in 1962, down more than 95 percent from the levels of the previous decade. And, in dozens of countries where the Salk vaccine had been shipped, the declines in polio cases were just as dramatic. Victory over polio was finally at hand, thanks to the effort of thousands of scientists, the donations of millions of people, and the work of one man who'd dedicated his life to solving puzzles and helping humanity—Jonas Salk.

"I think he always had faith in what the outcome would be," Dr. Salk's wife, Donna, said. "I think his confidence was supreme. Not in himself, but his confidence in the fact that there had to be an answer to this. And if one approached it in the appropriate way, the answer would reveal itself. As I say that, I can almost hear him saying it. That was his style of speaking: 'The answer would reveal itself.' I never doubted him."[29]

September 23, 1976
Human Nature and Sugar Cubes

Dr. Albert Sabin completed work on the live-poliovirus vaccine in 1958. He took the vaccine to the Soviet Union for a nationwide trial, and the vaccine succeeded in defeating polio there. In 1961, the U.S. Public Health Service approved Dr. Sabin's vaccine for use in the United States, and it quickly displaced the use of the Salk vaccine.

Many physicians in the United States preferred Dr. Sabin's "Oral Polio Vaccine," or OPV, to Dr. Salk's "Inactivated Polio Vaccine," or IPV, because it was easier to administer to children: The Sabin vaccine was injected into a sugar cube and then eaten. They also preferred the Sabin vaccine because children who took it would "shed" the weakened live virus in their stools and potentially infect other children who might not have been vaccinated. Spreading the weakened virus in this way spread immunity to non-vaccinated children and adults. With polio epidemics eliminated, the next problem facing the country was that parents no longer made it a priority to get their children vaccinated. Parents developed a false sense of security. The National Foundation for Infantile Paralysis found itself in the unexpected position of having to convince people to get their children vaccinated. The foundation ran television and radio ads, conducted "Vaccination Day" campaigns at schools, and hired movie stars to convince parents to get their children vaccinated.

"They almost had a psychological immunity because of the existence of the vaccine," said Charles Massey, president of the March of Dimes. "So we had the crazy job of convincing people that had been praying for a vaccine, 'Hey, use it.' We went through three years of promoting immunization campaigns, for example."[30]

In my time, people are not much different. Poliovirus has been eradicated in the United States, but it still exists in some parts of the world. It would only take one case of polio from another country to bring the disease back if we were not protected by vaccine. But some people don't get vaccinated. Some people refuse protection . . .[31]

Despite the arguments in favor of the Sabin vaccine, Dr. Salk spoke out against it. Dr. Sabin's vaccine had live poliovirus in it, and it carried the risk of causing polio, Dr. Salk said. Besides, he argued, it did not make sense to use a potentially dangerous live-virus vaccine when a safe killed-virus vaccine had already been developed and had already shown so much success.

By 1976, the numbers were on Dr. Salk's side of the argument: There had been 140 new cases of polio in the United States since 1962, and all of the cases could be traced to the Sabin Oral Polio Vaccine. On September 23, 1976, Dr. Salk and three other medical scientists testified in Congress against the continued use of the Sabin vaccine. "At the present time," Dr. Salk said, "the risk of acquiring polio from the live-virus vaccine is greater than from naturally occurring viruses . . ."[32]

Although Dr. Salk made his point in 1976, it wasn't until the year 2000—in my time—that the Department of Health and Human Services recommended that only Salk vaccine be used in the United States. On January 1, 2000, the department announced: "Oral polio vaccine (OPV) is no longer recommended. Until recently, OPV was recommended for most children in the United States. For a few people, about one in 2.4 million, OPV actually causes polio. Since the risk of getting polio in the United States is now extremely low, experts believe that using oral polio vaccine is no longer worth the slight risk. The polio shot (IPV) does not cause polio."[33]

With the War on Polio over in most countries, and his vaccine a success, Dr. Salk was asked what he would do next. He said matter-of-factly: "The greatest reward for a job well done is the opportunity to do more."[34]

In 1963, Dr. Salk founded the Salk Institute for Biological Studies in San Diego, California. He dedicated the new research institute to "doing more." He assembled the best and brightest people in medical research from around the world and gave them the equipment, funding, and facilities to work on some of the toughest biological puzzles facing mankind. Dr. Salk and his team of researchers tackled multiple sclerosis, cancer, and AIDS. Their work continues into my time.

Dr. Jonas Salk died on June 23, 1995. He was eighty-one. On that day, his friend Dr. Francis Crick said: "Few have made one discovery that has benefited humanity so greatly. Jonas was a man who, right to his last day, was actively in pursuit of another."[35]

Dr. Jonas Salk will always be remembered as the man who invented the polio vaccine—the "Man Who Saved the Children." I'll remember him for something else, too. I'll remember him for his perseverance and the strength of his character. Dr. Salk relied on reason and science to overcome the skepticism of his critics—to the benefit of all of us. Dr. Salk dedicated his life to making the world a better place.

When he was asked what advice he would give to others who wanted to make a difference in the world, Dr. Salk said: "I was once given the advice, 'Do what makes your heart leap.' And that's what I have done. I wanted to be a scientist and a healer, so I used science for healing. It was good advice and I give it to you."[36]

Thank you, Dr. Salk.

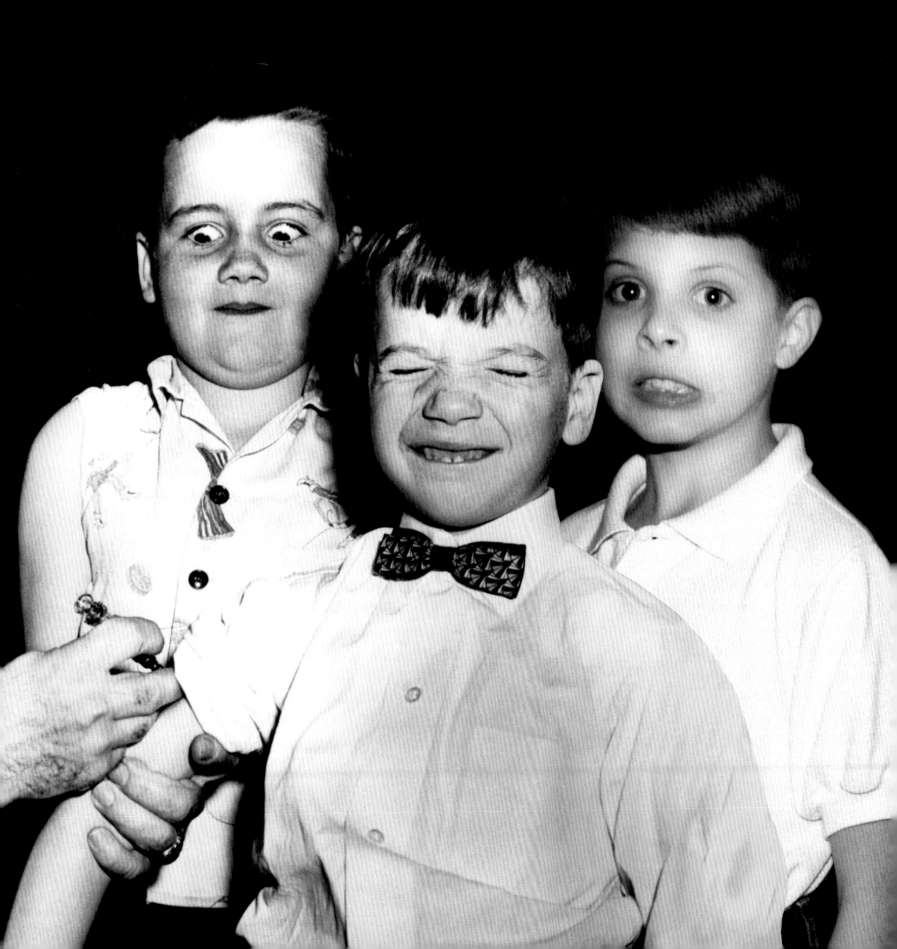

"This time, like all times, is a very good one if we but know what to do with it."

RALPH WALDO EMERSON (1803–1882),
AMERICAN LECTURER, POET, AND ESSAYIST

IN ANTHONY'S TIME ⁂

I tumbled out of the Picture Frame and into my bedroom. I wasn't sure how long I had been gone, but it felt good to be home. It felt good to be back in my own room. My room was just as I'd left it, except that the broken alarm clock by my bed was working again. It ticked forward from 8:46:40 A.M., the time it had displayed for three years. I only kept the clock because of the CD player that was built into it. The CD player worked just fine.[1]

An icon flashed on the screen of my PC. I had mail. I glanced at it and saw it was from Miraja, my email pen pal in Afghanistan. My school had set up the email pen pal program with kids in other countries. Miraja's school was new—the U.S. Army built it after the war—and allowing girls in school was new, too, in Afghanistan. Her school had only one computer and her Internet connection didn't always work, so I rarely got a message from her. She wanted to know how I was doing, and she asked if I had eaten any hot dogs lately. She put the "laughing face" symbol in her email after the word "hot dog." I told her once that I liked hot dogs, but she didn't know what a hot dog was at the time. She thought I meant a dog that was hot from standing too long in the sun, and now she kept kidding me about it. I'd answer her later.

how much I loved to eat them while they were warm and the sugary icing was still melting on top. I was happy to be home. I was happy to be with my family again. I was just plain happy.

I ran back toward the house, threw open the front door, skipped down the hallway, and burst into the kitchen. I wolfed down a half-dozen warm, sticky cinnamon rolls as I told my family the incredible story of where I had been, what I had seen, and whom I had met. I ate two hot dogs for lunch. I rode my bike through the park with my friends. I played catch with my dad in the backyard. I defeated Godzilla on my Xbox, once and for all. I annoyed my sister every chance I got. And I went to bed that night unafraid of the future, because I knew what I was going to do with my time. I knew what I was going to do the next day, and the day after that, and the day after that.

As you know, since that first night that the Picture Frame called to me, I've taken other trips into the past. I have seen many things: good things and bad things, funny things and sad things, some wonderful things and some horrible things, and even some things best left forgotten. No matter how many trips I take into the past, the lesson of history never seems to change. Time is precious. It is given to you only once, and you never know how much you have. If you use your time to achieve, to contribute, and to do what is right, then you will be using your time wisely. And if you try to do all the good that you can, for all the people that you can, for as long as you can—and you trust in God to guide you—then you will be happy.[14]

Since that day, I've been trying to do just that.

"And surely I am with you always, until the very end of time."[15]

WAKE UP, AMERICA !

CIVILIZATION CALLS
EVERY MAN WOMAN AND CHILD !

"Men occasionally stumble over the truth, but most of them pick themselves up and hurry off as if nothing ever happened."

SIR WINSTON CHURCHILL (1874–1965), BRITISH STATESMAN AND AUTHOR

THE REST OF ANTHONY'S STORY ⟨⟩

Notes

Chapter 1: The Magic Picture Frame

1. Birth records, school transcripts, and physical examinations confirm Anthony to be twelve years old, but a careful analysis of Anthony's narrative reveals that he spent thirty-four years in the past. Scientists theorize that the Picture Frame created a time paradox, resulting in a discrepancy between Anthony's physical age (twelve) and his experiential age (forty-six).

Chapter 2: The Men on the Moon

1. Stars don't twinkle when viewed in outer space, because there is no atmosphere. Stars appear to twinkle when viewed from the surface of the earth, because Earth's atmosphere is turbulent—windy and always moving—causing the light from the stars to shift and bend and bounce. The phenomenon is called stellar scintillation.

    And Anthony is alluding to the first words spoken by astronaut Neil Armstrong on the moon. When Armstrong stepped onto the surface of the moon, he said: "That's one small step for man, one giant leap for mankind." Some people believe that Armstrong intended to say "a man," but NASA's transcript of the Apollo 11 radio transmissions do not include the "a."

2. Anthony is referring to: *The Fly* [1958, NR], and *Stargate* [1994, PG-13].

3. Anthony says that he saw the earth rise above the horizon of the moon, but in reality, that is not possible. The moon spins on its axis in such a way that, as it orbits the earth, it always presents the same face to the earth. As a result, when viewed from any single place on the moon, the earth remains in about the same spot in the sky at all times.

4. "Apollo 11 Technical Air-to-Ground Voice Transcription," NASA Manned Spacecraft Center, Houston, TX, July 1969, time code 04:13:43:16. Asterisks denote clipping of words and phrases. Reprinted courtesy of NASA. Hereafter cited as: Transcript: Courtesy NASA. Note: First voice is Buzz Aldrin; second voice is Neil Armstrong.

5. The Apollo 11 mission patch depicts an eagle carrying an olive branch to the surface of the moon; the Apollo 11 crew contributed to the design of the patch. Astronaut Jim Lovell, Neil Armstrong's backup for the Apollo 11 mission, introduced the idea of using an eagle on the patch. Astronaut Michael Collins sketched the first concept of an eagle flying over the lunar surface. The original drawing had an olive branch in the eagle's beak, but the astronauts decided that the eagle looked too menacing that way, so in the final drawing the olive branch was placed in the eagle's talons. The Apollo 11 mission patch became the basis for the design of the Eisenhower/Apollo 11 silver dollar coin, minted from 1971 to 1974.

    ✓ **Anthony Recommends:** *Space Mission Patches*, by Gregory Vogt [0761316132, NF, MS+].

6. Transcript: Courtesy NASA, time code 04:13:49:42.

7. Transcript: Courtesy NASA, time code 04:14:14:05.

8. Anthony is experiencing Newton's First Law of Motion, also called the Law of Inertia. The law states: An object in motion will stay in motion, with constant speed and direction, until it encounters an outside force. So, if the moon's gravity (an outside force) were zero, Anthony would float in a straight line forever, far out into space. The Law of Inertia is one of Isaac Newton's Three Laws of Motion. The three laws describe force, acceleration, and momentum (Anthony's momentum is equal to his mass multiplied by his velocity; his momentum would be the same on Earth). Newton's First Law of Motion owes much to the experiments conducted by Galileo Galilei in the early part of the 17th century. Galileo, experimenting by rolling a ball up and down an inclined surface, surmised that a force—friction—caused the ball to slow down and stop. Galileo theorized that if the frictional force were reduced to zero, the ball would roll forever without stopping.

    ✓ **Anthony Recommends:** *Galileo*, by Paul Hightower [0766018709, NF, MS+]; *Isaac Newton*, by Margaret Anderson [0766018725, NF, MS+]; *The Isaac Newton School of Driving*, by Barry Parker [0801874173, NF, HS+].

Gregory Olsen announced that he would pay the Russians $20 million to become the third space tourist; his trip is scheduled for April 2005. In September 2004, British entrepreneur Richard Branson announced that he would create a company called Virgin Galactic that would one day offer trips into outer space; William Shatner, a star of the *Star Trek* TV series and motion pictures, said he would buy a ticket.

Anthony thinks space tourism is a great idea, but he also knows that America needs serious, specially trained astronauts to explore the "final frontier." You can become an astronaut by working hard in school, excelling in math and science, staying physically fit, and applying to NASA. Joining the Boy Scouts or the Girl Scouts can also help. According to NASA, 70 percent of U.S. astronauts have been scouting alumni. Candidates for commander/pilot astronaut positions should have at least one thousand hours flying time in jet aircraft, plus at least a bachelor's degree in engineering, biological science, physical science, or mathematics. Candidates for mission specialist astronaut positions should have advanced master's degrees or doctorates. All astronaut candidates must pass rigorous physical tests.

✓ **Anthony Recommends:** The Official NASA Astronaut Selection Web site [www.nasajobs.nasa.gov/astronauts].

28. Transcript: Courtesy NASA, time code 04:14:25:09.

29. Transcript: Courtesy NASA, time code 04:14:41:25.

30. Seamstresses using needle and thread and pots of glue assembled the high-tech Apollo 11 spacesuits by hand; the seamstresses got to know the astronauts personally because the spacesuits were made to fit the astronauts individually.

✓ **Anthony Recommends:** *U.S. Space Gear,* by Lillian Kozloski [1560983825, NF, MS+].

31. On January 28, 1986, Space Shuttle *Challenger* exploded shortly after liftoff, killing all aboard. In his address to the nation that day, President Reagan said: "And I want to say something to the schoolchildren of America who were watching the live coverage of the shuttle's takeoff. I know it is hard to understand, but sometimes, painful things like this happen. It's all part of the process of exploration and discovery. It's all part of taking a chance and expanding man's horizons. The future doesn't belong to the fainthearted; it belongs to the brave. The *Challenger* crew was pulling us into the future, and we'll continue to follow them." [Source: "Address to the Nation on the *Challenger* Disaster," 1/28/1986, courtesy Reagan Library/NARA.]

32. *The Dream of Spaceflight,* by Wyn Wachhorst [0465090575, NF, HS+], page xiv. Reprinted by permission of Buzz Aldrin.

33. *First on the Moon,* by Neil Armstrong, Michael Collins, Edwin Aldrin [156852398X, NF, HS+], page 193. Reprinted by permission of Konecky & Konecky.

34. Courtesy NASA History Office.

35. Courtesy CR: 9/16/1969.

36. *Carrying the Fire,* by Michael Collins [081541028X, NF, HS+], page 352. Excerpt from "To a Husband Who Seeks the Stars" and excerpt from *Carrying the Fire* by Michael Collins copyright © 1976 by Michael Collins. Reprinted by permission of Farrar, Straus and Giroux, LLC.

37. "Special Message to the Congress on Urgent National Needs," 5/25/1961, courtesy JFK Library/NARA.

38. *First on the Moon,* by Neil Armstrong, Michael Collins, Edwin Aldrin [156852398X, NF, HS+], page 32. Reprinted by permission of Konecky & Konecky.

39. Transcript: Courtesy NASA, time code 04:15:02:08.

40. The aurora borealis can be seen from many locations in North America.

✓ **Anthony Recommends:** *Northern Lights,* by Calvin Hall [1570612900, NF, MS+].

41. Transcript: Courtesy NASA, time code 04:15:11:15.

42. The first person to hit a golf ball on the moon was astronaut Alan Shepard, during the Apollo 14 mission. Shepard attached a golf club head to a lunar soil sampler scoop handle, and then used the makeshift golf club to hit the longest golf ball drive in history; the drive was estimated at over 400 yards. As the ball sailed out of sight, Shepard was heard to say: ". . . miles and miles and miles." The absence of an atmosphere on the moon helped Shepard break distance records, but on Earth, a golf ball's aerodynamic efficiency (how easily the ball moves through the air) makes all the difference in how far it will fly. When Anthony said that there was NASA technology in the longest-flying golf balls, he was referring to the Wilson Ultra 500 Series golf balls introduced in 1995. A Wilson company engineer who had once worked for NASA came up with the golf ball design that optimized lift and range: 500 dimples arranged in a pattern of 60 spherical triangles.

✓ **Anthony Recommends**: *Inventions from Outer Space,* by David Baker [0375409793, NF, MS+]; *It Came from Outer Space,* by Marjolijn Bijlefeld [0313322228, NF, MS+].

43. "Address at Rice University on the Nation's Space Effort," 9/12/1962, courtesy JFK Library/NARA.

44. Courtesy CR: 9/16/1969.

45. In 1977, NASA launched the twin spacecraft, *Voyager 1* and *Voyager 2.* The five-year mission was to conduct studies of Jupiter and Saturn. After the spacecraft completed the mission, NASA reprogrammed the Voyager twins to explore deeper regions of space. In Anthony's time, the Voyager twins are headed out of the solar system. Aboard each Voyager spacecraft is a gold-coated phonograph record inscribed with the music, images, and sounds of the planet Earth, including the following: directions to the planet Earth; diagrams and medical images of human anatomy; a description of human DNA; photographs of nature, cities, and human endeavor; recordings of greetings in all the major human languages; sounds of the animals on earth; recordings of music. The last human voice on the Voyager recording is that of Carl Sagan's five-year-old son, Nick, saying: "Hello from the children of planet Earth."

✓ **Anthony Recommends:** *Beyond,* by Michael Benson [0810945312, NF, MS+]; *Murmurs of Earth,* by Carl Sagan [0345315367, NF, MS+]; *Star Trek: The Motion Picture* [1979, PG]; The NASA/Jet Propulsion Laboratory Voyager Web site [http://voyager.jpl.nasa.gov].

46. In Anthony's time, support for space adventures has waned and the importance of bold space exploration seems to have been forgotten. In Anthony's time, no child has seen a man walk on the moon, and NASA sends astronauts on space shuttle missions that the public barely notices. About the situation, former astronaut Buzz Aldrin wrote: "A lasting human presence in space won't result from sudden leaps like Apollo; it has to move outward on a broad base of permanent support. But what we lack at present is less the technology than the vision." [Source: *The Dream of Spaceflight,* by Wyn Wachhorst (0465090575, NF, HS+), page xiv. Reprinted by permission of Buzz Aldrin.]

On January 14, 2004, President George W. Bush announced "a new plan to explore space and extend a human presence across our solar system." He outlined a plan for America to "return to the moon by 2020, as a launching point for missions beyond." The president said: "Mankind is drawn to the heavens for the same reason we were once drawn into unknown lands and across the open sea. We choose to explore space because doing so improves our lives, and lifts our national spirit. So let us continue the journey." [Source: "President Bush Announces New Vision for Space Exploration Program," 1/14/2004, courtesy The White House.]

47. Courtesy CR: 9/16/1969.

48. Transcript: Courtesy NASA, time code 04:15:39:13.

49. As the Apollo 11 astronauts climbed the lunar module's ladder, Neil Armstrong reminded Buzz Aldrin to leave behind some items that he had been carrying in his spacesuit pocket. The items were as follows: an Apollo 1 mission patch, a solid gold olive branch, a silicon message disk, and two Soviet cosmonaut medals. The Apollo 1 mission patch honored the American astronauts who died in the 1967 Apollo 1 fire. The gold olive branch signified that the Americans had "come in peace for all mankind." The silicon message disk carried goodwill statements by Presidents Eisenhower, Kennedy, Johnson, and Nixon, a listing of the leadership of the U.S. Congress, the names of NASA's management team, and messages from leaders of seventy-three countries around the world; the disk was inside the aluminum capsule that Anthony saw on the surface of the moon. The Soviet cosmonaut medals had once belonged to Yuri Gagarin, the first man in space, and Vladimir Komarov, who died aboard Soyuz 1 in 1967; American astronaut Frank Borman obtained the medals from Gagarin's widow. Two additional items that Anthony did not see were brought to the moon, and then returned to Earth: a stamped envelope postmarked on route by the Apollo 11 crew, and a piece of wood and fabric from the Wright brothers' airplane that made history's first powered flight on December 17, 1903.

50. Transcript: Courtesy NASA, time code 04:16:06:16.

51. *A Man on the Moon,* by Andrew Chaikin [0140272011, NF, HS+], page 204. From *A Man on the Moon* by Andrew Chaikin, copyright © 1994 by Andrew Chaikin. Used by permission of Viking Penguin, a division of Penguin Group (USA) Inc.

52. Anthony didn't know it, but after the Apollo 11 astronauts lifted off from the moon, President Nixon quietly discarded a speech he thankfully wouldn't have to give—the speech had been prepared in case the Apollo 11 mission met with disaster. If tragedy occurred, NASA planned to close down communications with the astronauts and let them die on the moon in un-televised peace, or commit suicide, while the president addressed the American people with the words:

"Fate has ordained that the men who went to the moon to explore in peace will stay on the moon to rest in peace...." [Source: "In Event of Moon Disaster," 1969, courtesy Nixon Library/NARA.]

53. Anthony is quoting Tycho Brahe (1546–1601), the Danish astronomer.

54. *The Last Man on the Moon,* by Eugene Cernan [0312199066, NF, HS+], page 347. Copyright © 1999 by Eugene Cernan. From *The Last Man on the Moon* by Eugene Cernan. Reprinted by permission of St. Martin's Press, LLC.

55. Courtesy CR: 9/16/1969.

Chapter 3: To America I Will Go

1. The A/G Vulcan Shipyard in Stettin, Germany, built the SS *Konig Albert* in 1889. The steam-powered, twin-screw ship weighed 10,484 gross tons, cruised at a speed of 15.5 knots, and was 521 feet long and 60 feet wide. The ship carried 2,175 passengers: 257 in first class, 119 in second class, and 1,799 in third class, or steerage. The ship was assigned to the transatlantic crossing in 1905. Seized by the Italian government in 1915, and renamed the *Ferdinando Palasciano,* the ship served as a transport for the Italian Navy during World War I. The ship was scrapped in 1926.

2. In 1910, the U.S. Government placed undercover agents on transatlantic ships to learn more about the conditions immigrants faced. About sleeping berths, the agents reported: "The mattress, and the pillow if there is one, is filled with straw or seaweed.... The berth, 6 feet long and 2 feet wide, and with 2½ feet of space above it, is all the space to which the steerage passenger can assert a definite right." About ship ventilation: "When to this very limited space and much filth and stench is added inadequate means of ventilation, the result is almost unendurable.... In many instances persons, after recovering from seasickness, continue to lie in their berths in a sort of stupor, due to breathing air whose oxygen has been mostly replaced by foul gases.... In two steamers the open deck was always filled long before daylight by those who could no longer endure the foul air between decks." [Source: "Report of the Immigration Commission on Steerage Conditions," U.S. Congress, 12/5/1910.]

3. To the immigrants who landed there, Ellis Island was both an "Island of Hope" and an "Island of Tears." The island represented hope because it was the doorway to America, and a new life filled with opportunity. But the island was also a tearful place because some people were denied entry into the United States; they were turned away at America's "Golden Door."

As Anthony observed, the Statue of Liberty was the first glimpse that immigrants arriving by ship had of America. The Statue of Liberty represented America's promise of acceptance, freedom, and opportunity. In 1883, American writer Emma Lazarus wrote a sonnet entitled *The New Colossus* to express her belief in America as a refuge for the oppressed of other nations. In 1903, the sonnet was inscribed on a bronze plaque and mounted inside the base of the Statue of Liberty. The last few lines of the sonnet are the most famous:

> Give me your tired, your poor,
> Your huddled masses yearning to breathe free,
> The wretched refuse of your teeming shore.
> Send these, the homeless, the tempest-tost to me,
> I lift my lamp beside the Golden Door!

The Statue of Liberty was a gift from the people of France. The plan was to present the statue to the United States in 1876, in time to commemorate the centennial of the American Declaration of Independence, but lack of funds delayed the statue's completion until 1885. French sculptor Frederic Auguste Bartholdi designed the statue; French engineer Alexandre Gustave Eiffel helped build it. When the statue was completed, it was disassembled, packed into 214 separate crates, put aboard a steamship, and sent to America where it was reassembled on its pedestal on Liberty Island in New York Harbor. The model for the Statue of Liberty was Bartholdi's mother, Charlotte.

✓ **Anthony Recommends:** *Liberty for All,* by Lee Iacocca [0966333713, NF, MS+]; *The Statue of Liberty Encyclopedia,* by Barry Moreno [0684862271, NF, MS+]; *Ken Burns' America: The Statue of Liberty* [1996, D, NR].

4. Immigration law in the early 1900s was designed to prevent people from entering the country who might become a burden to American taxpayers. The medical officials at Ellis Island were instructed to examine immigrants for diseases and disabilities. Because thousands of immigrants came through Ellis Island every day, the doctors had to develop a shorthand code for their diagnosis—the chalk marks that Anthony saw. Some of the codes included: *PG* for pregnant, *K* for hernia, *FT* for feet, *L* for lameness, *H* for heart trouble, *F* for facial rash, *E* for eye disease, and *X* for suspected mental disability. A chalk mark usually meant that the immigrant would be detained on Ellis Island until a more detailed examination could be performed, but an immigrant marked with an *X* or an *E* stood a good chance of being

sent back to their home country. Only 2 percent of new arrivals were denied entry for medical reasons, but it was a heartbreaking experience when it happened to only one member of a family traveling together. The family would have to decide whether to return home together, or split up and allow some members of the family to enter the United States. Anthony reported that he saw a family make just such a decision. First, he saw a mother marked both X and E taken from the line and led to an examination room. Then, he saw the father write instructions on the children's paper tags. Most likely, the parents had decided to let their children continue on to America alone, wearing their father's written instructions to someone who would be waiting for them in New York City.

5. The medical officials at Ellis Island used buttonhooks to upturn the eyelids of new arrivals and inspect for signs of the highly contagious eye disease called trachoma; the examination hurt. Even in Anthony's time, trachoma is the world's leading cause of preventable blindness. It is estimated that six million people are blind from the disease, mostly in the poorer regions of the world where people have limited access to clean water and health care.

6. Anthony is referring to the Great Hall, also called the Registry Room, on the second floor of the Ellis Island Federal Immigration Station building. The Great Hall was 200 feet long, 100 feet wide, and 56 feet high; the room was large enough to process 5,000 new arrivals every day. In 1907, there was a large U.S. flag hanging on the wall. Anthony's observation is correct: There were forty-five stars on the U.S. flag in 1907.

   ✓ **Anthony Recommends:** *Stars & Stripes Forever,* by Richard Schneider [0060525371, NF, MS+]; *Stars and Stripes Forever* [John Philip Sousa, 1896].

7. Questioning new arrivals and documenting their intentions in the United States was the primary duty of immigration officials at Ellis Island, and it was a big job. From 1901 to 1910, 8,795,386 people immigrated to the United States, mostly through Ellis Island. From 1892 to 1954, Ellis Island officials processed and documented more than 22 million immigrant, passenger, and crew arrivals.

8. Passenger Manifest: SS *Konig Albert,* Left Naples 8/23/1907, Arrived New York 9/5/1907.

9. The final staircase had three exits: The first exit was designated "New York Outside," and led to a ferry to New York City where an immigrant's sponsor would be waiting; the second exit was designated "New York Detained," and led to a holding area where immigrants would remain until a sponsor arrived to claim them; the third exit was designated "Railroads," and led to a ferry that would take the new arrivals to Hoboken, NJ, to catch trains for all points west. The immigrants called the final staircase the "Stairs of Separation," because they might never again see any of the people with whom they had crossed the Atlantic Ocean. In 1907, nearly one million immigrants walked down the Stairs of Separation.

10. At the turn of the 20th century, immigrants referred to America as a place "where the streets are paved with gold," meaning that the United States was a place where jobs could be found and money could be made. Francesco's humorous twist on the original saying was also a popular immigrant anecdote at the time; he was not the first to make the comment.

11. "Wop" and "Dago" were derogatory terms applied to Italian immigrants. The term Wop probably came from the "Without Passport" notation that immigration officials put on the entry papers of immigrants who had fled their home country without getting a valid passport. The term Dago may have had its origins in the fact that many Italian immigrants applied for day-labor jobs; hence, "day-go." Each successive wave of immigrants had to deal with undeserved discrimination and prejudice in the New World, not only from Americans, but from immigrants of other nationalities as well. At the turn of the 20th century, however, discrimination against Italians was especially bad; in 1910, Italian immigrants were some of the lowest paid workers in America.

   Perhaps the worst case of discrimination—and violence—against Italian immigrants occurred in 1891 in New Orleans. A gang of men had shot and killed David Hennessy, the city's chief of police. Before he died, Hennessey reportedly said the word "Italians." The police quickly rounded up dozens of suspects, and suspicion finally fell on ten Italian immigrants. But at their trial, all ten suspects were acquitted for lack of evidence. Not satisfied, newspaper editors and politicians fanned the flames of prejudice, blaming Italians in general for a number of the city's ills, not just the murder of Chief Hennessey. On March 14, 1891, an angry mob of several thousand citizens of New Orleans stormed the jail and hanged and shot the ten innocent men, plus one man being held for a lesser and unrelated crime. Eight of the murdered men were naturalized American citizens, and three were Italian citizens. The incident sparked an official protest from the government of Italy (diplomatic relations with the United States were severed), requiring President Benjamin Harrison to intervene.

12. In the early 1900s, America's system of free enterprise and capitalism provided an opportunity that was unknown elsewhere in the world: The opportunity for a family to become wealthy in a single generation. Immigrants took advantage of the opportunity and started businesses in America. Here are some examples of Italian immigrants who succeeded:

In 1890, nineteen-year-old Domenico DeDomenico emigrated from Italy and settled in California. He started a pasta company called Gragnano Products in 1912. In 1934, the company was renamed the Golden Grain Macaroni Company and later became famous for its Rice-A-Roni products.

In 1889, twelve-year-old Amadeo Obici emigrated from Italy. In 1904, he opened a fruit stand in New York City, offering bags of roasted peanuts for a nickel each. His roasted peanuts were so popular, that in 1906, Amadeo Obici established the Planters Peanut Company.

In 1900, Vincent Taormina emigrated from Sicily and settled in New Orleans. He began a small importing business, bringing the foods of Italy to America. In 1927, his successful business merged with another food company to form the Progresso Italian Food Corporation.

In 1915, seventeen-year-old Hector Boyardi emigrated from Italy and settled in Cleveland, OH, where he became a chef and opened a restaurant. Hector's spaghetti sauce was so popular that he packaged it in milk bottles for his customers to take home. Later, when Hector combined his bottled spaghetti sauce with pasta and offered the combination as a "cook-at-home" meal, he had the makings of a new company. Hector "Americanized" his name and called his new company Chef Boyardee.

In Anthony's time, America is still the place where families can become wealthy in a single generation: 80 percent of America's millionaires are first-generation rich. And starting a business is still the best and most popular way to become wealthy: The self-employed make up less than 20 percent of the workers in America, but they account for more than two-thirds of America's millionaires; twenty million Americans operate sole-proprietorships; and small companies (companies with less than five hundred employees) employ half of the American workforce, or about sixty million people. In Anthony's time, small businesses create three out of four new jobs in America annually.

✓ **Anthony Recommends:** *101 Marvelous Money-Making Ideas for Kids,* by Heather Wood [0812520602, NF, MS+]; *Whiz Teens in Business,* by Danielle Vallee [0966339320, NF, MS+]; *The Millionaire Next Door,* by Thomas Stanley [0671015206, NF, HS+]; *The Young Entrepreneur's Guide to Starting a Business,* by Steve Mariotti [0812933060, NF, HS+].

13. Passenger Manifest: SS *Sant Anna,* Left Naples 8/4/1910, Arrived New York 8/17/1910.

14. Passenger Manifest: SS *Konig Albert,* Left Naples 4/19/1912, Arrived New York 5/3/1912.

15. Hell's Kitchen was the New York City district west of 8th Avenue, between 33rd Street and 59th Street. In the late 1890s, tenements sprang up in Hell's Kitchen to house the immigrant workers who settled in the area. Poverty and close quarters bred ill will between neighbors of different nationalities, and riots and gang violence were not uncommon. In 1912, Antonio Gaetano was living with his father in a tenement located at 506 33rd Street. Antonio described his childhood in Hell's Kitchen in a 1977 interview: "Back then, you couldn't go outside, or walk to school, if you didn't know how to take care of yourself. Your lunch would be taken from you. Your money would be taken, if you had any. Learning the art of self-defense was a must. You had to show everyone how tough you were, or they wouldn't leave you alone. But after I learned how to fight, they would just say, 'Ah, there goes Tony,' and they wouldn't bother me any more." Antonio took up boxing, a sport he continued into the 1920s; he boxed under the auspices of the Golden Gloves Association of America.

Anthony and Antonio probably didn't walk the entire distance to school. They probably walked to a nearby station and took the train. In March 1900, ground was broken in Manhattan for an electric-powered subway. Twelve thousand men built the subway for the Inter-Borough Rapid Transit Company (IRT) using the "cut-and-cover" method: A trench was cut to accommodate a 55-foot-wide and 15-foot-high tunnel, the rails were laid and stations built, the finished work was enclosed in steel beams, and a shallow layer of fill was placed over the trench. When the subway opened in 1904, people paid a nickel each to ride the fastest city transportation system in the world: "City Hall to Harlem in 15 minutes!" was the slogan.

✓ **Anthony Recommends:** *Evolution of New York City Subways,* by Gene Sansone [0801868866, NF, MS+]; *New York City Subway,* by Tom Range [0738510866, NF, MS+].

16. Gennaro Lombardi emigrated from Naples, Italy, in 1895, when he was twenty years old. In 1897, Lombardi opened a grocery store at 53 Spring Street, where he made pizzas for hungry Italian immigrant workers. Lombardi's store was officially established as the first pizzeria in America when it obtained a New York City mercantile license in 1905. In Anthony's time, Lombardi's pizzeria still turns out some of the best pizza in America, using a coal-fired, 900°F brick oven.

Antonio Ferrara emigrated from Italy in the late 1800s. In 1892, he opened Caffé A. Ferrara, at 195 Grand Street in New York City. Ferrara's quickly became famous for the wide variety and outstanding freshness of its coffee, cookies, and cakes. Sfogliatella Napoletana is a delicate, layered, clamshell-shaped pastry, usually filled with semolina farina, ricotta cheese, candied fruits, and nuts. During World War II, American servicemen with Italian ancestry requested that Ferrara's cookies be sent to them in Europe. It was the beginning of Ferrara's mail-order business. In Anthony's time, Ferrara's still sells the most exquisite Italian pastries in the United States.

✓ **Anthony Recommends:** Lombardi's Pizzeria [New York, NY, 212-941-7994, www.lombardispizza.com]; Ferrara's Café [New York, NY, 212-226-6150, www.ferraracafe.com].

17. Anthony is describing Pizza Margherita, prepared in the classic Neapolitan style. In 1889, Queen Margherita of Italy asked Raffaele Esposito, the owner of a restaurant near the palace in Naples, to cook a pizza dinner for the royal family. Raffaele prepared three pizzas: Pizza alla Mastunicola, a pungent cheese and lard pizza; Pizza alla Marinara, a seafood pizza with anchovies; and Pizza alla Mozzarella, a cheese pizza. On a patriotic impulse, Raffaele placed bright green leaves of basil on top of the cheese pizza to match the colors of the Italian flag—red, white, and green. Raffaele named the new pizza, Pizza Margherita, in honor of the Queen.

Like most Americans, Anthony has eaten a lot of bad pizza, but the situation in America is improving. In 1984, Antonio Pace, the owner of one of the oldest Pizza restaurants in Naples, Italy, founded the Association for True Neapolitan Pizza. The Association published specifications for True Neapolitan Pizza and began a formal program of training pizza chefs and certifying pizza restaurants in the United States and around the world. To eat a pizza that is similar to the pizza Anthony ate in 1913, look for a pizza restaurant that displays the sign: "Vera Pizza Napoletana [Certified True Neapolitan Pizza]." The specifications for True Neapolitan Pizza include: Pizza dough must consist of only flour, natural yeast, and water; the dough must be kneaded by hand or with an approved mixer; the dough must be formed by hand without the help of a rolling pin or any other mechanical device; the pizza must be round, no more than 14 inches in diameter, no thicker than 0.1 inches in the middle and with a crust of about 0.8 inches; toppings for the pizza must be sparing, but should include imported Italian tomatoes, olive oil, and buffalo mozzarella cheese; the pizza must be cooked in a bell shaped, wood-fired, stone oven; the oven temperature must be between 800°F and 900°F.

✓ **Anthony Recommends:** Pizza, by Rosario Buonassisi [1552093212, NF, MS+]; Pizza: A Slice of Heaven, by Ed Livine [0789312050, NF, MS+]; Pizza Napoletana, by Pamela Johns, [1580080855, NF, MS+]; Lou Monte Sings Songs for Pizza Lovers [Collectables, 1999]; That's Amore [Dean Martin, 1954].

18. Antonio Gaetano Family Archive (hereafter cited as: AGFA).

19. It is difficult for people in Anthony's time to imagine the hardships and the terror endured by World War I soldiers in the trenches. Charging across No Man's Land into withering machine gun fire was futile and deadly, but daily living in the trenches had its own special horrors. In the trenches, soldiers had to contend with unceasing artillery shelling (causing the mentally debilitating condition called "shell shock"), being surrounded by poorly buried dead bodies, poison gas attacks, trench cave-ins, rats, lice, malaria-carrying mosquitoes, poor sanitation, shortages of drinkable water, hunger, poor nutrition and poor hygiene (causing the gum disease called "trench mouth"), puddles of standing water (causing rotted boots and the disease called "trench foot"), and extremes of weather.

The only good thing to come out of trench warfare was the trench coat: The fashionable trench coat worn in Anthony's time is a descendant of the gabardine military coats worn by British, Canadian, and French soldiers during World War I. Invented in England in 1880 by Thomas Burberry, gabardine is a breathable fabric made from wool yarn that is waterproofed before weaving. In 1901, Burberry was commissioned by England's War Office to design a new service uniform for British officers; he designed a full-length gabardine military coat. In 1914, Burberry adapted the design of the coat to accommodate the military equipment of World War I, and the trench coat was born. The World War I trench coat had cuff straps on the sleeves, epaulettes to hold gloves and a service cap, and a belt with small brass D-rings to secure grenades, side arms, and swords.

✓ **Anthony Recommends:** World War I Trench Warfare: 1914–1916 and World War I Trench Warfare: 1916–1918, by Stephen Bull [1841761974 and 1841761982, NF, MS+].

20. Antonio Gaetano attended DeWitt Clinton High School (DWCHS) in Manhattan, NY, at the same time as Thomas Waller (DWCHS Class of 1917) and Richard Rodgers (DWCHS Class of 1919). Thomas "Fats" Waller became a jazz musician and composer and is credited with writing over 450 jazz tunes; one of his most famous is Ain't Misbehavin' [1929]. Richard Rodgers became a composer and is famous for

lunch, and about Frank Hardart's drip coffee that only cost a nickel a cup. Businessmen in a rush used the Automat's stand-up counters; eating at the counters was known as having a "perpendicular lunch." In the 1940s, the Horn & Hardart Company marketed the Automat experience to families as a way to "give mom a break" from making dinner. There are no Automats in Anthony's time; the last Automat closed in 1991, succumbing to the competition of fast-food restaurants.

✓ **Anthony Recommends:** *The Automat,* by Marianne Hardart [0609610740, NF, MS+]; *Easy Living* [1937, NR]; *That Touch of Mink* [1962, NR]; *Radio Days* [1987, PG]; *Dark City* [1998, R]; *Lunching at the Automat* [Irving Berlin, 1932].

32. The phrase "tickling the ivories" stems from the earlier use of ivory for piano keys. Companies imported elephant tusks from Africa and cut them into thin pieces for use as piano keys ("ivories"), and sold them to piano manufacturers. When the African elephant became an endangered species, the practice was stopped. In Anthony's time, piano keys are made from enamel, plastic, and wood.

Anthony is describing a pneumatically driven "reproducing" player piano. Carefully arranged holes in a roll of paper told the piano what keys to depress and what tempo and volume to use to reproduce the performance of the original pianist. Anthony had only to pump the pedals to power the piano's playing mechanisms by suction. Before World War I, families bought pianos for entertainment: At parties and family gatherings, one family member played the piano while the others sang or danced. The player piano extended the popularity of the piano because it eliminated the need for costly lessons and musical ability. In the years after World War I, sales of player pianos declined as affordable radios became available, and the audio quality of phonographs improved.

✓ **Anthony Recommends:** *Piano,* by David Crombie [0879303727, NF, MS+].

33. Steeplechase Park at Coney Island was the brainchild of George Cornelius Tilyou, a real-estate developer turned showman in the late 1800s. Tilyou's amusement park featured "never-seen-before" rides and attractions, including: the Steeplechase Horse Race, the Human Pool Table, the Human Niagara, the Mixer, Noah's Ark, the Ocean Roller Coaster, and the Grinder. Many of Tilyou's rides would be considered too dangerous in Anthony's time. The Grinder, for example, was a huge sausage machine where people entered one end, squeezed through soft rollers, and were spit out at the other end.

George Tilyou died in 1914 and his son, Edward, ran the park at the time Anthony was there.

✓ **Anthony Recommends:** *Coney Island,* by John Berman [0760738874, NF, MS+]; *Coney Island Walking Tour,* by Charles Denson [0966698207, NF, MS+]; *Fatty at Coney Island* [1917, NR]; *The Crowd* [1928, NR]; *When Strangers Marry* [1944, NR]; *Little Fugitive* [1953, NR]; *Annie Hall* [1977, PG]; *The American Experience: Coney Island* [1993, D, NR].

34. Anthony is referring to *Mary Poppins* [1964, NR].

35. The invention of the hot dog is credited to Charles Feltman in 1874, but Nathan Handwerker made the hot dog famous. In 1912, at the age of twenty, Nathan Handwerker immigrated to the United States and went to work in Charles Feltman's Coney Island restaurant, splitting rolls for hot dogs and sausage sandwiches. In 1916, Handwerker left Feltman's restaurant and opened his own hot dog stand on Coney Island. Handwerker used his own special recipe and offered his hot dogs at the incredibly low price of five cents apiece (half the price of a Feltman hot dog). But people didn't think that a five-cent hot dog was safe to eat and they refused to buy them, so Handwerker surrounded his hot dog stand with people dressed in white gowns. "If doctors eat my hot dogs," Handwerker said, "you know they're good!" There was some controversy over whether or not the people in white gowns were really doctors, but Handwerker's hot dogs became popular and famous nonetheless. In Anthony's time, delicious Nathan's Famous hot dogs are available throughout the United States.

✓ **Anthony Recommends:** *America Eats: History on a Bun* [2001, D, NR].

36. The Palisades Amusement Park was located in Cliffside Park, Fort Lee, NJ. The park opened in 1898 and closed in 1971. The park was famous for having the world's largest saltwater pool.

37. "Prices of Stocks Crash in Heavy Liquidation," *New York Times,* 10/24/1929.

38. 1930 Census: Bay 38th Street, Brooklyn, New York, 5/3/1930. NARA.

39. Construction of the Empire State Building began in January 1930. The project was conceived by John Raskob, a member of the board of directors at General Motors. Raskob's goal was to outdo automotive competitor Walter Chrysler, who's 1,046-foot-tall Chrysler Building was already under construction and on the way to becoming the world's tallest building. The Empire State Building was completed in just 410 days, and it reached 103 floors, and 1,454 feet, into the sky.

The original plan called for a dirigible mooring mast atop the building, but, during tests, pilots found it impossible to safely navigate the wind currents near the building. When the Empire State Building was officially opened on May 1, 1931, President Herbert Hoover flipped a switch in Washington, D.C., remotely turning on the building's lights for the first time. On July 28, 1945, a B-25 bomber accidentally crashed into the 78th floor of the Empire State Building, causing a fire, but the building survived the impact. In Anthony's time, the Empire State Building's observation deck still offers a great view.

✓ **Anthony Recommends:** *The Empire State Building,* by John Berman [0760738890, NF, MS+]; *An Affair to Remember* [1957, NR]; *Sleepless in Seattle* [1993, PG]; *Modern Marvels: Empire State Building* [1994, D, NR]; The Empire State Building [New York, NY, www.esbnyc.com].

40. Encampments of out-of-work and homeless people during the Great Depression were called "Hoovervilles," especially during President Hoover's time in office.

Anthony is referring to the Bonus Army Expeditionary Force of 1932, a group of 20,000 World War I veterans. President Hoover ordered General Douglas MacArthur to remove the Bonus Army marchers from Washington's streets by force. MacArthur, assisted by Major Dwight Eisenhower and Major George Patton, exceeded his orders and proceeded to force the protesters out of Washington, D.C., entirely; he also burned down their tents and huts on the outskirts of the city. The incident contributed to President Hoover's defeat in the next election.

41. "On the Bank Crisis," 3/12/1933, courtesy FDR Library/NARA.

42. Ibid.

43. Anthony is referring to *King Kong* [1933, NR].

44. Hoover Dam is situated in Black Canyon on the Colorado River, near Las Vegas, NV. Construction on the dam was begun in 1930, during the Hoover administration. President Hoover named the dam after himself, hoping to show that he was doing something about unemployment in the early years of the Great Depression. In 1933, President Roosevelt changed the name to Boulder Dam, no doubt for political reasons. On April 30, 1947, a resolution restoring the original name of the dam was passed by Congress and signed by President Truman. It took less than five years to build Hoover Dam, but the engineering challenges were astounding. The river was diverted by drilling four tunnels, each 50 feet in diameter, through the solid rock walls of the Black Canyon. Men were lowered by cable over the edges of the canyon walls to strip away loose rock. Concrete was poured twenty-four hours a day, seven days a week, for two years, to fill the enormous forms of the 726-foot-high dam; 582 miles of one-inch steel pipe, carrying ice water from a specially constructed refrigeration plant, were embedded in the three million cubic yards of concrete to dissipate the heat generated as the concrete cured. Five thousand men and their families settled in the Nevada desert to complete the project. In Anthony's time, Hoover Dam is a National Historic Landmark and is considered one of America's Seven Modern Civil Engineering Wonders.

✓ **Anthony Recommends:** *American Experience: Hoover Dam* [1999, D, NR]; *Modern Marvels: Building Hoover Dam* [1999, D, NR]; Hoover Dam [702-597-5970, www.usbr.gov/lc/hooverdam].

45. Anthony is referring to the photographs taken by Dorothea Lange. Lange worked for the U.S. Government and was assigned to document the plight of displaced farm families and migrant workers during the Great Depression. Anthony is describing the photograph commonly referred to as "Migrant Mother, Nipomo, California," but its original caption was: "Destitute Pea Pickers in California; a 32-Year-Old Mother of Seven Children." The photograph was taken in February 1936. In a 1960 interview, Dorothea Lange talked about the famous photograph: "I saw and approached the hungry and desperate mother, as if drawn by a magnet. I do not remember how I explained my presence or my camera to her, but I do remember she asked me no questions. I made five exposures, working closer and closer from the same direction. I did not ask her name or her history. She told me her age, that she was thirty-two. She said that they had been living on frozen vegetables from the surrounding fields, and birds that the children killed. She had just sold the tires from her car to buy food. There she sat in that lean-to tent with her children huddled around her, and seemed to know that my pictures might help her, and so she helped me. There was a sort of equality about it." [Source: "The Assignment I'll Never Forget: Recollections of Dorothea Lange," *Popular Photography,* February 1960. Reprinted by permission of *Popular Photography.*]

✓ **Anthony Recommends:** *The Photographs of Dorothea Lange,* by Dorothea Lange [0810963159, NF, MS+].

46. In 1866, William Breyer hand-cranked his first gallon of ice cream in his home in Philadelphia, PA; he sold the ice cream to his neighbors from a horse-drawn wagon. Breyer opened his first ice cream store in 1882 and his first ice cream manufacturing plant in 1896. The plant where Salvatore Vincenzo worked opened in 1925. In Anthony's time,

11. "The Papa of the Phonograph: An Interview with Edison, The Inventor of the Talking Machines," *New York Daily Graphic*, 4/2/1878. Courtesy Edison Papers: TAED #MBSB10472.

12. "Dolls That Really Talk: The Wonderful Toys Which Mr. Edison Is Making for Nice Little Girls," *New York Sun*, 11/22/1888. Courtesy Edison Papers: TAED #SC88130A.

13. "The Smoke of an Electric Lamp," *Scientific American*, 7/12/1879. Courtesy Edison Papers: TAED #SM012111C.

14. "Edison's Newest Marvel: Sending Cheap Light, Heat, and Power by Electricity," *New York Sun*, 9/16/1878. Courtesy Edison Papers: TAED #MBSB20889.

15. "Letter: Edison to Theodore Puskas," 10/5/1878. Courtesy Edison Papers: TAED #LB003394.

16. "A Night with Edison," *New York Herald*, 12/31/1879. Courtesy Edison Papers: TAEM #94:557.

17. *Menlo Park Reminiscences*, by Francis Jehl [0766126471, NF, HS+], page 357. Reprinted by permission of the Henry Ford Museum.

18. Francis Jehl's journals corroborate Anthony's story that the lamp lasted for about forty-five hours, but Charles Batchelor's notes indicate that the lamp lasted for only fourteen hours. Batchelor wrote that "lamp number 9" was "on from 1:30 AM till 3 PM 13½ hours and was then raised to 3 gas jets for 1 hour then cracked glass & busted." [Source: "Batchelor, Charles: Technical Notes and Drawings, Carbon, Glass, Ceramics; Incandescent Lamp," 10/22/1879. Courtesy Edison Papers: TAED #N052105.]

    October 21 became known as "Edison Day," and on anniversaries of October 21, 1879, parades were held and children studied Thomas Edison's achievements in school. The largest celebration occurred in 1929, the fiftieth anniversary known as "Light's Golden Jubilee." On that day, Edison and Jehl reenacted their Menlo Park experiment at the opening of the reconstructed Menlo Park laboratory on the grounds of the Henry Ford Museum in Greenfield Village, Dearborn, MI.

19. Electrifying Manhattan—and the world—turned out to be a lot more complicated than most people thought in 1879, and it was Nikola Tesla, not Thomas Edison, who invented the best way to do it. Tesla immigrated to the United States in 1884 at the age of twenty-eight, and he began working for Edison on the recommendation of Charles Batchelor. Edison tasked Tesla with making his electric generators more efficient. Tesla succeeded, but quit in disgust, claiming that Edison refused to pay him for his work. It was the beginning of a battle between the two men. Edison's electrical distribution system was based on direct current (DC), but Tesla had an idea for alternating current (AC). Edison's DC system had limitations: Electricity could not be transmitted through copper wires more than a mile, and only a single voltage could be transmitted in a wire. Edison's solutions to these problems turned out to be impractical: Edison proposed that electrical power be generated as near as possible to where it was needed, requiring hundreds of power stations to be built in a single city. Edison also proposed that separate wires be used to carry the different voltages needed by different appliances, requiring several wires to be strung to each home. Tesla's AC system didn't have these problems. Edison wasn't going to easily surrender the potential profits from his patented DC system, however, so he set out to discredit Tesla's AC system, which was backed by the Westinghouse Company. First, Edison set up demonstrations of electrocutions of stray animals using alternating current to prove that alternating current was more dangerous than direct current. Then, Edison's team invented the electric chair for the Department of Corrections of the State of New York using alternating current to drive the point home that alternating current was deadly to humans, too. But in the end, Tesla's AC system proved superior to Edison's DC system and was widely adopted. Even Edison's General Electric Company switched to AC.

20. "Letter: Francis Upton to Elijah Upton," 12/28/1879. Courtesy Edison Papers: TAED #MU041.

21. "Letter: Francis Upton to Lucy Winchester Upton," 11/7/1878. Courtesy Edison Papers: TAED #MU001.

22. Ibid.

23. "Vaudeville" was the term for a form of live entertainment that was popular in the United States from the mid-1890s until the early 1930s. A vaudeville show typically had jugglers, comedians, trained animals, dancers, acrobats, magicians, and short dramatic segments. The first movies were shown in vaudeville theaters. Then, on November 26, 1905, John Harris and Harry Davis of Pittsburgh, PA, opened the first theater exclusively created for the showing of motion pictures; their first attraction was *The Great Train Robbery,* and admission was a just nickel. Word got around quickly and other entrepreneurs followed suit; "Nickelodeons" sprang up all over the country.

    ✓ **Anthony Recommends:** *Vaudeville*, by Judy Alter [0531203581, NF, MS+]; *Vaudeville* [1997, D, NR].

24. Butch Cassidy was born Robert Leroy Parker in 1866. Cassidy's "Hole-in-the-Wall" gang robbed trains and banks in South Dakota, Idaho, Montana, Wyoming, and Colorado. Eventually, the gang was wanted in so many states that Butch Cassidy fled to South America with his partner Harry Longabaugh ("The Sundance Kid"), and Harry's wife, Etta. Cassidy and Longabaugh robbed banks in Chile, Bolivia, and Peru. Legend has it that Butch Cassidy and the Sundance Kid were killed in a gunfight with Bolivian soldiers in 1908, but some people say that the two men were seen in the United States after 1908.

✓ **Anthony Recommends:** *Butch Cassidy and the Sundance Kid* [1969, PG].

25. Edwin Porter joined Thomas Edison's staff in 1895. Porter revolutionized early filmmaking: He invented the technique of "dramatic editing"—splicing together scenes shot at different times and in different places. Porter used the technique to produce the first documentary film in the United States: *The Life of an American Fireman* [1903]. In the film, Porter spliced together scenes of an actual house fire with scenes of live actors playing the parts of a mother and child caught in the blaze.

26. "Patent Caveat Number 110," submitted by Thomas Edison on 10/8/1888, courtesy the Edison National Historic Site.

A patent caveat is a written notification to the United States Patent Office stating that the writer is working on an invention and intends to file an official patent application. A patent caveat records the date of invention and protects the inventor from patent infringements. Thomas Edison's patent caveat became the basis for two final patents: Patent #589,168, granted August 31, 1897, for the Kinetographic Camera, and Patent #493,426, granted March 14, 1893, for "An Apparatus for Exhibiting Photographs of Moving Objects."

✓ **Anthony Recommends:** The U.S. Patent and Trademark Office Web site [www.uspto.gov]. To see scanned images of Edison's patents—just go to the U.S. Patent and Trademark Office Web site and type in the patent numbers provided in this note. Also: The Thomas Alva Edison Papers Project Web site [http://edison.rutgers.edu/patents.htm].

27. *The Diary and Observations of Thomas Edison,* by Dagobert Runes [0802224342, NF, MS+], page 74. Reprinted by permission of The Philosophical Library, New York. Original Source: "The Story of the Motion Picture: Edison, Its Great Inventor, Tells How the Idea Came to Him and How He Worked It Out," by Hugh Weir, *McClure's Magazine,* November 1922, Volume 54, Number 9, page 81.

28. Ibid.

In 1880, George Eastman perfected a process for making dry plates for photography and founded the Eastman Dry Plate and Film Company. Eastman's vision was to make photography simple and to place the power of the camera in everyone's hands. In 1888, Eastman introduced the "Kodak," a point-and-shoot camera with pre-loaded film inside. Eastman's company processed the film and printed the pictures when people mailed the camera back to him with all the exposures used. Eastman renamed his company in 1892 as the Eastman Kodak Company. In 1900, Eastman introduced a camera simple enough for children to use, called the "Brownie."

✓ **Anthony Recommends:** *George Eastman,* by Lynda Pflueger [076601617X, NF, MS+]; *Kodak Cameras,* by Brian Coe [1874707375, NF, MS+]; *The Wizard of Photography* [2000, D, NR].

29. *The Diary and Observations of Thomas Edison,* by Dagobert Runes [0802224342, NF, MS+], page 74. Reprinted by permission of The Philosophical Library, New York. Original Source: "The Story of the Motion Picture: Edison, Its Great Inventor, Tells How the Idea Came to Him and How He Worked It Out," by Hugh Weir, *McClure's Magazine,* November 1922, Volume 54, Number 9, page 81.

30. Born Phoebe Anne Oakley Mozee on August 13, 1860, in Patterson Township, OH, Annie Oakley grew up to become the star attraction of Buffalo Bill's Wild West Show in the late 1800s. Annie was an extraordinary markswoman. She was famous for being able to hit a dime tossed into the air at ninety feet, a playing card's thin edge at ninety feet, and for having shot (with a .22 rifle) 4,472 out of 5,000 glass balls thrown into the air. Annie married Frank Butler, a marksman she beat in a shooting contest when she was just sixteen years old. Frank became part of Annie's act; she would shoot the ashes off of a cigarette he held in his mouth from twenty paces. Annie Oakley died in 1926, at the age of sixty-six. She is remembered for breaking down barriers to women in society, and for overcoming adversity in her younger days. Annie grew up poor, learned to shoot to put food on the table for her family, and suffered abuse in a foster home. Annie's motto was: "Aim at a high mark and you will hit it. No, not the first time, not the second, and maybe not the third. But keep on aiming and keep on shooting, for only practice will make you perfect. Finally, you'll hit the bull's-eye of success." [Source: Generally attributed to Annie Oakley.]

✓ **Anthony Recommends:** *Annie Oakley and Buffalo Bill's Wild West,* by Isabelle Sayers [0486241203, NF, MS+]; *Bulls-Eye,* by Sue Macy [0792270088, NF, MS+]; *Annie Get Your Gun* [1950, NR].

9. The term "G.I." is derived from the words "Government-Issued." Government-Issued products (food, clothing, office supplies, and weapons) were those produced according to U.S. military specifications and issued to American soldiers. During World War II, people associated the term with the soldiers themselves, and began calling American soldiers G.I.s. In Anthony's time, G.I. Joe, the military-themed doll, represents all American soldiers.

✓ **Anthony Recommends:** *G.I. Joe,* by John Michlig [0811818225, NF, MS+]; *Government Issue: Collector's Guide,* by Henry Enjames [2913903878, NF, MS+].

10. "A Pure Miracle," by Ernie Pyle, 6/12/1944. Reprinted by permission of the Scripps Howard Foundation.

Ernie Pyle was one of America's most famous and beloved war correspondents. Pyle set a new journalistic standard during World War II by moving among the soldiers on the front lines. His reporting gave the American people a closeness to war that they had never experienced before. Pyle never glorified war, but he explained combat in terms of the sacrifices that American soldiers made on behalf of the people back home. Pyle wrote of the American warrior with a "heart-of-gold," of the American soldier fighting the "good fight" against evil, and of the American soldier fighting for a "just and moral cause." Ernie Pyle died on April 18, 1945, while reporting on the Battle of Okinawa in the Pacific.

✓ **Anthony Recommends:** *Ernie's War,* by Ernie Pyle [0394549236, NF, MS+]; *The Story of G.I. Joe* [1945, NR].

11. Ernie Pyle's style of reporting must have seemed strange to Anthony, because Ernie Pyle made it clear which side he was on. In Anthony's time, during the War on Terror, many Americans wonder where the loyalties of some journalists lie.

After the World Trade Center attack on September 11, 2001, journalists from the Reuters international news service refused to describe Osama bin Laden and his murderous disciples as "terrorists." The journalists pointed to the official Reuters editorial policy, which stated: "As part of a long-standing policy to avoid the use of emotive words, we do not use terms like 'terrorist.' . . . We do not characterize the subjects of news stories but instead report their actions, identity and background so that readers can make their own decisions based on the facts." But the definition of the word "terrorist" is: "A person who uses or favors violent and intimidating methods of coercing a government or community." The term is clearly descriptive, not "emotive." [Sources: "Editorial Policy," Reuters, 1/9/2004. Reprinted by permission of Reuters. And: *The 2003 Oxford Pocket American Dictionary of Current English,* edited by Frank Abate (0195150821, NF, MS+), reprinted by permission of Oxford University Press.]

In the United States, ABC News barred its journalists from wearing American flag lapel pins because it didn't want to be seen taking sides in the War on Terror. An ABC News spokesman said: "We cannot signal how we feel about a cause, even a justified and just cause, through some sort of outward symbol. Overseas, it could be perceived that we're just mouthpieces for the U.S. government, and that can place our journalists in danger." [Source: "ABC News Bans Flag Pins," *The Washington Post,* 9/25/2001.]

In February 2003, just before the American invasion and liberation of Iraq, CBS News aired an interview with Iraqi dictator Saddam Hussein, the despicable mass murderer, torturer of women and children, and supporter of international terrorism. Many Americans scratched their heads during the televised interview, wondering what could possibly be learned about Saddam that wasn't already known, and why they should believe anything that Saddam had to say. At the end of the interview, CBS News anchorman Dan Rather told Saddam: "I would very much like to see you in the future, Mr. President." [Source: "Transcript: Saddam Hussein Interview," *60 Minutes II,* 2/26/2003.]

On April 13, 2004, during a nationally televised presidential press conference, viewers across the country were astonished to hear members of the American press corps ask repeatedly whether or not President George W. Bush thought he should apologize for the tragedy of 9/11. The questions included: "Do you feel a sense of personal responsibility for September 11, 2001?" and "Do you believe the American people deserve an apology from you, and would you be prepared to give them one?" The president responded: "Here's what I feel about that. The person responsible for the attacks was Osama bin Laden. That's who's responsible for killing Americans." [Source: "Transcript: President's Press Conference," 4/13/2004, courtesy The White House.]

✓ **Anthony Recommends:** *Citizen Kane* [1941, NR]; *Call Northside 777* [1948, NR]; *All the President's Men* [1976, PG]; *Absence of Malice* [1981, PG]; *The Insider* [1999, R]; *Shattered Glass* [2003, PG-13].

12. Interview with John Ellery: Courtesy D-Day Museum.

13. When Anthony uses the term "human shields" to describe the Allied soldiers invading Normandy, he uses the term differently than most people in his time. In Anthony's time, three hundred people from

thirty countries, including about twenty Americans, called themselves human shields and traveled to Iraq shortly before the war. But the human shields in Anthony's time never intended to shield the Iraqi people from Saddam Hussein; the human shields went to Iraq to prevent the invasion and liberation of Iraq by American armed forces. Once inside Iraq, the human shields were surprised to discover that the Iraqi authorities insisted on posting them at military sites, electric plants, water treatment plants, and oil refineries—and not at hospitals and schools as they had planned. When the human shields heard firsthand accounts of Saddam's atrocities, they became even more disillusioned and some of them returned home. The Americans who traveled to Iraq as human shields did so illegally; they violated U.S. sanctions in place preventing business with Iraq. Upon returning to the United States, the American human shields were fined by the U.S. Treasury Department and threatened with imprisonment. The U.S. military, in a coalition with dozens of other nations, removed Saddam Hussein from power and liberated Iraq in April 2003.

14. Anthony did not mention the little French girl's name, so it's not possible to know what became of her. In later life, she may very well have honored her liberators and the sacrifices they made for her freedom. But many Americans living in Anthony's time would express some doubt about the loyalties of the French people in general, and their willingness to fight evil in the world. In Anthony's time, France stands accused of obstructing the free world's efforts to end Saddam Hussein's evil regime in Iraq. Evidence suggests that France placed business interests ahead of its concern for the suffering Iraqi people, and ahead of the security of its American ally. There is evidence that French government officials conducted secret negotiations with Saddam Hussein, assuring him that France would use its power in the United Nations to prevent the United States from invading Iraq and ending his regime. The purported payoff to France was lucrative oil production and business contracts, and bribes. The money for the bribes came from the United Nations Oil-for-Food Program, a program that allowed Iraq to sell its oil on the open market only if the money was used by Saddam to feed starving Iraqi children—but Saddam used the money for bribes instead. Because of the corruption of the U.N. Oil-for-Food Program, Iraqi children died—the food never got to them. In March 2003, the displeasure many Americans felt toward the French erupted into an American boycott of French products.

15. World War II pitted the Axis powers (Germany, Italy, Japan, Hungary, Romania, and Bulgaria) against the Allied powers (The United States, Great Britain, France, the Soviet Union, Australia, Belgium, Brazil, Canada, China, Denmark, Greece, the Netherlands, New Zealand, Norway, Poland, South Africa, and Yugoslavia). The Soviet Union was communist country, ruled by a brutal dictator named Joseph Stalin. Stalin was every bit as evil as Adolph Hitler—Stalin was responsible for mass murder and tens of millions of deaths in the Soviet Union. The United States allied with the Soviet Union to destroy German Nazism, however, because Nazism was the greater threat at the time. After World War II, the Soviet Union and the United States came into direct conflict because the leaders of the Soviet Union sought to spread communism around the globe. The United States and the Soviet Union engaged in a "cold war" that lasted several decades. The United States prevailed and Soviet communism ended in the early 1990s with the financial collapse of the Soviet Union.

✓ **Anthony Recommends:** *Invasion of the Body Snatchers* [1956, NR]; *The Manchurian Candidate* [1962, NR]; *From Russia with Love* [1963, NR]; *The Bedford Incident* [1965, NR]; *Ice Station Zebra* [1968, G]; *Colossus: The Forbin Project* [1970, NR]; *The Missiles of October* [1974, NR]; *War Games* [1983, PG]; *The Hunt for Red October* [1990, PG]; *CNN Perspective Presents: Cold War* [1998, D, NR]; *The Berlin Airlift* [1999, D, NR]; *Biography: Joseph Stalin* [2000, D, NR]; *I Am David* [2004, PG]; *Secret Agent Man* [Johnny Rivers, 1965].

16. "1992 Interview: Holocaust Survivor Ruth Webber Describes the Auschwitz Crematoria," United States Holocaust Memorial Museum, Washington, D.C. Reprinted by permission of Ruth Webber.

Ruth Webber was born in 1935, in Ostrowiec, Poland. She was four years old when the Germans invaded Poland and occupied her town. Her family was forced into a ghetto. Ruth hid in the nearby woods, and sometimes within the ghetto itself. When the ghetto was liquidated, Ruth's parents were split up. Ruth was captured and sent to a succession of concentration camps, and finally to Auschwitz-Birkenau. After the war, Ruth lived in an orphanage until she was reunited with her mother. Later, Ruth Weber immigrated to the United States.

17. "1992 Interview: Holocaust Survivor Lily Malnik Describes the Death March from Auschwitz-Birkenau to Bergen-Belsen," United States Holocaust Memorial Museum, Washington, D.C. Reprinted by permission of Lily Applebaum Lublin Malnik.

Lily was twelve years old and living with her mother in Brussels, Belgium, when the German Army invaded the city in 1940. In 1944, Lily was deported to Auschwitz-Birkenau because she was Jewish. Lily survived because she was lucky enough to be chosen to work in

"World Islamic Front Statement," 2/23/1998; "A Letter to America," 11/24/2002.]

23. The six marines were: John Bradley, from Appleton, WI; Franklin Sousley, from Hilltop, KY; Harlon Block, from Rio Grande Valley, TX; Ira Hayes, from Gila River Indian Reservation, AZ; Rene Gagnon, from Manchester, NH; and, Mike Strank, from Franklin Borough, PA. The photographer's name was Joe Rosenthal. Rosenthal's photograph became one of the most famous images of World War II; the photo was used for War Bond promotions, printed on a United States postage stamp, and became the model for the Marine Corps War Memorial in Arlington, VA.

The code that Anthony heard was in the Navajo language. The Japanese were skilled at breaking codes, so the military created a code based on the Navajo language. Navajo is not a written language, it has no alphabet or symbols, and it is only spoken on the Navajo lands in the American Southwest. The code was developed in 1942 by twenty-nine marines from the Navajo Nation. In combat, the "Navajo Code Talkers" spoke the code over the radio to relay important strategic and tactical battlefield information. The Japanese heard the messages, but they could not understand them. The Navajo Code Talkers served in all six marine divisions and fought in all the battles in the Pacific from 1942 to 1945. World War II combat veterans have said that the battle on Iwo Jima would not have been won without the help and bravery of the Navajo Code Talkers. The top secret Navajo Code was declassified by the U.S. Government in 1969. On July 26, 2001, President George W. Bush presented the Navajo Code Talkers with a Congressional Gold Medal, honoring their service to the country in World War II. On the back of the medal are the words: "Diné Bizaad Yee Atah Naayéé' Yik'eh Deesdlíí" ["The Navajo Language Was Used to Defeat the Enemy"]. Other Native American Code Talkers also contributed to American success in World War II (and World War I), including: Comanche, Choctaw, and Sioux.

✓ **Anthony Recommends:** *Unsung Heroes of World War II,* by Deanne Durrett [0816036039, NF, MS+]; *Warriors,* by Kenji Kawano [0873585135, NF, MS+]; *The Navajo Code Talkers* [2002, D, NR]; *Windtalkers* [2002, R]; Monument Valley Navajo Tribal Park [Arizona, 928-871-6647, www.navajonationparks.org]; The Navajo Code Talkers Memorial [Window Rock, AZ, 505-998-3274, www.navajocodetalkers.org].

24. Attributed to Frank Caldwell, 1st Parachute Division, 26th Marines, 5th Marine Division, in *Into the Rising Sun,* by Patrick K. O'Donnell [0743214803, NF, HS+], page 251. Copyright © 2002 by Patrick K.

O'Donnell. Reprinted with permission of The Free Press, a Division of Simon & Schuster Adult Publishing Group. All rights reserved.

25. Attributed to General Erskine, 3rd Marine Division Commander, in *Into the Rising Sun,* by Patrick K. O'Donnell [0743214803, NF, HS+], page 227. Copyright © 2002 by Patrick K. O'Donnell. Reprinted with permission of The Free Press, a Division of Simon & Schuster Adult Publishing Group. All rights reserved.

26. Anthony is referring to the Manhattan Project, America's top-secret military project to build an atomic bomb. In 1939, Albert Einstein wrote a letter to President Roosevelt warning him that the research going on in universities in America and Germany might lead to the development of an atomic bomb. Then, the U.S. military confirmed that Germany was working on an atomic bomb and intended to use it to win the war. The army placed General Leslie Groves in overall charge of the urgent project to develop America's nuclear bomb; American physicist J. Robert Oppenheimer was chosen to lead the scientific research team. The Manhattan Project was carried out in three secret locations that were not revealed until after the war had ended: Hanford, WA, Los Alamos, NM, and Oak Ridge, TN. At 5:29:45 A.M., on July 16, 1945, the first nuclear bomb was exploded at the military's secret Trinity Test Site in Alamogordo, NM. The Manhattan Project scientists were unsure of what would happen when the bomb exploded. They thought that the explosion might ignite the atmosphere and burn the entire surface of the earth. Seconds after the explosion, as he watched an enormous mushroom cloud boil up into the sky, Oppenheimer said: "Now I am become Death, destroyer of worlds."

✓ **Anthony Recommends:** *100 Suns,* by Michael Light [1400041139, NF, MS+]; *Picturing the Bomb,* by Rachel Fermi [0810937352, NF, MS+]; *The House on 92nd Street* [1945, NR]; *The Day after Trinity* [1980, D, NR]; *Fat Man and Little Boy* [1989, PG-13]; *Trinity and Beyond* [1995, D, NR]; *Infinity* [1996, PG].

27. Anthony is referring to the Boeing B-29 Superfortress Model Kit #5711, 1/48th Scale, by Revell-Monogram [www.revell-monogram.com]. Also the Boeing B-29A Superfortress *Enola Gay* Model Kit #14488, 1/144th Scale, by Minicraft [www.minicraftmodels.com].

28. U.S. bombers were heavily armed, but many were still shot down by enemy aircraft. Bombers had to be escorted and protected on their missions by other fighter aircraft. The very best escort fighter group during World War II was the 332nd Red Tail Fighter Group; the group never lost a single U.S. bomber to enemy aircraft attack. The group's success was due to the extraordinary talent of its combat fighter

pilots, plus a unique combat rule that forbade the pilots to chase their enemy until shot down. The Red Tail pilots stayed close to the bombers they escorted, denying the enemy any advantage. The Red Tail pilots broke combat flying records during World War II, and they broke down barriers, too. Also known as the "Tuskegee Airmen," the Red Tail fighter pilots were America's first Black combat airmen. Their patriotism drove them to overcome the extreme prejudice that existed in the racially segregated U.S. military during World War II. No one wanted to give them a chance, and no one believed they could fly. But their talent ultimately made them a legend.

The 332nd Fighter Group was organized and commanded by Colonel Benjamin Oliver Davis. After the war, Colonel Davis helped plan the desegregation of the Air Force. In 1950, Davis commanded a fighter wing in the Korean War. In 1959, Davis became the first Black officer to reach the rank of major general; he was promoted to lieutenant general in 1965. Davis served as the U.S. assistant secretary of transportation in the 1970s. Davis' father, Benjamin Oliver Davis, was the first Black general in the U.S. Army; President Franklin Delano Roosevelt promoted him to the rank in 1940.

✓ **Anthony Recommends:** *Red-Tail Angels,* by Pat McKissack [0802782922, NF, MS+]; *The Tuskegee Airmen,* by Lynn Homan [0738500453, NF, MS+]; *Nightfighters* [1994, D, NR]; *The Tuskegee Airmen* [1995, PG-13]; Tuskegee Airmen National Museum [Detroit, MI, 313-843-8849, www.tuskegeeairmen.org].

29. Anthony is right: A horrible power was let loose on August 6, 1945, and life was never the same. After World War II, both the United States and the Soviet Union embarked on programs to create, test, and deploy thousands of nuclear weapons. First, the two "Superpowers" aimed their nuclear missiles at each other's cities, threatening each other with annihilation if a war broke out. The military policy was officially called "Mutually Assured Destruction," or MAD, because if either side started a war, both sides would certainly lose. Living under the constant threat of nuclear attack took a psychological toll on people: Some people decided to "live for today," thinking the world could end at any moment. Some people built bomb shelters in their suburban backyards. Schoolchildren practiced ducking under their desks when air raid sirens blew. Teenagers swarmed to movies about monsters created by nuclear fallout.

When missiles became more accurate and spy satellites revealed where missile silos were hidden, the United States and the Soviet Union changed their tactic: They targeted their missiles on each other's silos, instead of each other's cities, believing that a surprise "first strike" could prevent the other side from retaliating. Because

the retargeting of the missiles suggested that a nuclear war was winnable, America's policy of MAD was changed to a policy called "Launch-on-Warning." The new policy meant that if the United States detected a nuclear missile launch in the Soviet Union (a missile launch "warning"), then all the American missiles would be launched immediately to avoid having them destroyed in their silos by the inbound Soviet missiles. The Soviet Union quickly adopted the same policy. Launch-on-Warning is not MAD, but it still sets up a dangerous situation because thousands of missiles could be launched in response to a mistaken warning of attack. It almost happened in 1980: The Soviet warning system mistakenly reported that America had launched a missile attack, because someone had placed a war game simulation tape into the computer. The mistake was corrected after a few tense minutes.

In Anthony's time, there is less room for a mistake like the one made in 1980 because a nuclear missile can be launched from a submarine very close to shore. There would be just seconds to decide if the threat was real, and how to respond. In Anthony's time, the U.S. Department of Defense is experimenting with a new way to protect America from missile attack. Called the Strategic Defense Initiative, or "Star Wars" by some, the new system would use lasers, radar, mirrors, and interceptors to destroy inbound missiles while they are still in flight. In effect, the system would be a missile shield.

✓ **Anthony Recommends:** *Face to Face with the Bomb,* by Paul Shambroom [0801872022, NF, MS+]; *Duck and Cover* [1951, D, NR]; *Godzilla* [1954, NR]; *Strategic Air Command* [1955, NR]; *Dr. Strangelove* [1964, NR]; *Fail-Safe* [1964, NR]; *The War Game* [1967, D, NR]; *The China Syndrome* [1979, PG]; *The Atomic Café* [1982, D, NR]; *Testament* [1983, PG]; *The Day After* [1983, NR]; *Crimson Tide* [1995, R]; *K-19 The Widowmaker* [2002, PG-13]; *99 Red Balloons* [Nena, 1983].

30. In the last months of World War II, the United States had almost unchallenged air supremacy over Japanese skies. As Anthony stated, the destruction of Japanese cities by U.S. bombers was horrific. In the summer of 1945, for example, the U.S. Army Air Force issued a report estimating the level of destruction of Japanese cities: Tokyo 51 percent, Nagoya 31 percent, Kobe 51 percent, Yokohama 44 percent, Osaka 26 percent, Kawasaki 68 percent, and Hitachi 72 percent. The devastation of Tokyo, one of Japan's largest cities, was wrought by multiple B-29 firebombing missions, like the one on March 9, 1945, when 334 B-29s dropped 8,519 napalm bombs on the city. The ancient city of Kyoto was deliberately spared attack. In all air raids combined, there were an estimated 315,922 casualties, 126,762 dead, and 1,439,115 buildings destroyed. American military planners were

4. Lou Gehrig's mother was right about one thing: Engineering is a noble and honorable profession that usually pays very well. That's because engineers solve problems and build things of value. You may not realize it, but almost everything around you that makes your life easier and more fun was designed and built by engineers: Bridges, roads, roller coasters, video games, baseballs, computer software, artificial organs, microwave ovens, skyscrapers, toasters, and even the Disney theme parks. To become an engineer and earn your share of the "big bucks," you must study hard in school and excel at math and science. You must also develop a good imagination, because engineers are often asked to create "something" out of "nothing." Most of all, you must possess an "engineering mind." Fortunately, that's an easy thing to assess. Just answer this question: When you see a good design, do you still have to change it? If your answer is "yes," there is a lucrative engineering career waiting for you!

Engineering students at the Georgia Institute of Technology (Georgia Tech) in Atlanta, Georgia, often tell the story of George P. Burdell—an engineer of myth and legend. According to the story, in 1916, George P. Burdell enrolled in every engineering class offered at Georgia Tech, and just four years later earned degrees in chemical, textile, civil, mechanical, and industrial engineering. Burdell also played on every sports team at Georgia Tech, and set many athletic records for the school. On October 17, 1916, Burdell, playing quarterback, led Georgia Tech's football team to a stunning 222–0 victory over Cumberland University. In track and field, Burdell was unbeatable in the 50-yard dash, javelin, pole-vault, and high-jump events. In the 1920s, Burdell became a millionaire many times over, designing and building skyscrapers in New York City. Burdell lost all of his money in the stock market crash of 1929. In the 1930s, Burdell again enrolled at Georgia Tech and earned advanced engineering degrees in several disciplines, including a Ph.D. in civil engineering. When World War II broke out, Burdell joined the U.S. Army Air Service and flew B-17 bombing missions over Germany. Later in the war, Burdell served as an engineering officer in the U.S. Navy. Burdell was qualified to serve aboard navy ships because he had successfully completed Georgia Tech's drownproofing class years before. Drownproofing was a required class for Georgia Tech freshmen, and involved being tied up with rope, laden with weights, and being thrown into the deep end of an Olympic-size swimming pool for hours at a time. Burdell never drowned—he was certified "drownproof." After World War II, Burdell returned to Atlanta and started his second construction company. Burdell built many buildings in the Atlanta area, but his most famous was The Big Chicken, in Marietta, GA, at the intersection of Highway 120 and U.S. 41. Rising 56 feet above the ground, the massive sheet metal chicken had eyes that rotated and a beak that opened and closed. Upon completion of the chicken, Burdell was hailed far and wide as a "Helluva Engineer." Burdell was famous—but he shied away from the spotlight and became a recluse. In 1997, George P. Burdell was hit by a car and killed, as he was crossing North Avenue in Atlanta, while on his way to the Varsity restaurant for a Frosted Orange. The car that hit Burdell was described by witnesses to be a "Ramblin' Wreck." Although the story of George P. Burdell is fiction, some people believe that there really was a George P. Burdell—and some people believe he is still alive. In 2004, some engineering students at Georgia Tech claimed to have seen a very healthy and enthusiastic George P. Burdell enrolling in several graduate-level thermodynamics classes at the school. And, after all, somebody built The Big Chicken.

✓ **Anthony Recommends:** *Is There an Engineer Inside You?* by Celeste Baine [0971161399, NF, MS+]; *The Seventy Wonders of the Modern World,* by Neil Parkyn [0500510474, NF, MS+]; *Walt Disney Imagineering,* by The Imagineers [0786883723, NF, MS+]; *Georgia on My Mind* [Ray Charles, 1960]; *Ramblin Wreck* [Frank Roman, 1911]; The Georgia Institute of Technology [Atlanta, GA, 404-894-2000, www.gatech.edu]; The Big Chicken [Marietta, GA, www.roadsidegeorgia.com]; The Varsity Restaurant [Atlanta, GA, 404-881-1706, www.thevarsity.com].

5. "Mom's Boys" were: Benny Bengough (catcher), Joe Dugan (third base), Mark Koenig (shortstop), Tony Lazzeri (second base), and Babe Ruth (right field).

6. *A Yankee Century,* by Harvey Frommer [0425186172, NF, HS+], page 61. Reprinted by permission of Harvey Frommer.

In 1926, the New York Yankees took the pennant. In 1927, the New York Yankees won the World Series with a sweep of four straight games (5–4, 6–2, 8–1, and 4–3). In 1928, the New York Yankees won the World Series again, with another four game sweep.

7. Rouladen is a traditional German dish of thin rolls of steak filled with bacon, onions, pickles, and red cabbage. Pickled eels, of course, are exactly that. According to Eleanor Gehrig, Lou's wife, pickled eels were the "specialty of the house" at the senior Gehrig home and Babe Ruth loved eating them. In her autobiography, Eleanor Gehrig wrote: "Ruth would wolf down [the pickled eels] between innings of games, especially when he happened to be in a hitting slump and needed some supernourishment." [Source: *My Luke and I,* by Eleanor Gehrig

(0690011091, NF, HS+), page 130. TM 2004 Estate of Eleanor Gehrig by CMG Worldwide, www.LouGehrig.com. Reprinted with permission.]

8. TM 2004 Estate of Eleanor Gehrig by CMG Worldwide, www.LouGehrig.com. Reprinted with permission.

9. *Secrets of Baseball Told by Big League Players,* by Rogers Hornsby [1557094314, NF, MS+], page 48.

10. Ibid., page 47.

11. *Lou Gehrig: An American Classic,* by Richard Bak [0878338837, NF, MS+], page 138. Reprinted by permission of Richard Bak.

12. *Iron Horse,* by Ray Robinson [0060974087, NF, MS+], page 169. Reprinted by permission of W. W. Norton & Company, New York.

13. Ibid.

14. *Lou Gehrig: An American Classic,* by Richard Bak [0878338837, NF, MS+], page 146. Reprinted by permission of Richard Bak.

15. Ibid., page 138.

16. Ibid., page 141.

17. Ibid.

18. Ibid.

Joe DiMaggio played his first game for the New York Yankees in 1936. He hit twenty-nine home runs his first season. DiMaggio became a three-time Yankee MVP (Most Valuable Player) and was inducted into the National Baseball Hall of Fame in 1955. Joe DiMaggio married actress Marilyn Monroe in 1954. In 1972, DiMaggio became famous to a new generation of Americans as "Mr. Coffee" when he agreed to do national advertising for the Mr. Coffee coffee-making machine. Joe DiMaggio died in 1999. He is remembered as one of the greatest baseball players of all time.

✓ **Anthony Recommends:** *Joe DiMaggio,* by David Jones [0313330220, NF, MS+]; *The Promise,* by Joe Carrieri [096447011X, NF, MS+]; *Mrs. Robinson* [Simon & Garfunkel, 1968].

19. Anthony lives in a time when children routinely see television news reports of their sports heroes engaging in outrageous public behavior, drug use, gun violence, sexual promiscuity, and even murder. Young sports fans also see their heroes brawl on the playing field: On January 20, 2004, a fight broke out between players of the Indiana Pacers and the Detroit Pistons that even involved people in the stands. Bad sportsmanship and misbehavior on the playing field is legendary among hockey players, but it was relatively new to basketball. Drug use in professional athletics has become so prevalent in Anthony's time, that President George W. Bush was moved to condemn the practice in his State of the Union Address on January 20, 2004: "The use of performance-enhancing drugs like steroids in baseball, football, and other sports is dangerous, and it sends the wrong message—that there are shortcuts to accomplishment, and that performance is more important than character." The use of steroids by Major League Baseball players may be responsible for some of the extraordinary batting averages and home run records in Anthony's time. In December 2004, members of Congress warned Major League Baseball commissioners and team managers that if they didn't "clean up their act," they would impose mandatory drug testing on the players. Congress conducted hearings on the issue in early 2005, and the Major League Baseball Commissioners agreed to test players for steroid use.

In Anthony's time, some celebrity athletes say that criticism of their behavior is unfair, and that they should not be viewed as role models. But most people believe that national celebrity carries with it an automatic obligation to set a good example, even off the field, because children are watching. Lou Gehrig was aware that his behavior had an effect on the public, and he tried to send a positive message at all times. In 1938, Lou Gehrig said: "I'm not trying to pretend that ball players have any altruistic mission in life. Frankly, we play baseball for a living. It's our job. Yet, I do think we accomplish more than just our own selfish purposes. I do feel we contribute to the spirit of the country and its mental attitude towards life. . . ." [Source: *Iron Horse,* by Ray Robinson (0060974087, NF, MS+), page 242. Reprinted by permission of W. W. Norton & Company, New York.]

✓ **Anthony Recommends:** *Champions of Faith,* by Thomas O'Toole [1580510914, NF, MS+]; *Competitor's Edge,* by Dave Branon [0802478190, NF, MS+]; *Good Sports,* by Joel Brown [1887432620, NF, MS+]; *The Heart of a Champion,* by Frank Deford [1559718374, NF, MS+].

20. Anthony is quoting American sportswriter Grantland Rice (1880–1954).

21. Anthony is quoting New York sportswriter Ed Farrell.

22. Lou Gehrig's record of 2,130 consecutively played professional baseball games stood until Cal Ripken, Jr., broke it in 1995. Other records set by Lou Gehrig: Lou was the first baseball player to hit four home

runs in a single game (June 3, 1932); Lou holds the record for the most grand slams in a career (twenty-three); Lou Gehrig was the first athlete to have his number (#4) retired. In 1939, Lou Gehrig was inducted into the Baseball Hall of Fame.

23. TM 2004 Estate of Eleanor Gehrig by CMG Worldwide, www.Lou Gehrig.com. Reprinted with permission.

24. *Iron Horse,* by Ray Robinson [0060974087, NF, MS+], page 252. Reprinted by permission of W. W. Norton & Company, New York.

25. Ibid., page 258.

   Amyotrophic Lateral Sclerosis (ALS), often called Lou Gehrig's Disease in Anthony's time, is a degenerative nervous-system disorder that causes muscle atrophy and paralysis. The disease occurs more often in men than in women, and usually after the age of forty. Victims of the disease usually die within two to five years of being diagnosed, although there have been exceptions. Most ALS patients first experience weakness in the hands, progressing to weakness in the legs, and then more general muscular atrophy. Death generally occurs due to atrophy of the respiratory muscles. There is no cure for ALS, but new drugs have been shown to have a modest effect in prolonging ALS survival. Treatments under study include the following: growth factors that might stimulate nerve recovery, medicines that alter the immune system, and drugs that control seizures.

   ✓ **Anthony Recommends:** *ALS: Lou Gehrig's Disease,* by Mary Wade [0766015947, NF, MS+].

26. Dr. William Worrall Mayo immigrated to the United States from England in 1846 and served in the Union Army as a surgeon during the Civil War. After the war, Dr. Mayo and his two sons, William J. Mayo and Charles Mayo, formed a medical practice in Rochester, MN. It was the nation's first "group" medical practice, bringing together physicians of different specialties to solve the medical problems of patients. The Mayo Clinic also pioneered the integration of medical research and education with medical practice. By Lou Gehrig's time, the Mayo Clinic was known nationwide as the place to go to have difficult and complex medical problems diagnosed and treated by the world's best physicians. Anthony must have met one of Dr. William Worrall Mayo's sons. In Anthony's time, there are three Mayo Clinic locations: Rochester, MN, Jacksonville, FL, and Scottsdale, AZ.

27. *Iron Horse,* by Ray Robinson [0060974087, NF, MS+], page 261. Reprinted by permission of W. W. Norton & Company, New York.

28. TM 2004 Estate of Eleanor Gehrig by CMG Worldwide, www.Lou Gehrig.com. Reprinted with permission.

29. Ibid.

30. Ibid.

31. Ibid.

32. It was rumored that a feud developed between Lou Gehrig and Babe Ruth in 1934, when Lou's mother made an unkind comment about Babe's wife, Claire. If the rumor was true, the feud apparently ended when Babe Ruth hugged Lou Gehrig on July 4, 1939.

33. It was Fiorello La Guardia, the mayor of New York, who offered Lou Gehrig the job as a parole officer and swore him into public service on January 2, 1940. Lou's job was to interview the criminals held in New York jails and help determine their release dates. One day, Lou interviewed Thomas Rocco Barbella, a troubled young man from the Lower East Side of Manhattan. Barbella had been jailed for street fighting and for the theft of baseball equipment from Yankee Stadium. Lou recommended extra time for Barbella in reform school. Barbella didn't like Gehrig's suggestion, but years later he admitted that his chance meeting with Lou Gehrig had a positive effect on his life. Barbella took a new name, Rocky Graziano, and became one of America's best professional boxers. In 1991, Rocky Graziano was inducted into the International Boxing Hall of Fame in Canastota, NY.

   ✓ **Anthony Recommends:** *Somebody Up There Likes Me* [1956, NR].

34. *My Luke and I,* by Eleanor Gehrig [0690011091, NF, HS+], page 228. TM 2004 Estate of Eleanor Gehrig by CMG Worldwide, www.LouGehrig .com. Reprinted with permission.

35. Ibid., page 159.

36. Ibid.

37. *Lou Gehrig: An American Classic,* by Richard Bak [0878338837, NF, MS+], page 142. Reprinted by permission of Richard Bak.

38. *My Luke and I,* by Eleanor Gehrig [0690011091, NF, HS+], page 228. TM 2004 Estate of Eleanor Gehrig by CMG Worldwide, www.LouGehrig .com. Reprinted with permission.

39. Ibid., page 229.

Chapter 8: The Vaccine

1. Marco Polo was an Italian adventurer, merchant, and author born in the year 1254. He traveled the Silk Road to China and spent twenty-four years in Asia, becoming an expert on Asian culture, commerce, and geography. His adventures inspired Christopher Columbus to set sail for the Far East. Anthony is not referring to Marco Polo the man, however, he is referring to Marco Polo the children's game. The game is played in a swimming pool. One child who is "it" closes his eyes and shouts "Marco," and the other children in the pool respond by shouting "Polo." With eyes closed, the child who is "it" must find and tag one of the other children, locating the other children by the sounds of their voices only.

   The Frisbee traces its roots to the Frisbie Pie Company of Bridgeport, CT. College students in the early 1900s tossed and caught the baking company's empty pie tins, and invented games with the flying tins. In 1948, Walter Frederick Morrison invented a plastic version of the Frisbie pie tin that could fly farther. He sold the rights to his design to the Wham-O toy company in 1957. Wham-O manufactured millions of the flying discs, calling them Pluto Platters. In 1964, Wham-O improved the toy's design, changed the name to Frisbee, and patented the aerodynamic design. Mattel, the world's largest toy company, bought Wham-O in 1994. In Anthony's time, Ultimate Frisbee is a recognized sport that is a cross between football, basketball, and soccer; Frisbee Golf is also popular.

   ✓ **Anthony Recommends:** *Marco Polo: A Photographer's Journey,* by Michael Yamashita [885440005X, NF, MS+]; *The Complete Book of Frisbee,* by Victor Malafronte [0966385527, NF, MS+]; *The Adventures of Marco Polo* [1938, NR]; The U.S. Patent and Trademark Office Web site [Frisbee patent #3,359,678, www.uspto.gov].

2. From a U.S. Board of Health warning sign posted during the polio epidemic of 1916.

3. Optical microscopes are limited by the physics of light to about 1000x magnification. They are not powerful enough to see something as small as poliovirus. The electron microscope uses a narrow beam of electrons to resolve an image, and can provide more than 1,000,000,000x magnification. Electron microscopes were developed in the late 1930s; poliovirus was first seen by an electron microscope in the early 1950s. Another type of electron microscope, called a scanning tunneling microscope, developed in the 1980s, can see individual atoms.

   ✓ **Anthony Recommends:** *Hidden Beauty,* by France Bourely [0810935473, NF, MS+]; *Hidden Worlds,* by Stephen Kramer [0618055460, NF, MS+]; *Journeys in Microspace,* by Dee Breger [0231082525, NF, MS+].

4. *Polio's Legacy,* by Edmund Sass [076180143X, NF, HS+], page 55. Reprinted by permission of University Press of America. Note: Interview with Marilyn R., who contracted polio in 1949.

5. Anthony is quoting from "She Was a Phantom of Delight," the poem written by William Wordsworth in 1804.

6. "On the President's First Birthday Ball for Crippled Children," 1/30/1934, courtesy FDR Library/NARA.

7. Ibid.

8. Ibid.

9. Ibid.

10. Information from: "Active Immunization Against Poliomyelitis," by Maurice Brodie, M.D., and William H. Park, M.D., *Journal of the American Medical Association,* 10/5/1935.

11. Eddie Cantor was a star of stage and screen in the 1920s and 1930s, and of radio and television in the following years. In a meeting with President Roosevelt to discuss the plan to raise money to fight polio, Cantor coined the term "March of Dimes." Eddie Cantor died in 1964.

    ✓ **Anthony Recommends:** *Whoopee!* [1930, NR]; *Roman Scandals* [1933, NR]; *Kid Millions* [1934, NR].

12. "On the President's Fifth Birthday Ball for Crippled Children," 1/29/1938, courtesy FDR Library/NARA.

    In October 2001, President George W. Bush asked the children of America to donate one dollar each to provide food and medicine to the children in Afghanistan who had suffered under the oppressive Taliban regime; the "America's Fund for Afghan Children" was modeled after the March of Dimes campaign of 1938.

13. By 1939, more than 2.5 million dimes had been mailed to the White House. In 1938, the dime bore the face of the Roman God Mercury, the Winged Messenger. In Anthony's time, the dime bears the portrait of FDR. The U.S. Mint put FDR's portrait on the dime in 1946 to commemorate his involvement in the March of Dimes fundraising campaign of 1938. After President Ronald Reagan died in 2004, a bill was introduced in Congress to replace FDR's portrait on the dime

5. Excerpts from Interim Iraqi Prime Minister Ayad Allawi's address to the U.S. Congress, in Washington, D.C., on 9/23/2004.

6. On January 20, 2005, in his Second Inaugural Address, President George W. Bush said: "The only force powerful enough to stop the rise of tyranny and terror, and replace hatred with hope, is the force of human freedom. . . . So it is the policy of the United States to seek and support the growth of democratic movements and institutions in every nation and culture, with the ultimate goal of ending tyranny in our world. This is not primarily the task of arms, though we will defend ourselves, and our friends, by force of arms when necessary. Freedom, by its nature, must be chosen, and defended by citizens, and sustained by the rule of law and the protection of minorities. And when the soul of a nation finally speaks, the institutions that arise may reflect customs and traditions very different from our own. America will not impose our own style of government on the unwilling. Our goal instead is to help others find their own voice, attain their own freedom, and make their own way."

On January 30, 2005, more than 60 percent of eligible Iraqis turned out to vote in the nation's first free elections in decades. They defied the terrorists. In his State of the Union Address on February 2, 2005, President George W. Bush commented on the courage and unity of the Iraqi people: "Across Iraq, often at great risk, millions of citizens went to the polls and elected 275 men and women to represent them in a new Transitional National Assembly. A young woman in Baghdad told of waking to the sound of mortar fire on Election Day, and wondering if it might be too dangerous to vote. She said, 'Hearing those explosions, it occurred to me—the insurgents are weak, they are afraid of democracy, they are losing. So I got my husband, and I got my parents, and we all came out and voted together.' Americans recognize that spirit of liberty, because we share it. In any nation, casting your vote is an act of civic responsibility; for millions of Iraqis, it was also an act of personal courage, and they have earned the respect of us all."

7. Excerpts from: "Radio Address of the President," 9/11/2004, courtesy The White House.

8. Ibid.

9. Anthony is quoting George Washington, from: "Fifth Annual Address to Congress," 12/3/1793.

10. Excerpts from: "Radio Address of the President," 9/11/2004, courtesy The White House.

11. Excerpt from: "Second Inaugural Address," by President George W. Bush, 1/20/2005, courtesy The White House.

12. Anthony is referring to the following events:

Superman: In 2004, DC Comics released an alternate history comic book about Superman growing up in the communist Soviet Union and working for Joseph Stalin.

Army: About twenty-five hundred American soldiers applied for conscientious objector status during the Persian Gulf War in 1990–1991, and several hundred American soldiers applied for conscientious objector status during the Iraq War in 2003–2004. A conscientious objector is a person who refuses to serve in the military for moral reasons, religious reasons, or reasons of conscience—a person who claims that they can't take another life in battle. But all of the soldiers who applied for conscientious objector status had volunteered to join the U.S. Army.

Energy: Oil prices rose to record levels in 2004 because the demand for imported oil increased dramatically worldwide (especially in China), and Islamic terrorists destroyed oil pipelines in the Middle East. Gasoline prices rose to record levels, too. Even with America's oil supplies threatened, and oil and gasoline prices at an all-time high, members of Congress were unable to reach an agreement to drill for oil in Alaska and make America more energy independent, until March 2005. The decision to drill for oil in Alaska's Arctic National Wildlife Regufe was narrowly reached, by a vote in the Senate of 51–49.

POWs: In 2003–2004, the U.S. military released some of the POWs it captured in the War on Terror, only to see them return to the battlefield.

Modesty: In 2004, an eleven-year-old girl in Seattle, WA, wrote to executives at Nordstrom department store complaining that much of the children's clothing they sold required her to display her belly button and underwear in public. The children's clothing at Nordstrom was typical of fashions offered at most department stores, and was based on the provocative apparel worn by much older female rock stars on stage.

Environmental Groups: In 2003, a radical environmental group burned cars and SUVs on a Los Angeles–area car dealer lot, and the FBI implicated "Eco-Terrorists" in the destruction of private home construction sites in several states.

Food: In 2004, Burger King introduced a hamburger without a bun in response to the low-carbohydrate diet craze sweeping the nation, and pizza restaurants responded by cutting off crusts.

Abortion: In 2004, presidential candidate John Kerry said he believed that "life begins at conception," but a first-trimester abortion is not murder because the embryo is "not a person yet." His opinion reflected the stance of pro-choice advocates that human life begins at conception, but "personhood" is a legal quality that the unborn are endowed with later, and only "persons" can be murdered. In 2004, the U.S. Department of Health and Human Services reported that from 1970–2001, approximately 42,301,576 legal abortions were performed in the United States. [Source: "Abortion Surveillance—United States, 2001, Morbidity and Mortality Weekly Report," U.S. Centers for Disease Control, 11/26/2004, Vol. 53, No. SS–9.]

Movies: In 2004, the best movie about marriage was *The Incredibles* [2004, PG], and the only movie to deal with the subject of Islamic terrorism was *Team America World Police* [2004, R]. Anthony recommends the *The Incredibles*; he does not recommend *Team America World Police*.

Immigration: "Immigrants" are people lawfully admitted for permanent residence in the United States. Unauthorized immigrants, or "illegal aliens," are people who enter the United States without permission; their presence in the United States violates the law. In 2002, the U.S. Department of Homeland Security reported that there were approximately 7 million unauthorized immigrants living in the United States, and that 67 percent of them, or 4,690,000 people, had entered the United States without being stopped or questioned. They had entered the country illegally by sneaking across the border. In 2003, the Department of Homeland Security said that it apprehended 1,046,422 illegal aliens, but experts said that nearly 3 million people illegally entered the United States that year. [Source: "Yearbook of Immigration Statistics," U.S. Department of Homeland Security, 2002, 2003.]

Most people agree that allowing so many people to cross the borders of the United States without questioning their intentions is dangerous, especially after 9/11. But in Anthony's time, there are elected government officials and private organizations that actually encourage illegal border crossing by offering benefits to illegal aliens. In Anthony's time, jobs, elementary school education, drivers licenses, in-state college tuition, bank accounts, food stamps, health care, and even home ownership, are all offered to illegal aliens. Some city councils are even considering letting illegal aliens vote in elections because they have children in public schools. The states of Washington, California, New York, Illinois, Oklahoma, Texas, and Utah provide in-state college tuition rates to illegal aliens; other states are considering the same tuition policy. Several states grant drivers licenses to illegal aliens, ignoring the fact that driver's licenses are used as a form of ID nationwide. In a few instances, illegal aliens received expensive organ transplant surgery free of charge, and they were placed ahead of tax-paying Americans on the waiting list for the scarce organs. Realtors and lenders in several cities have been known to help illegal aliens purchase homes. Several American cities have become sanctuaries for illegal aliens: In 2003, Seattle's City Council passed an ordinance preventing the city's police from questioning the immigration status of people they meet on the streets. For aliens crossing America's southwest border illegally, water-stations are provided to make the trip through the desert easier. Humanitarian groups placed the water stations along known illegal alien smuggling routes in the Arizona desert.

In April 2005, a group of U.S. citizens calling themselves "Minutemen" went to the U.S.-Mexico border to observe illegal aliens entering the country and turn them over to the U.S. Border Patrol. The Minutemen proved that illegal immigration could be stopped by placing more guards on America's borders, but President George W. Bush derided the efforts of the Minutemen by calling them "vigilantes."

Toxin: In 2003, more than two million Americans received Botulinum Toxin-A injections to temporarily improve their appearance.

Christmas: Christmas is a celebration of the birth of Jesus Christ, the Son of God. Christmas Day is a federal holiday, and the president of the United States lights the national Christmas tree on the White House lawn every Christmas season.

Fat Children: In 2003, the U.S. Department of Health and Human Services reported that 16 percent of American children were overweight, resulting in a consumer backlash against fast-food restaurants even though the remedy is a personal choice to "eat a balanced diet, eat less, and exercise more."

Skin Color: In June 2003, the United States Supreme Court ruled that colleges and universities could legally discriminate based on skin color and race in student admission procedures. While saying that treating people differently based on race was not an injustice, the court simultaneously concluded that "race-conscious admissions policies must be limited in time," and that it expected that "25 years from now, such programs will no longer be necessary."

Marriage: The dictionary definition of marriage is "the legal union of a man and a woman in order to live together and often to have children." On September 21, 1996, President Bill Clinton signed the Defense of Marriage Act into federal law, with the approval of both houses of the U.S. Congress. The Defense of Marriage Act states: "the word marriage means only a legal union between one man and one

Chapter 3: To America I Will Go

PART THREE
THE GREAT DEPRESSION

Books:

- ❏ *Children of the Dust Bowl,* by Jerry Stanley [0517880946, NF, MS+]
- ❏ *Dear Mrs. Roosevelt,* by Robert Cohen [0807854131, NF, MS+]
- ❏ *Depression Era Recipes,* by P. Wagner [0934860556, NF, MS+]
- ❏ *Everyday Fashions of the Thirties,* by Stella Blum [048625108X, NF, MS+]
- ❏ *Franklin Delano Roosevelt,* by Russell Freedman [0395629780, NF, MS+]
- ❏ *Growing Money,* by Gail Karlitz [0843177020, NF, MS+]
- ❏ *Little Orphan Annie in the Great Depression,* by Harold Gray [0486237370, F, MS+]
- ❏ *Posters of the WPA,* by Chris Denoon [0295965436, NF, MS+]
- ❏ *Six Days in October,* by Karen Blumenthal [0689842767, NF, MS+]
- ❏ *Stories and Recipes from the Great Depression,* by Rita Van Amber [0961966319, NF, MS+]
- ❏ *The Homecoming,* by Earl Hamner [089966945X, F, MS+]
- ❏ *The New Deal and the Great Depression,* by Lisa Wroble [0766014215, NF, MS+]

....

- ❏ *Down and Out in the Great Depression,* by Robert McElvaine [0807840998, NF, HS+]
- ❏ *FDR,* by Joseph Alsop [0517202964, NF, HS+]
- ❏ *Of Mice and Men,* by John Steinbeck [0140177396, F, HS+]
- ❏ *Riding the Rails,* by Errol Uys [0415945755, NF, HS+]
- ❏ *Teenvestor,* by Emmanuel Modu [0399527605, NF, HS+]
- ❏ *The Grapes of Wrath,* by John Steinbeck [0142000663, F, HS+]
- ❏ *The Great Depression,* by T. H. Watkins [0316924547, NF, HS+]

Movies:

- ❏ *The Public Enemy* [1931, NR]
- ❏ *Gold Diggers of 1933* [1933, NR]
- ❏ *Looking Forward* [1933, NR]
- ❏ *Turn Back the Clock* [1933, NR]
- ❏ *Stand Up and Cheer* [1934, NR]
- ❏ *Blondie* [1938, NR]
- ❏ *Of Mice and Men* [1939, NR]
- ❏ *The Wizard of Oz* [1939, NR]
- ❏ *The Grapes of Wrath* [1940, NR]
- ❏ *It's a Wonderful Life* [1946, NR]
- ❏ *Sunrise at Campobello* [1960, NR]

- ❏ *Bonnie and Clyde* [1967, R]
- ❏ *The Homecoming* [1971, NR]
- ❏ *Paper Moon* [1973, PG]
- ❏ *The Sting* [1973, PG]
- ❏ *Brother, Can You Spare a Dime?* [1975, D, NR]
- ❏ *Eleanor and Franklin* [1976, NR]
- ❏ *Phar Lap* [1983, PG]
- ❏ *Places in the Heart* [1984, PG]
- ❏ *The Journey of Natty Gann* [1985, PG]
- ❏ *The Untouchables* [1987, R]
- ❏ *Wall Street* [1987, R]
- ❏ *1939 New York World's Fair* [1992, D, NR]
- ❏ *King of the Hill* [1993, PG-13]
- ❏ *Riding the Rails* [1997, D, NR]
- ❏ *Breadline* [1997, D, NR]
- ❏ *Surviving the Dust Bowl* [1998, D, NR]
- ❏ *The Great Depression* [1998, D, NR]
- ❏ *Our Daily Bread: Films of the Great Depression* [1999, D, NR]
- ❏ *Jazz: A Film by Ken Burns* [2000, D, NR]
- ❏ *O Brother, Where Art Thou?* [2000, PG-13]
- ❏ *The Legend of Bagger Vance* [2000, PG-13]
- ❏ *Seabiscuit* [2003, PG-13]
- ❏ *Cinderella Man* [2005, PG-13]

Music:

- ❏ *Big Rock Candy Mountain* [Harry McLintock, 1920s]
- ❏ *Billboard Pop Memories: 1930s* [Rhino, 1994]
- ❏ *Brother Can You Spare a Dime?* [New World, 2001]
- ❏ *Cotton Club* [Gallerie, 2001]
- ❏ *Duke Ellington: 1926–1949* [Proper Box, 2001]
- ❏ *Essential George Gershwin* [Sony, 2003]
- ❏ *FDR: Nothing to Fear* [Jerden, 1995]
- ❏ *Happy Days Are Here Again* [Jack Yellen, 1929]
- ❏ *Hobo's Lullaby* [Arlo Guthrie, 1974]
- ❏ *Louis Armstrong: 1930–1932* [JSP, 2000]
- ❏ *Nipper's Greatest Hits: The 30's* [RCA, 1990]
- ❏ *The Great Depression: 1930s* [Sony, 1933]
- ❏ *Woody Guthrie: Dust Bowl Ballads* [Buddha BMG, 2000]

Places:

- ❏ The Franklin Delano Roosevelt Memorial [Washington, D.C., 202-426-6841, www.nps.gov/fdrm] traces twelve years of American history through a sequence of four outdoor rooms, each room devoted to one of FDR's terms in office. Book: *The Franklin Delano Roosevelt Memorial*, by Lawrence Halprin [0811817067, NF, MS+].

❏ Franklin Delano Roosevelt Home and Presidential Library [Hyde Park, NY, 800-FDR-VISIT, www.fdrlibrary.marist.edu].

❏ Herbert Hoover Presidential Library [West Branch, IA, 319-643-5301, http://hoover.archives.gov].

❏ New York Stock Exchange [11 Wall Street, New York, NY, 212-656-3000, www.nyse.com]. See the 16-foot tall bronze statue of a charging bull, located across the street from the exchange.

❏ United States Department of the Treasury [Washington, D.C., www.ustreas.gov].

❏ Congress founded the Federal Reserve [Washington, D.C., www.federalreserve.gov] in 1913 to provide the nation with a stable monetary and financial system.

❏ Junior Achievement [www.ja.org]. Learn how to manage your money, how to start your own business, how to obtain financial aid for college, and much more.

Chapter 3: To America I Will Go

PART FOUR
AN AMERICAN IN AMERICA

Books:

❏ *America on My Mind*, by Globe Pequot Press [0762723602, NF, MS+]
❏ *America 24/7*, by Rick Smolan [0789499754, NF, MS+]
❏ *FDR's Four Freedoms Speech*, by Julia Hargrove [1573102202, NF, MS+]
❏ *Freedom: A History of US*, by Joy Hakim [0195157117, NF, MS+]
❏ *I Am an American: Essays*, by Robert Benjamin [083691449X, NF, MS+]
❏ *I Like Being American*, by Michael Leach [0385507437, NF, MS+]
❏ *In Defense of Liberty: The Bill of Rights*, by Russell Freedman [0823415856, NF, MS+]
❏ *Johnny Tremain*, by Esther Forbes [0440442508, F, MS+]
❏ *My Fellow Americans: Speeches of America's Presidents*, by Michael Waldman [1402200277, NF, MS+]
❏ *Norman Rockwell's America*, by Christopher Finch [0810980711, NF, MS+]
❏ *Norman Rockwell's Four Freedoms*, by Stuart Murray [0517202131, NF, MS+]
❏ *101 Reasons to Be a Proud American*, by Brenda Star [1884886175, NF, MS+]
❏ *Proud to Be an American*, by Arnold Schwarzenegger [Speech: Republican National Convention, 8/31/2004]
❏ *Proud to Be an American*, by Carol Stout [1886161089, NF, MS+]

❏ *Songs Sung Red, White, and Blue*, by Ace Collins [0060513047, NF, MS+]
❏ *The American Heritage Book of Great American Speeches*, by Suzanne McIntire [0471389420, NF, MS+]
❏ *The Coming American*, by Sam W. Foss [Poem, 1894]
❏ *The Declaration of Independence and Other Documents*, by John Grafton [0486411249, NF, MS+]
❏ *The Pocket Patriot*, by George Grant [1581820925, NF, MS+]
❏ *The U.S. Constitution: Fascinating Facts About It*, by Terry Jordan [1891743007, NF, MS+]
❏ *We Are Americans*, by Dorothy Hoobler [0439162971, NF, MS+]

....

❏ *Founding Fathers: Uncommon Heroes*, by Steven Allen [1879033763, NF, HS+]
❏ *My America: By 150 Americans*, by Hugh Downs [0743240898, NF, HS+]
❏ *The Melting Pot: A Drama in Four Acts*, by Israel Zangwill [0881431702, NF, HS+]
❏ *The Story of America*, by Allen Weinstein [0789489031, NF, HS+]
❏ *The New Dictionary of Cultural Literacy*, by E. D. Hirsch [0618226478, NF, MS+]
❏ *The Words We Live By*, by Linda Monk [0786867205, NF, HS+]
❏ *What's So Great About America*, by Dinesh D'Souza [0142003018, NF, HS+]

Movies:

❏ *America* [1924, NR]
❏ *Mr. Smith Goes to Washington* [1939, NR]
❏ *Yankee Doodle Dandy* [1942, NR]
❏ *Johnny Tremain* [1957, NR]
❏ *1776* [1972, G]
❏ *Biography: George Washington* [1995, D, NR]
❏ *Biography: Thomas Jefferson* [1995, D, NR]
❏ *The Patriot* [2000, R]
❏ *Freedom: A History of US* [2002, D, NR]
❏ *America's Heart & Soul* [2004, D, PG]
❏ *John Ratzenberger: Made in America* [TV Series, D, NR]

Music:

❏ *America* [Samuel Smith, 1831]
❏ *America* [Simon & Garfunkel, 1968]
❏ *America the Beautiful* [Ray Charles, 1972]
❏ *An American Child* [Phil Vassar, 2002]
❏ *God Bless America* [Kate Smith, 1939]
❏ *Fanfare for the Common Man* [Aaron Copland, 1942]

- *The Thin Red Line* [1998, R]
- *American Experience: MacArthur* [1999, D, NR]
- *Heroes of Iwo Jima* [2001, D, NR]
- *Pearl Harbor* [2001, PG-13]
- *The Great Raid* [2005, R]
- *Flags of Our Fathers* [2006, R]

Music:

- *A Hard Rain's a-Gonna Fall* [Bob Dylan, 1963]
- *Goodbye, Mama, I'm Off to Yokohama* [J. Fred Coots, 1942]
- *Praise the Lord and Pass the Ammunition* [Frank Loesser, 1941]
- *Remember Pearl Harbor* [Sammy Kaye, 1941]
- *The Son of a Gun Who Picks on Uncle Sam* [E. Y. Harburg, 1942]
- *We Did It Before and We Can Do It Again* [Cliff Friend, 1942]
- *What Have They Done to the Rain?* [The Searchers, 1964]

Places:

- The USS *Arizona* Memorial [Pearl Harbor, Honolulu, HI, 808-422-0561, www.nps.gov/usar] is the final resting place for many of the ship's 1,777 crewman who lost their lives on December 7, 1941.
- The design of the Marine Corps War Memorial, also known as the Iwo Jima Memorial [Arlington, VA, 703-289-2500, www.nps.gov/gwmp/usmc.htm], is based on the photograph taken by Joe Rosenthal on Iwo Jima in 1945.
- The National Museum of the Marine Corps [Quantico, VA, 800-397-7585, www.usmcmuseum.org] preserves the American flag that was raised on Mount Suribachi in 1945.
- Military Historical Tours [Alexandria, VA, 800-722-9501, www.miltours.com] arranges tours of the World War II military cemetery on Iwo Jima.
- This book can guide you to the World War II historical sites in the Pacific: *The 25 Best World War II Sites: Pacific Theatre*, by Chuck Thompson [0966635264, NF, MS+].
- The *Enola Gay* is on display at the National Air and Space Museum's Steven F. Udvar-Hazy Center [Dulles International Airport, Chantilly, VA, 202-633-1000, www.nasm.si.edu/museum/udvarhazy]. Book: *America's Hanger*, by Smithsonian [0974511307, NF, MS+].
- Official Web site of Brigadier General Paul W. Tibbets, USAF Retired [www.theenolagay.com].
- The National Museum of Nuclear Science and History [Albuquerque, NM, 505-245-2137, www.atomicmuseum.com] has exhibits on the Manhattan Project and the men who built the bomb.
- Trinity Test Site [White Sands Missile Range, near Socorro, NM, 505-678-1134, www.wsmr.army.mil]. The exact spot where the first atomic bomb was exploded is open to the public twice a year, on the first Saturday of April and October. Radiation levels are low, but visits are limited to one hour for safety.
- Hiroshima Peace Memorial Museum and Park [Hiroshima, Japan, www.pcf.city.hiroshima.jp].

Chapter 6: For Your Tomorrow

PART FOUR
SACRIFICE

Books:

- *Design for Victory: WWII Posters*, by Harry Rubenstein [1568981406, NF, MS+]
- *Everyday Fashions of the Forties*, by JoAnne Olian [0486269183, NF, MS+]
- *From Foxholes and Flight Decks: Letters*, by Rod Gragg [0312287151, NF, MS+]
- *Grandma's Wartime Kitchen*, by Joanne Hayes [0312253230, NF, MS+]
- *Medal of Honor: Portraits*, by Nick Del Calzo [1579652409, NF, MS+]
- *Norman Rockwell's World War II*, by Susan Meyer [0963101102, NF, MS+]
- *Rosie the Riveter*, by Penny Coleman [0517885670, NF, MS+]
- *Since You Went Away: Letters*, by Judy Litoff [0700607145, NF, MS+]
- *Slacks and Calluses*, by Constance Bowman [156098368X, NF, MS+]
- *The Victory Garden*, by Lee Kochenderfer [0440417031, F, MS+]
- *V for Victory: America's Home Front*, by Stan Cohen [092952151X, NF, MS+]
- *V Is for Victory: American Home Front*, by Sylvia Whitman [0822517272, NF, MS+]
- *World War II Home Front Collectibles*, by Martin Jacobs [0873418530, NF, MS+]

....

- *Americans Remember the Home Front*, by Roy Hoopes [0425186644, NF, HS+]
- *A Separate Peace*, by John Knowles [0743253973, F, HS+]
- *Don't You Know There's a War On?* by Richard Lingeman [1560254653, NF, HS+]
- *Dr. Seuss Goes to War*, by Richard Minear [156584565X, NF, HS+]
- *The Bedford Boys*, by Alex Kershaw [0306811677, NF, HS+]
- *The United States of America's Congressional Medal of Honor Recipients and Their Official Citations*, by R. J. Proft [0964459035, NF, HS+]
- *When the Stars Went to War*, by Roy Hoopes [0679414231, NF, HS+]

Movies:

- *Women in Defense* [1941, D, NR]
- *Pride of the Marines* [1945, NR]

- ❏ *The Best Years of Our Lives* [1946, NR]
- ❏ *The Man in the Gray Flannel Suit* [1956, NR]
- ❏ *Summer of '42* [1971, R]
- ❏ *A Soldier's Story* [1984, PG]
- ❏ *The Assault* [1986, PG]
- ❏ *Home Front U.S.A.* [1998, D, NR]
- ❏ *The Life and Times of Rosie the Riveter* [2002, D, NR]
- ❏ *American Valor* [2003, D, NR]

Music:

- ❏ *Eternal Father, Strong to Save* [Dykes/Whiting, 1861]
- ❏ *Marines' Hymn* [Marine Corps, 1800s]
- ❏ *Reckless Talk* [Woody Guthrie, 1942]
- ❏ *Rosie the Riveter* [Redd Evans and John Loeb, 1942]
- ❏ *When the Lights Go on Again All Over the World* [Vaughn Monroe, 1943]
- ❏ *Where Have All the Flowers Gone?* [Pete Seeger or Kingston Trio, 1961]

Places:

- ❏ The National World War II Memorial [Washington, D.C., 800-639-4WW2, www.wwiimemorial.com] honors the sixteen million who served in the armed forces of the United States during World War II, the more than four hundred thousand who died, and all who supported the war effort from home. Book: *The World War II Memorial*, by Douglas Brinkley [1588342107, NF, MS+].
- ❏ Arlington National Cemetery [Arlington, VA, 703-607-8000, www.arlingtoncemetery.org]. Visit the Tomb of the Unknowns, where unknown soldiers of World War I, World War II, the Korean War, and the Vietnam War are interred. Visit Audie Murphy's gravesite, in Section 46 near Memorial Drive; it's one of the most visited.
- ❏ This book can guide you to the World War II historical sites in the United States: *World War II Sites in the United States*, by Richard Osborne [0962832413, NF, MS+].
- ❏ The Official Audie Murphy Memorial Web site [www.audiemurphy.com].
- ❏ Veterans of Foreign Wars (VFW) Web site [www.vfw.org].
- ❏ U.S. Department of Veterans Affairs Web site [www.va.gov].
- ❏ Rosie the Riveter World War II Home Front National Historical Park [Richmond, CA, 510-232-5050, www.rosietheriveter.org].

Chapter 7: The Luckiest Man

Books:

- ❏ *Baseball's Golden Age*, by Neal McCabe [0810991195, NF, MS+]
- ❏ *Baseball's Sad Lexicon: Tinkers to Evers to Chance*, by Franklin Pierce Adams [Poem, 1910]
- ❏ *Baseball in Art and Literature*, by David Colbert [073700102X, NF, MS+]
- ❏ *Casey at the Bat*, by Ernest Thayer [0689854943, F, MS+]
- ❏ *Classic Baseball Photographs*, by Donald Honig [0765110555, NF, MS+]
- ❏ *Classic Baseball: Photos*, by Walter Iooss [0810942585, NF, MS+]
- ❏ *Collecting Baseball Cards*, by Thomas Owens [0761317082, NF, MS+]
- ❏ *Glove Affairs*, by Noah Liberman [1572434201, NF, MS+]
- ❏ *Iron Horse*, by Ray Robinson [0060974087, NF, MS+]
- ❏ *Lou Gehrig*, by Kevin Viola [0822517949, NF, MS+]
- ❏ *Lou Gehrig: An American Classic*, by Richard Bak [0878338837, NF, MS+]
- ❏ *Lou Gehrig: A Quiet Hero*, by Frank Graham [0395068347, NF, MS+]
- ❏ *New York Yankees: First 25 Years*, by Vincent Luisi [0738509132, NF, MS+]
- ❏ *Secrets of Baseball Told By Big League Players*, by Rogers Hornsby [1557094314, NF, MS+]
- ❏ *The Joy of Keeping Score*, by Paul Dickson [0156005166, NF, MS+]
- ❏ *Why Is the Foul Pole Fair?* by Vince Staten [0743233840, NF, MS+]

- ❏ *A Yankee Century*, by Harvey Frommer [0425186172, NF, HS+]
- ❏ *Babe Ruth's Own Book of Baseball*, by George Herman Ruth [0803289391, NF, HS+]
- ❏ *My Luke and I*, by Eleanor Gehrig [0690011091, NF, HS+]
- ❏ *The Games Do Count*, by Brian Kilmeade [0060736739, NF, HS+]
- ❏ *The Wonder Team: 1927 Yankees*, by Leo Trachtenberg [0879726784, NF, HS+]

Movies:

- ❏ *Rawhide* [1938, NR]
- ❏ *Knute Rockne, All American* [1940, NR]
- ❏ *The Pride of the Yankees* [1942, NR]
- ❏ *It Happens Every Spring* [1949, NR]
- ❏ *Take Me Out to the Ball Game* [1949, NR]
- ❏ *The Stratton Story* [1949, NR]
- ❏ *Angels in the Outfield* [1951, NR]
- ❏ *Jim Thorpe, All American* [1951, NR]
- ❏ *Brian's Song* [1971, G]
- ❏ *The Other Side of the Mountain* [1975, PG]
- ❏ *One on One* [1977, PG]
- ❏ *Something for Joey* [1977, PG]
- ❏ *A Love Affair: Eleanor and Lou Gehrig Story* [1978, NR]
- ❏ *Breaking Away* [1979, PG]
- ❏ *The Abbott & Costello Show: Who's on First?* [1981, NR]
- ❏ *The Natural* [1984, PG]
- ❏ *Eight Men Out* [1988, PG]
- ❏ *Field of Dreams* [1989, PG]

- ❏ *Home Front: Flags Across America,* by Peter Elliott [0972328009, NF, MS+]
- ❏ *One Nation: America Remembers 9/11,* by *Life* magazine [0316525405, NF, MS+]
- ❏ *Portraits 9/11/01,* by the *New York Times* [0805072225, NF, MS+]
- ❏ *The World Trade Center Remembered,* by Sonja Bullaty [0789207648, NF, MS+]
- ❏ *Understanding September 11th,* by Mitch Frank [0670035823, NF, MS+]
- ❏ *Voices from the Front: Gulf War II,* by Frank Schaeffer [078671462X, NF, MS+]

....

- ❏ *After: The September 12 Era,* by Steven Brill [0743237099, NF, HS+]
- ❏ *American Soldier,* by Tommy Franks [0060731583, NF, HS+]
- ❏ *A Table in the Presence,* by Carey Cash [0849918235, NF, HS+]
- ❏ *Dawn over Baghdad,* by Karl Zinsmeister [1594030502, NF, HS+]
- ❏ *Escape from Slavery,* by Francis Bok [0312306237, NF, HS+]
- ❏ *Escape in Iraq,* by Thomas Hamill [088317314X, NF, HS+]
- ❏ *Hating America: The New World Sport,* by John Gibson [0060580100, NF, HS+]
- ❏ *Let's Roll,* by Lisa Beamer [0842374183, NF, HS+]
- ❏ *Never Forget,* by Mitchell Fink [0060514337, NF, HS+]
- ❏ *No True Glory,* by Bing West [0553804022, NF, HS+]
- ❏ *Report from Ground Zero,* by Dennis Smith [067003116X, NF, HS+]
- ❏ *Shadow War,* by Richard Miniter [0895260522, NF, HS+]
- ❏ *The 9/11 Commission Report,* by the National Commission on Terrorist Attacks [0393326713, NF, HS+]
- ❏ *We Will Prevail,* by George W. Bush [0826415520, NF, HS+]
- ❏ *Why We Fight,* by William Bennett [0895261340, NF, HS+]

Movies:
- ❏ *The FBI Story* [1959, NR]
- ❏ *Black Sunday* [1977, R]
- ❏ *Raid on Entebbe* [1977, NR]
- ❏ *On Wings of Eagles* [1986, NR]
- ❏ *The Delta Force* [1986, R]
- ❏ *The Taking of Flight 847* [1988, NR]
- ❏ *The Hijacking of the Achille Lauro* [1989, NR]
- ❏ *Voyage of Terror: The Achille Lauro* [1990, NR]
- ❏ *Without Warning: Terror in the Towers* [1993, NR]
- ❏ *Courage Under Fire* [1996, R]
- ❏ *Executive Decision* [1996, R]
- ❏ *Air Force One* [1997, R]
- ❏ *Path to Paradise* [1997, NR]
- ❏ *Jinnah* [1998, D, NR]
- ❏ *The Siege* [1998, R]

- ❏ *One Day in September* [1999, D, R]
- ❏ *Three Kings* [1999, R]
- ❏ *Uncle Saddam* [2000, D, NR]
- ❏ *National Geographic: Afghanistan Revealed* [2001, D, NR]
- ❏ *Behind Enemy Lines* [2001, PG-13]
- ❏ *Beneath the Veil: The Taliban* [2001, D, NR]
- ❏ *Black Hawk Down* [2001, R]
- ❏ *World Trade Center: In Memoriam* [2001, D, NR]
- ❏ *In Memoriam: New York City, 9/11/01* [2002, D, NR]
- ❏ *Live from Baghdad* [2002, NR]
- ❏ *9/11* [2002, D, NR]
- ❏ *Baghdad Bob* [2003, D, NR]
- ❏ *DC 9/11* [2003, D, NR]
- ❏ *National Geographic: 21 Days to Baghdad* [2003, D, NR]
- ❏ *Osama* [2003, PG-13]
- ❏ *Tears of the Sun* [2003, R]
- ❏ *The Guys* [2003, PG]
- ❏ *The Horrors of Hussein* [2003, D, NR]
- ❏ *Biography: Osama bin Laden* [2004, D, NR]
- ❏ *FahrenHYPE 9/11* [2004, D, NR]
- ❏ *Hotel Rwanda* [2004, PG-13]
- ❏ *IMAX: Fighter Pilot, Operation Red Flag* [2004, D, NR]
- ❏ *Day 4* [2005, TV: 24, NR]
- ❏ *Gunner Palace* [2005, D, R]
- ❏ *Occupation: Dreamland* [2005, D, NR]
- ❏ *Syriana* [2005, R]

Music:
- ❏ *A Hard Day's Night* [The Beatles, 1965]
- ❏ *Amazing Grace* [John Newton, 1779]
- ❏ *American Soldier* [Toby Keith, 2003]
- ❏ *Back Home Again* [John Denver, 1974]
- ❏ *Courtesy of the Red White and Blue* [Toby Keith, 2003]
- ❏ *Have You Forgotten?* [Darryl Worley, 2003]
- ❏ *In America* [Charlie Daniels, 2003]
- ❏ *It Can't Rain All the Time* [Jane Siberry, 1993]
- ❏ *It's the End of the World* [REM, 1987]
- ❏ *Mansions of the Lord* [Nick Glennie-Smith, 2002]
- ❏ *Nothing Man* [Bruce Springsteen, 2002]
- ❏ *One Nation under God* [Frog & Scorpion, 2003]
- ❏ *Osama Yo-Mama* [Ray Stevens, 2001]
- ❏ *Paradise* [Bruce Springsteen, 2002]
- ❏ *People Got to Be Free* [Young Rascals, 1969]
- ❏ *Political Science* [Randy Newman, 1999]
- ❏ *Ragged Old Flag* [Johnny Cash, 1974]
- ❏ *Rejoice in the Sun* [Joan Baez, 1971]

- *Sympathy for the Devil* [The Rolling Stones, 1970]
- *The Ballad of Mike Moran* [The Chamber-Made Brigade, 2001]
- *The Boy in the Bubble* [Paul Simon, 1986]
- *The End* [The Doors, 1967]
- *The Times They Are a-Changin'* [Bob Dylan, 1964]
- *The World Don't Bother Me* [John Mellencamp, 2004]
- *This Ain't No Rag, It's a Flag* [Charlie Daniels, 2003]
- *This Is the Time* [Billy Joel, 1986]
- *Those Were the Days* [Mary Hopkins, 1968]
- *Where Were You?* [Song; Alan Jackson, 2002]

Places:

- A new skyscraper, the Freedom Tower, is being built on the site of the destroyed World Trade Center [Lower Manhattan Development Corporation, New York, NY, 212-962-2300, www.renewnyc.com]. The Freedom Tower will reach 1,776 feet into the air and will include a permanent memorial to the innocent and heroic victims of the terrorist attacks of September 11, 2001. Groundbreaking took place on July 4, 2004, and a 20-ton cornerstone was laid with the inscription: "To honor and remember those who lost their lives on September 11, 2001 and as a tribute to the enduring spirit of freedom—July Fourth 2004." The Freedom Tower is scheduled for completion in 2008 or 2009.
- A memorial to the victims of the terrorist attack on the Pentagon, and those who lost their lives on American Airlines Flight 77, is scheduled for completion in 2005 or 2006. The memorial will be located at the southwest corner of the Pentagon Reservation [Pentagon Tour Office, Arlington, VA, 703-697-1776, www.defenselink.mil].
- Flight 93 National Memorial [Somerset, PA, www.flight93memorial project.org]. In 2002, Congress directed the National Park Service to "commemorate the passengers and crew of Flight 93 who, on September 11, 2001, courageously gave their lives thereby thwarting a planned attack on the Nation's Capital."
- The New York City Fire Department Museum [New York, NY, 212-691-1303, www.nycfiremuseum.org].
- The National Fallen Firefighters Memorial [Emmitsburg, MD, 301-447-1365, www.firehero.org].
- Arlington National Cemetery [Arlington, VA, 703-607-8000, www .arlingtoncemetery.org]. Pay tribute to those who have died defending America in the War on Terror.
- The U.S. Department of Homeland Security Web site [www.dhs.gov].
- The Federal Bureau of Investigation (FBI) [Washington, D.C., www .fbi.gov] publishes the names and photographs of the "Most Wanted Terrorists."
- The U.S. State Department [Washington, D.C., www.state.gov] publishes two lists: "The State Department's List of State Sponsors of Terrorism" and the "The State Department's List of Terrorist Organizations."
- Until Al-Qaeda is defeated, the threat of another terrorist attack in the United States is real. But don't be afraid. Be ready. Do your part in the War on Terror. Visit the Web site: www.ready.gov.
- National Guard Memorial Museum [Washington, D.C., 202-408-5887, www.ngef.org].
- Minuteman National Historical Park [Boston, MA, 978-369-6993, www.nps.gov/mima]. See Concord's North Bridge, the place where Colonial "Minutemen" fired the "shot heard round the world," and American Colonists first took up arms in defense of liberty.

Anthony's Extra Credit List

Books:

- *Children's History of the 20th Century,* by DK [0789447223, NF, MS+]
- *Don't Know Much About American History,* by Kenneth C. Davis [0064408361, NF, MS+]
- *Inaugural Address,* by President John F. Kennedy [Speech, 1/20/1961]
- *Jonathan Livingston Seagull,* by Richard Bach [0380012863, NF, MS+]
- *My Dear Young Friends,* by Pope John Paul II [0884897486, NF, MS+]
- *Second Inaugural Address,* by President George W. Bush [Speech, 1/20/2005]
- *The Book of Virtues,* by William Bennett [0671683063, F, MS+]
- *The Five People You Meet in Heaven,* by Mitch Albom [0786868716, NF, MS+]
- *The Timetables of American History,* by Laurence Urdang [0743202619, NF, MS+]
- *What It Felt Like,* by Henry Allen [0375420630, NF, MS+]
- *What Your 6th Grader Needs to Know,* by E. D. Hirsch [0385411200, NF, MS+]

. . . .

- *A Patriot's History of the United States,* by Michael Allen [1595230017, NF, HS+]
- *Animal Farm,* by George Orwell [0451526341, NF, HS+]
- *Becoming a Critical Thinker,* by Sherry Diestler [0130289221, NF, HS+]
- *Legacies,* by Stephen D. Lubar [156098886X, NF, HS+]
- *Letters of the Century,* by Lisa Grunwald [0385315902, NF, HS+]
- *Lord of the Flies,* William Golding [0399501487, NF, HS+]
- *More Than Money,* by Neil Cavuto [0060096438, NF, HS+]
- *1984,* by George Orwell [0451524934, NF, HS+]
- *The Power of Positive Thinking,* by Norman Vincent Peale [0449911470, NF, HS+]
- *Up from Slavery,* by Booker T. Washington [0486287386, NF, HS+]

❑ *Voices of War*, by Library of Congress [0792278380, NF, HS+]

❑ *Witness to America*, by Stephen Ambrose [0062716115, NF, HS+]

Movies:

❑ *Boys Town* [1938, NR]

❑ *Abe Lincoln in Illinois* [1940, NR]

❑ *The Ox-Bow Incident* [1943, NR]

❑ *My Darling Clementine* [1946, NR]

❑ *A Christmas Carol* [1951, NR]

❑ *High Noon* [1952, NR]

❑ *Houdini* [1953, NR]

❑ *Shane* [1953, NR]

❑ *The Robe* [1953, NR]

❑ *Bad Day at Black Rock* [1955, NR]

❑ *The Searchers* [1956, NR]

❑ *The Ten Commandments* [1956, NR]

❑ *Twelve Angry Men* [1957, NR]

❑ *Inn of the Sixth Happiness* [1958, NR]

❑ *Inherit the Wind* [1960, NR]

❑ *The Magnificent Seven* [1960, NR]

❑ *King of Kings* [1961, NR]

❑ *The Man Who Shot Liberty Valance* [1962, NR]

❑ *To Kill a Mockingbird* [1962, NR]

❑ *Lilies of the Field* [1963, NR]

❑ *In the Heat of the Night* [1967, NR]

❑ *To Sir, with Love* [1967, NR]

❑ *Jesus of Nazareth* [1977, NR]

❑ *Oh, God!* [1977, PG]

❑ *A Woman Called Moses* [1978, NR]

❑ *Chariots of Fire* [1981, PG]

❑ *Gandhi* [1982, PG]

❑ *Never Cry Wolf* [1983, PG]

❑ *Tender Mercies* [1983, PG]

❑ *Stand and Deliver* [1987, PG]

❑ *Wings of Desire* [1988, PG-13]

❑ *Glory* [1989, R]

❑ *The Long Walk Home* [1990, PG]

❑ *Class Action* [1991, R]

❑ *Defending Your Life* [1991, PG]

❑ *Gettysburg* [1993, PG]

❑ *Searching for Bobby Fischer* [1993, PG]

❑ *The Straight Story* [1999, G]

❑ *Men of Honor* [2000, PG-13]

❑ *Master and Commander* [2003, PG-13]

❑ *Spellbound* [2003, D, G]

❑ *Whale Rider* [2003, PG-13]

❑ *Ladder 49* [2004, PG-13]

❑ *The Passion of the Christ* [2004, R/Recut 2005, NR]

❑ *Millions* [2005, PG]

❑ *The Five People You Meet in Heaven* [2005, NR]

Music:

❑ *Abraham, Martin and John* [Dick Holler, 1968]

❑ *Auld Lang Syne* [Robert Burns, 1788]

❑ *Carry on Wayward Son* [Kansas, 1976]

❑ *Don't Worry, Be Happy* [Bobby McFerrin, 1988]

❑ *Don't You Forget About Me* [Billy Idol, 1985]

❑ *Every Time You Go Away* [Darryl Hall, 1985]

❑ *Father and Son* [Cat Stevens, 1970]

❑ *Golden Years* [David Bowie, 1983]

❑ *Help Pour Out the Rain* [Buddy Jewel, 2003]

❑ *I Melt with You* [Modern English, 1992]

❑ *In My Life* [The Beatles, 1965]

❑ *I've Loved These Days* [Billy Joel, 1976]

❑ *I Wish* [Stevie Wonder, 1976]

❑ *Learning to Fly* [Tom Petty, 1991]

❑ *Old Souls* [Jessica Harper, 1970]

❑ *Ooh La La* [The Corrs, 1998]

❑ *Simple Man* [Lynyrd Skynyrd, 1973]

❑ *Teach Your Children* [Crosby, Stills, Nash & Young, 1970]

❑ *Thanks for the Memories* [Bob Hope, 1938]

❑ *The Best Is Yet to Come* [Frank Sinatra, 1960]

❑ *The Wedding Song* [Noel Paul Stookey, 1971]

❑ *Time* [Pink Floyd, 1973]

❑ *Time of Your Life* [Green Day, 1998]

❑ *Wait for Me* [Rebecca St. James, 2003]

❑ *What a Wonderful World* [Louis Armstrong, 1967]

❑ *Where Have All the Cowboys Gone?* [Paula Cole, 1996]

Places:

❑ National Museum of American History [Washington, D.C., 202-633-1000, www.si.edu].

❑ Library of Congress American Memory Web site [www.memory.loc.gov].

❑ The fresco, the *Last Judgment*, painted by Michelangelo in 1541, is located in the Sistine Chapel [The Vatican, Rome, Italy, www.vatican.va]. The thought-provoking and visually arresting painting is centered around the figure of Jesus Christ, and depicts Heaven, Earth, and Hell at the moment the verdict of the Last Judgment is uttered according to Mathew 25:31–46, The Holy Bible, King James Version. Movie: *The Agony and the Ecstasy* [1965, NR].

THANK YOU!

———————◆•◈•◆———————

Thank you for purchasing a copy of *Anthony and the Magic Picture Frame*. We hope you found the story fun and exciting—and the notes and lists educational and stimulating. It's important to understand the past—we must know where we came from in order to decide where we are going.

Do you know someone who would like a copy of *Anthony and the Magic Picture Frame*? Would you like to buy additional copies of the book?

WHERE TO BUY ADDITIONAL COPIES OF THE BOOK

———————◆•◈•◆———————

To find out where to buy additional copies of *Anthony and the Magic Picture Frame*, just visit our Web site, or contact us by e-mail.

Web site: www.magicpictureframe.com

E-mail: publisher@magicpictureframe.com

Magic Picture Frame Studio, LLC
P.O. Box 2603
Issaquah, WA 98027-0119